Ordinary

Th
obj
pas
pre
fan
me
the
of
dai
the

ref
Ra
bio
cul
aes
life
rou
fin
life
sen

sui
and

Be
of Sussex, UK. He is the author of *A Passion for Cultural Studies* (2009),
Michel de Certeau: Analysing Culture (2006), *Cityscapes: Cultural Readings in
the Material and Symbolic City* (2005), *Everyday Life and Cultural Theory* (2002)
and *The Everyday Life Reader* (2002).

For Wendy Bonner, love of my life

Ordinary Lives

Studies in the Everyday

Ben Highmore

 Routledge
Taylor & Francis Group

LONDON AND NEW YORK

First published 2011
by Routledge
2 Park Square, Milton Park, Abingdon, Oxon, OX14 4RN

Simultaneously published in the USA and Canada
by Routledge
270 Madison Ave, New York, NY 10016

Routledge is an imprint of the Taylor & Francis Group, an informa business

© 2011 Ben Highmore

Typeset in Goudy by Taylor & Francis Books
Printed and bound in Great Britain by TJ International Ltd, Padstow, Cornwall

British Library Cataloguing in Publication Data
A catalogue record for this book is available from the British Library

Library of Congress Cataloging in Publication Data
Highmore, Ben, 1961–
Ordinary lives : studies in the everyday / Ben Highmore.
p. cm.
Includes bibliographical references and index.
1. Anthropology. 2. Aesthetics. I. Title.
GN25.H55 2011
301--dc22
2010012689

ISBN13: 978-0-415-46186-3 (hbk)
ISBN13: 978-0-415-46187-0 (pbk)
ISBN13: 978-0-203-84237-9 (ebk)

Contents

Acknowledgements

Thanks are due to Simon During for supporting this project in a number of ways. Michael Gardiner and Gregory Seigworth are my mentors and fellow travellers in the misadventures of the everyday: thanks as ever. Working with Janice Winship on her course on 'the culture of the everyday' reinvigorated my enthusiasm for this project and got me thinking in a more practical way about the everyday. Thanks to Ellie Harrison and all the artists involved in her *Day-to-Day Data* project. In no particular order (apart from alphabetical) the following have all been helpful in minor or major ways: Sara Ahmed, Ien Ang, Caroline Bassett, Paul Betts, Mark Bhatti, Paul Bowman, Ian Buchanan, Michael Bull, Adrian Carton, Constance Classen, Paola Di Cori, Jean Duruz, Marian Füssel, Danielle Gallegos, Rosalind Galt, Melissa Gregg, Jerome Hansen, Ramaswami Harindranath, Richard Hornsey, David Howes, Nick Hubble, Margaretta Jolly, Kate Lacey, Claire Langhamer, Scott McCracken, Andy Medhurst, Michael Morris, Sally Munt, Felicity Newman, Kate O'Riordan, Wendy Parkins, Elspeth Probyn, Louise Purbrick, Raiford Quins, Adam Ranson, Rhona Richman Kenneally, Polly Ruiz, Johanne Sloan, Will Straw, Deborah Sugg Ryan, Imre Szeman, Lizzie Thynne and Amanda Wise. Michelle Henning and Gillian Swanson are my immediate writing-support group, and much else besides. I benefited from a number of invitations to talk about this project: the invitations came from Marquard Smith, Ian Buchanan, Judith Ash, Michael Hviid Jacobsen, Gen Doy and Linda Kaljundi. The seminar that Linda Kaljundi invited me to in Tallin, Estonia, was especially productive in sharpening the focus of this inquiry. Routledge are, as always, a supportive and collegiate team. It is a pleasure to work with Natalie Foster, Charlie Wood and Emily Laughton. Chapter six owes a debt of gratitude to the Arts and Humanities Research Council (UK) for research funding from the strategic initiative 'Diasporas, Migration and Identities' programme.

This book tries to show how the confusions, routines, intricacies and surprises of daily life, that are felt so 'personally', are always connecting us to a realm of communal (and differentiated) life. Ordinary life is collective even when it is experienced as isolated and desolate. My ordinary life is far from isolated, far from desolate. It is collective in the most immediate, practical and affective way. So my last and greatest thanks have to go to those who are 'nearest and dearest' (as usual the cliché exceeds its worn familiarity); to Zeb, Molly and Wendy (to whom this book is dedicated).

Ben Highmore
April 2010

Permissions

But what sort of sense is constitutive of this everydayness? Surely this sense includes much that it is not sense so much as sensuousness, an embodied and somewhat automatic 'knowledge' that functions like peripheral vision, not studied contemplation, a knowledge that is imageric and sensate rather than ideational; as such it not only challenges practically all critical practice across the board of academic disciplines but is a knowledge that lies as much in the objects and spaces of observation as in the body and mind of the observer.

(Taussig 1992: 141–42)

Everyday life is a life lived on the level of surging affects, impacts suffered or barely avoided. It takes everything we have. But it also spawns a series of little somethings dreamed up in the course of things.

(Stewart 2007: 9)

Preface

This book is about ordinary, everyday life and it is also about aesthetics. Because these two terms might not seem immediately compatible it is worth me initially telegraphing an argument I will make in greater detail throughout the book. Once upon a time the word 'aesthetics' was less freighted with the task of policing the corridors of art or evaluating the experiences associated with it. Initially it pointed, with imprecision and unease, to a messy world of sensate perception, a world irreducible to rational meanings or ideation. Aesthetics gestured thought towards the great left-over: the bodily creature; the paths of often unruly emotions; the whole sensual world in all its baseness and brilliance. Emerging as a named area of inquiry only in the mid-eighteenth century, the history of aesthetics can be seen to follow a wayward path of increased intellectual specialisation, increasingly limiting itself to only certain kinds of experience and feeling, and becoming more and more dedicated to finely wrought objects. Once taken out of their lively solution, such discrete objects (artworks, powerful feelings of awe in the face of nature) were left beached on the shores of disciplinary knowledge. Marooned by an attention designed to praise and appraise them, art objects were often shorn of the very thing that aesthetics originally sought to engage with – the sensual, material entanglement with the socio-natural world.

The etymology of the term aesthetics stems from the Greek words *aisthêtikos* and *aisthêta*, and refers to a fundamentally empiricist approach to the world that privileges a concern with sensation and 'the network of physical perceptions' (Barilli 1993: 2). Such a root is lost when we associate aesthetics primarily with art, and it is lost when we find beauty parlours and cosmetic surgeons rebranded as 'aesthetic' technicians. But it is commonly maintained, albeit in its negative form, in the term anaesthetics – the practice of making insensate or blocking painful sensations. (It is also maintained in less everyday terms such as synaesthesia and hyperaesthesia.) If anaesthetics befuddles and dulls us, causing us to not feel pain or pleasure, it would make sense to see aesthetics as the inverse of this: our lively sensitivity to stimulus from without and within; our sensate connectivity to a world of things and other people; our responsiveness to a world of feelings.

Aesthetics was born out of Enlightenment philosophy's attempt to understand human 'nature'. Reason alone could not explain the way people lived and loved, the way they sympathised or remained unmoved. Much European philosophical thought, from the seventeenth through to the eighteenth and early nineteenth century, was concerned with the passions and their moral management. Passions included what we would more routinely call emotions, feelings and affects, but also included phenomena such as imitation. Sometimes the invocation of the passions was designed to loosen the shackles of religiosity, sometimes it worked in tandem with religious belief, most often it seems to pull both ways at once. It is easy enough to critique Enlightenment attitudes towards virtue and the good life and to find them promoting values that are heavily classed, gendered and racialised, but I can't help marvelling at the sheer ambition of such an attempt to understand the cultural creatureliness of human life.

If 'aesthetics' only fully emerges as a philosophical term in 1750 in the work of Alexander Baumgarten, it designates an arena in European philosophy that was by then already fully established: this is the intersection of passions, tastes, sentiments and morality. Classical, Enlightenment philosophy couldn't simply describe these intersections, it also felt the need to evaluate them. And it is, I will argue, the values, rather than the forms of attention, that are problematic for understanding the aesthetics of daily life. Some, if not most, of the evaluations from seventeenth, eighteenth and early nineteenth-century philosophy will appear odd, often aristocratic, thoroughly gendered and at times implicitly racial. But this is not something peculiar to aesthetic thinking. On the other hand classical aesthetics (before it ruinously narrows its purview by attending so obsessively and exclusively to art and beauty) is wonderfully attuned to the sociality of subjective experience and to the way that passions and affects circulate across our human and thingly world. This is a dynamic world view, where passions provoke actions, where sympathy attaches us to feelings, and where our most 'internal' feelings turn out to be a part of public culture. And it is this potential to attend to the dynamics of our interpersonal and transpersonal tunings that is so crucial for understanding the liveliness of ordinary life.

But if this means that at times we need to turn aesthetics away from the artwork and away from a consideration of beauty, it doesn't mean that we have to dispatch them to oblivion. In classical aesthetics (as in psychoanalysis) artworks are sometimes called upon to draw out a point and to enliven an account of a type of experience. If they are used as objects of contemplation then they have to take their place alongside shoes, gardens, rivers, houses, faces, plants and so on. As part of our artificial, object world, however, books, plays, music and paintings aren't just objects of contemplation, they are also part of the communal circulation of affects and passions. If this was true in the eighteenth century it is even more evident today. Novels, poetry and paintings are today coupled with films, TV shows, radio and the internet to mark out an increasingly expansive terrain where culture presents itself passionately. News stories of tragedy and peril are routinely piped into our homes and places of work; sadness and joy animate every story and every song that syncopates daily life. The cultural world is an ecology of optimism and pessimism, of pleasure and pain, and it makes communal subjects of us all.

Such objects don't require a narrow 'aesthetic appreciation', but need to be recognised as a central realm where the orchestration of sentiment and affect takes place. This ecology of 'presented passions' (what some would call the world of representation) is also the arena that has most insistently and viscerally attended to the patterns of everyday life. In *The Practice of Everyday Life* Michel de Certeau suggests that modernity witnesses increased intellectual specialisation. A classical inquiry about 'leading the good life', about passions and affects, becomes atomised and hardened into discrete enclaves of activity and reflection (psychology, sociology, economics, a narrowly defined aesthetics and so on). As a result everyday life (as the subject of intellectual reflection) gets remaindered, falling through the cracks between disciplines. There is, however, one place where everyday life becomes more and more vivid – literature:

> As indexes of particulars – the poetic or tragic murmurings of the everyday – ways of operating enter massively into the novel or the short story, most notably into the nineteenth-century realist novel. They find there a new representational space, that of fiction, populated by everyday virtuosities that science doesn't know what to do with and which become the signatures, easily recognised by readers, of everyone's micro-stories.
>
> (de Certeau 1984: 70)

What literature (and we could add here film, TV, pop music and so on) does so well, of course, is to describe the details of life and the pulsings of affect: the risings and fallings of hope, love, hatred and irritation; the minor and major disturbances of life set against and within a world of day-to-day habits, routines and collective sentiments.

While in this book art has to be held in abeyance so that it can return as socially vivid matter, so beauty needs to be deprioritised so that it can be recoded and revalued. It would simply be mean-spirited to permanently delete beauty from the realm of the daily. While few could claim that their daily life was suffused with beauty, many would, I hope, have some sense of beauty punctuating their daily life. Beauty might be a value that is routinely set against the sometimes bland consistency of everyday life: a lovely meal, a wonderful sunset, a dog running in the park, a football match played exquisitely. Beauty can animate the daily and structure our experiences of it through its relative rarity. Beauty can initiate a sudden effervescence that casts a light which illuminates some things while casting shadows over others. But beauty also circulates in ordinary life as a normative value (think of such magazines as *House Beautiful*, *Allure: The Beauty Expert* and so on) which is as likely to provoke envy as effervescence, as likely to produce anxiety as pleasure. Beauty is often a form of negative discrimination that propagates racial and age-specific values, reinforcing particular articulations of sexuality and gender. It is also tied to the increasingly unsustainable rhythms of commercial culture: three years ago that was beautiful, now it is dowdy. Aesthetics, once it has cut its ties with the automatic privileging of 'beauty', might be able to find new forms of beauty in what had previously been passed off as dowdy and dull, ugly and uninteresting, routine and irregular. It might involve learning to appreciate new forms of beauty that could be more sustainable, more precarious and more world-enlarging. Ordinary life maintains habitual values, but it is also where the body learns to like new things (new smells, new tastes, new sounds). The potential for opening up the senses to the unknown and new (the foreign, the different) is a way of moving away from a cross-cultural ecology that is driven by something as mealy-mouthed as 'tolerance' (and tolerance only has positive connotations when it is spoken in a culture deeply marred by hostility: who would accept 'being tolerated' as a positive value in any other situation?). Aesthetic contact with another culture involves the passions. In what follows my aesthetic approach favours description over evaluation in the hope that such an orientation might result in new appreciations of habit and routine and new forms of inclination and aversion.

In championing an older understanding of aesthetics, and in an endeavour to vitalise this so as to attend to ordinary life, this book finds its materials in a number of places. I use literature, film and TV, alongside philosophy and critical theory (and for the most part purposefully fail to see any essential differences between them). What I value in literature is often what I value most in theory: the ability to call forth an experience through (sometimes exorbitant) description. Rather than this dedifferentiating such a disparate stock of materials, it forfeits the often taken-for-granted demands of genre, focusing instead on the singularities and potential of a presentation. But this is not a book that provides a critical distance on debates so as to scrutinise them rigorously and critically for academic appraisal. My aim is generative: I want to mobilise aesthetics for the task of attending to ordinary life, and this means getting in among things. So while I use theory and literature I also theorise and present descriptions of everyday life that some might feel are far too literary. Literature and theory are rarely 'correct' or 'incorrect': instead both theory and literature put in play a set of values and accounts that we are invited to ascribe to or to recognise as in some ways true, adequate or productive. It is the test of recognition that I want to prize here. I am less interested in whether something can be generalised and applied universally, than if a description is recognisable and has a shape that is something like the shape of other experiences of the ordinary. This book is empirical (in the sense that Hume gave to the term) but it does not try to be representative (there are no focus groups, surveys, interviews, etc.). The book's task shares the ambition of classical aesthetics (to attend to human creaturely life) but also the modesty of literature (to attend to the singularities of ordinary existence). Such a task could only ever be partially successful: all I can hope is that any substantive achievements mitigate the falling-short that is the necessary outcome of attending to the ordinary. I have also stayed within the orbit of my local culture, which means that most of the examples are geographically English. In a globalised world this may seem peculiarly provincial – I hope that it doesn't and that this sort of necessarily close work could be extended into other geographies.

Chapter I

Introduction

How does everyday life feel to you? Do the habits and routines of the day-to-day press down on you like a dull weight? Do they comfort you with their worn and tender familiarity, or do they pull irritably at you, rubbing your face in their lack of spontaneity and event? When cleaning or cooking does time ricochet past in the half-light of the daydream or stutter and collapse in the stupor of drudgery? Can domestic routines become precious moments snatched from more thoroughly exhaustive work practices, or do their rhythms constantly signal their lack of value? And how, supposing we wanted to, would we call attention to such 'non-events', without betraying them, without disloyalty to the particularity of their experience, without simply turning them into 'events'?

Somewhere a clock is ticking like it always does, you are getting hungry like you always do, the telephone is ringing like it always will, and the TV is playing in an empty room. Somewhere someone is dying, someone is being born, someone is making love; somewhere a war is being fought. Midwives and morticians, paupers and princes, go about their everyday lives. Everything can become everyday, everything can become ordinary: it is our greatest blessing, our most human accomplishment, our greatest handicap, our most despicable complacency.

The almost glacial movement of dust settling is too slow to watch, it's a constant drift of particles building up and becoming visible: however much you polish and vacuum its presence is relentless. The everyday is the accumulation of 'small things' that constitute a more expansive but hard to register 'big thing'. But like fissures in a stream of constancy the everyday is also punctuated by interruptions and irruptions: a knock on the door, a stubbed toe, an argument, an unexpected present, a broken glass, a tear, a desperate embrace. Crowding round these syncopations is the background hiss of the ambient everyday. A mood, a rhythm, a feeling provides a stage on which the ordinary events and happenings of the everyday unfold. It is a field of experience constantly in flux: I was calm but now I am anxious; I was happy but now I am sad; I was daydreaming but now I am just bored; I was frustrated but now I am indifferent.

The everyday may be vague but it is not abstract. Abstractions, however, might allow some purchase on the amorphousness of what tends to pass, and what tends to get passed off in ordinary life. How could we say anything about the everyday that was both general and true without being fatuous, without resorting to platitudes? If everyday life is an endless field of singular moments held loosely in place by the threads of the overarching (power, governance, etc.) then how would we talk about *this* everyday life without excluding *that* one? One way out of this impasse is to suggest that everyday life is a thoroughly relational term and that rather than try and pinpoint its characteristic content we would do better to draw out its grammar, its patterns of association, its forms of connection and disconnection. Rather than analysing shopping, for instance, as a practice separate from other practices (dreaming, for instance) it might be more productive to look at the patterning of desire and routine as they connect and disconnect, and to try and describe the different intersections of memory, need, forgetfulness, humour and so on, as they are played out while buying the groceries.[1] The path I take in this book is to pursue a 'science of singularity' (de Certeau 1984: ix), which means that the particular is studied *as if* it could contribute to a more general account of the world. Of course much hangs on this 'as if': it signals that the contact with the concrete particular will necessarily be the ground for a provisional and contestable account of things.

Boredom, routine, habit and familiarity might characterise important aspects of ordinary life, but what is ordinariness without accident, without anxiety and joy, without surprise? How would we characterise the moods, rhythms and affects of the day-to-day? What are its orchestrations and intensities? How does daydreaming exhaust itself and turn into boredom? And how does boredom sometimes dissolve into spontaneity and exuberance? When Freud claimed that chronic toothache and being in love were mutually incompatible ('so long as he suffers, he ceases to love' [Freud 1914: 75]), he was participating in an age-old understanding of human nature where one passion (pain) blocks out another (love). Yet much of what constitutes ordinary life can't be written in such stark terms. The ordinary is as much characterised by confusion as clarity, as much by simultaneity and complexity as discrete and separable motifs. 'Confusion' isn't the obverse of rational clarity, but a radically different order: con-fusion is the fusing together of disparate material in ways that aren't reconciled into clear and discrete syntheses. The ordinary con-fuses thought and feeling as ideas and sensation, remembrances and hope, and myriad somatic perceptions, fall and rise in pressing their attention on us. The ordinary demands complexity because, at times, nothing is really in the foreground of experience. The dynamic simultaneity of desire (and its sublimations), of confidence (and its undoing), of concentration (and its dispersal) require a mode of description that is more tuned to orchestration than the ascription of meaning.

Nothing much

What's going on when nothing much is happening? If, when asked 'what have you been up to?' or 'what's been happening?' you reply 'nothing much' then what is this 'nothing much' referring to? 'Nothing much' is an odd formula: half of it sounds like the indignant cry of children when questioned by parents or anyone when questioned by the police ('what are you doing?' *nothing!* [spoken pleadingly or disdainfully, obstinately or innocently, as befits the scene]). The 'much' qualifies the 'nothing', and in the court of ordinary life there is never 'nothing' going on, just nothing 'much'. But perhaps this 'much' is really too much. When nothing much is going on then there is already too much to know where to begin. 'Nothing much', signals a reticence; sometimes this reticence is inviting (you know me, same old thing, the usual complaints, the usual interests); sometimes it is stand-off-ish (there's been nothing happening that concerns you). 'Nothing much' stands in relation to that which can be remarked upon: the trip to the cinema, the shopping excursion, the holiday, the job interview, the visit to a sick relative (the remarkable in the literal sense of the term). But when there is no remark to be made, no event to be marked out, then where would you possibly start, and where could you possibly end, in giving an account of the ordinary?

I take a break from work to enjoy the early summer sun. I take a cup of coffee outside. My head is full of essay marking and a list of things that I should do. I'm fairly sealed off, caught in a maze of preoccupations. The sun begins to warm my skin and clothes; the warmed skin presses 'its' attention on consciousness. I realise I had been staring at the ground, and now I look up and look around, noticing my surroundings for the first time since I had come outside. This is enough to momentarily stop the endless replaying of the cycle of 'to do' lists that had been looping round my mind. For some reason I start to think about my toes and to wiggle them. I realise that really I hardly ever think about my toes, nor do my toes alert 'me' to their presence. So what are my toes doing the rest of the time? Presumably they are firing all sorts of information across my nervous system, just as my skin continues to register the atmospheric conditions no matter if it is sunny or cloudy, warm or cool. The thought trails off as I suddenly remember that I have to organise a meal for the department where I work. Shit; I'm worried that I've left it too late, that few will come.[2] The sunlight bolts across the grass towards me as someone on the second floor opens their window and my eyes catch the glare. I've finished my coffee: the 'to do' list is playing again ...

If someone stopped me as I was coming inside and asked me 'what was happening' would they really want to hear all this? Most of the time, to be frank, I'd have to say that I haven't got a clue what's been going on, as the endless 'inner speech' is lost almost as soon as it appears. My coffee break could be described as drifting. Mine was a luxurious confusion of sense and sensation, of ideas and somatic registering, pitted with the demands of a work-a-day world. We all drift, even if the orchestrations of our drifting differ enormously. While Freud overstated the effects of one passion or feeling obliterating everything else, it is clearly the case that the qualities and conditions of our ordinary life will shape not just the pattern of such drifting but the central motifs that press upon our attention. The sense of being cold and hungry or in pain might or might not obliterate drifting: clearly though it would profoundly colour it.

The sense of drifting has been a key to some recent understandings of modernity. The sense that modernity disanchors the human subject and lets it loose on the high seas of modern life, where it will be tossed about on the waves of spectacular culture, is a central tenet of an understanding of modernity as post-traditional culture.[3] Alongside this is the sense that drifting is not simply the human subject facing the storm-clouds of industrial culture, but the human subject emptied out: not just adrift but drowned. This is Leo Charney:

> Everyone says modern life, coming out of the late nineteenth and early twentieth centuries, was about too much happening, things moving too fast, assaulting you, too much stimulation, too many distractions. … But they have it backward. Modernity's about the emptiness, the drift. All those things going on were a cover, to mask the emptiness. Once people realised life was empty and boring, they couldn't face it. They had to have all those things going on to make them forget, to deny it, make it go away, go back to a time before they knew that life was empty and boring.
>
> (Charney 1998: 13)

The existential loss that modernity generates is filled, for Charney, by the agitated spectacular culture of the modern (cinema, advertising, TV and so on). My argument is different from Charney's. I'm putting my money on a different orchestration of these terms. Here 'the drift' is the ordinary as it is continually hidden and obfuscated by a number of strong forces. One of these forces is exactly the same as Charney's: the spectacular extravaganzas of industrial culture. The ordinary everyday never stood much of a chance against the sensationalism of newspapers, cinema and advertising. However dull and repetitious soap operas and reality TV are, they have a clarity and vividness that often throws shadows over the day-to-day-ness of ordinary life. But alongside this, modernity witnesses the intellectual culture abandoning the ordinary everyday. When intellectual culture shatters into a vast array of technical specialisms, the ordinary, it seems, can only be grasped as problem, as trauma, as something in need of management. The drift, then, isn't the emptiness of the ordinary, but the ordinary submerged, hiding in an expanse of shadows.

Ordinary life, ordinary lives

To write a book entitled *Ordinary Lives* is to court criticism, if not derision, from the start. Whose life is ordinary? Doesn't the attempt to map the ordinary, to establish its contours, immediately throw open the doors to a hundred thousand complaints: But what about ... ? Why have you not included ... ? What happens to your ideas when you consider ... ? The insistence on the ordinary doesn't have to be pursued in the name of normative values, of ascertaining means and averages. The *Oxford English Dictionary* reunites the term with a range of meanings that exceed the reduced sense of ordinary as a depleted form of life. For instance while 'ordinary' is mainly used as an adjective there are plenty of examples of its use as a noun. In the eighteenth century, for instance, 'an ordinary' was a meal that was equivalent to the French term *plat de jour* (the dish of the day). So, in Henry Mackenzie's *The Man of Feeling* from 1771, two well-to-do men are walking by a park when 'they observed a board hung out of a window, signifying, "An excellent ORDINARY on Saturdays and Sundays." It happened to be Saturday and the table was covered for the purpose' (Mackenzie 2001 [1771]: 20, capitalisations in the original). There is no sense that the two men are going for the cheap or the measly option here. An ordinary in this sense was the meal on which most care and labour was lavished, that used the freshest produce and the best cuts of meat. It was also what you might eat as a regular customer of the café or restaurant. An 'ordinary' suggests both the care and effort of the cook or chef and a community of diners who know how to choose the best option because they respect the decisions and skills of their patron.

This sense of collectivity is central to thinking about the ordinary. While the everyday might be an endless succession of singularities it is not helpful to understand it as peopled by monads. The ordinary harbours an abundance that is distinct from material plenty: it is there when we talk about something as common, it is there when we talk about society, and it is there when we talk about 'us'. The ordinary brings with it one of the most optimistic but also most daunting phrases from science fiction and horror: you are not alone. And even in the midst of the most desperate isolation, the ordinary can take hold of what seems exceptional and connect it with other 'exceptions'. The ordinary speaks of commonality without necessarily intoning the ideological set pieces of 'the silent majority', or of universality. But the ordinary also carries with it the policing exertions of the normative and the governmentality of institutions who would set out to regulate and regularise your eating habits, your cleanliness, your work routines, your sleeping habits, your political affiliations, your sexual practices and your consumption. To be marked as 'extraordinary' in your ordinariness is to be marked out collectively, to become one of a collective of people similarly marked-out as 'deviants', 'perverts', as 'idlers', 'unhealthy' and so on. There is little solace in being marked this way, and such marking increasingly posits a virtual rather than an actual collective, but the history of the twentieth century is also a history of that marked collective coming together to exert their ordinariness as just that – ordinary.

In hierarchical societies, where social status is at a premium, and where novelty is seen as a positive value, what counts as ordinary is often denigrated and felt to be of lowly status. This sense of the term is instantiated in certain of the armed forces where to be an 'ordinary' is to be without rank, and in the Scottish higher education system where an 'ordinary' degree is the lower of two classes. Yet ordinariness, as this book hopes to demonstrate, is also a positive value, an accomplishment. For something to become ordinary you have to become used to it, it must be part of your regular life, your habitual realm. For midwives and funeral directors, ordinary life includes dealing with people at points in their life that are often far from ordinary and highly emotionally charged. One person's ordinary is another person's extraordinary. And yet the ordinary is never set in stone: ordinariness is a process (like habit) where things (practices, feelings, conditions and so on) pass from unusual to usual, from irregular to regular, and can move the other way (what was an ordinary part of my life, is no more). There is always the 'being ordinary' but there is also the 'becoming ordinary'.

For the literary critic and historian Raymond Williams, writing in 1961, to insist that culture is ordinary is to see it as alive, pulsing with the passionate energies of the time. Williams glosses his insistence on the ordinary in the following way: 'there are, essentially, no "ordinary" activities, if by "ordinary" we mean the absence of creative interpretation and effort' (Williams 1992 [1961]: 37). Williams' argument is about the relationship between art and society but is clearly aimed at making a much more general point about human culture in all its ordinariness:

> Art is ratified, in the end, by the fact of creativity in all our living. Everything we see and do, the whole structure of our relationships and institutions, depends, finally, on an effort of learning, description and communication. We create our human world as we have thought of art being created. Art is a major means of precisely this creation. Thus the distinction of art from ordinary living, and the dismissal of art as unpractical or secondary (a 'leisure-time activity'), are alternative formulations of the same error. If all reality must be learned by the effort to describe it successfully, we cannot isolate 'reality' and set art in opposition to it, for dignity or indignity. If all activity depends on responses learned by the sharing of descriptions, we cannot set 'art' on one side of a line and 'work' on the other; we cannot submit to be divided into 'Aesthetic Man' and 'Economic Man'.
>
> (Williams 1992 [1961]: 37–38)

It is, to my mind, a stunning argument that simultaneously enlivens the practice of art (and fundamentally connects it to the everyday) while ennobling ordinary life by recognising the process of reflection, cognition, description that is an essential aspect of day-to-day living. Creativity, Williams makes clear, is not some special realm of sensitivity and expression, but the daily business of making sense of the world around us, of reflecting on it, of narrating it and communicating to others, of learning about it and adopting and adapting the narrations and feelings available to us.

The quotation above echoes Raymond Williams' insistence, in 1958, that 'culture is ordinary'. What he had in mind was neither a sense of ordinary culture as representative of 'the average Joe or Josephine', nor of a commitment to a particular sphere of life (domestic life over public life, physical labour over intellectual work, for instance). For Williams 'ordinary' signalled a commitment to the messy, provisional and deeply corporeal 'whole ways of life' of a community, a culture. And while we may argue about the entanglement of 'community' and 'culture' in Williams' formulation, his use of the word 'whole' was never intended to signal consistency or coherency: the dedication was to life in its fractured, effervescent, unmanageable totality. 'Ordinary' is the world pulsing with life in its very singularity, existing across and in the interstices of the arbitrary and unhelpful distinctions we can't help making between 'labour' and 'love', 'private' and 'public', 'text' and 'context', 'art' and 'economics'. The term 'ordinary' is a flag raised as a commitment to a world in solution (and dissolution), a commitment to the heuristic, prespecialised *gestalt* of life – an unachievable goal, no doubt, but one worth striving for nonetheless.

To name something as ordinary is not without risk. At once the founding act of all that is worthwhile in cultural studies it also marks the source of all its troubles; it is the stigmata of the burden it (often unwittingly and unwillingly) carries. Inevitably bearing the freight of representing the fantasy of 'average' life, mobilising the term ordinary is as likely to alienate as to garner assent. Thus a customer review on the website for the online store Amazon can write of Kathleen Stewart's *Ordinary Affects*: 'I was disappointed. I was looking for a serious work on feeling and ordinary life. Instead what I found was a literary and post-modernist account of weirdness and banality in America. There are of course people who like that kind of thing.' This reviewer gave the book one star out of five. 'Ordinary', like the term cultural studies, seems to promise something it never intends to deliver; a promise of what it is constitutionally designed to renege upon.

Stewart's book conjures up a world of humdrum violence, banal perseverance and unexpected tenderness. Its atmosphere is simultaneously small-town gothic, blue-collar naturalism and main-street surrealism. The world that is painted is filled with correspondences and miscommunications, with mounting frustrations and outbreaks of intensity. Stewart is an anthropologist who studies that side of American life that is off the tourist map. Her book reads like a field diary of someone sensitised to a range of emotional ecologies as they are played out in the localised encounters of individuals, couples and small groups. There is no overarching sense of America here, but also no feeling that you could be anywhere else.

In one of the endorsements on the back of *Ordinary Affects*, Lauren Berlant claims that this is 'a profoundly pedagogic book'. Yet there is nothing explicit here that can simply be extracted and applied to something else, no easily borrowed system of thought or analysis, no quotable paragraph that would underwrite a methodology. Here the pedagogy is deep and performative. As you read the book you become more and more alert to your surroundings. Your skin begins to prickle with the apprehensions of the lives of others, of resonances of care and indifference, of anxiety and ease. It is the pedagogy that Walter Benjamin claims is characteristic of fairground rides, of the mechanism of cameras and the jarring attempts of crossing busy roads. It attunes and reattunes the human sensorium. I read the book on a train journey from the south west of England up to the north western coast (just below the Lake District). Passing through a dozen towns and cities of the English Midlands I saw countless down-at-heel Victorian terraced streets, peppered with corner shops, austere pubs and boarded-up petrol stations. For anyone spending any time in England this is a familiar sight. Yet by about Birmingham the streets began to change: their familiarity was unsettled and I was filled with feelings that new places generate when you first set out on your own. Arriving in an unfamiliar town as an apprentice adult, such streets were never 'mean' or 'impoverished', but the corridors of anticipation, possibility, trepidation and disappointment. I swooned with a strange admix of lonely-excitement that I hadn't felt for a couple of decades. The damp stone and brick of a forlorn landscape began to bristle with the possibility of adventure, with the possibility of endless somethings.

The thing-ness of some*thing* is Stewart's insistent object. Her guide is the action of listening-in, of observing, of passing-by and taking-part. She is in a café in Ohio watching and listening as an ill-matched couple strive to get through what looks like a first date. The man is tucking into a high-cholesterol plate of 'biscuits and gravy' while his companion eats a grapefruit and a cluster of vitamin supplements while outlining her extensive fitness regimes. Stewart's practice is descriptive and in a few paragraphs she evokes a meal of awkward exchanges, of embarrassment and disdain. Her final sentence assesses the situation without judging the participants: 'And things were happening, all right, even though "it" was so "not happening"' (2007: 31). The 'thing' of experience here is the materiality of disappointment, of condescension received and given, of wishing away time, of suffering the ill-ease of not getting along. And in our turn, as 'critical readers', what do we do? Do we judge Stewart's descriptions as adequate (or not), productive (or not), analytical (or not)? Such judgements seem to flounder in the face of a much more pressing and immediate question. Do we recognise this scene? Do we share the hunched-over mumbling awkwardness of the meeting or not? It is the judgement more usually reserved for fiction than academic work, but it is the one judgement that in the face of *Ordinary Affects*, really appears to matter.

The book you're now reading follows in the wake of the work of writers of such different temperaments and styles as Stewart and Williams. While Stewart's work (in *Ordinary Affects*) is primarily descriptive and observational, Williams' writing is historical, more theoretically expansive and more soberly analytical. I can't claim either the economical affectivity of Stewart or the historical erudition and critical acumen of Williams, but I can say that working across these dimensions is not without its awkwardness, its anxieties, but also its productivity and pleasures. *Ordinary Lives* pursues an attention to areas of routine and habit (but also their disruptions and emergence) across areas of work and domesticity, across leisure and necessity. In doing so there are three overlapping themes that are central to the entire book: aesthetics; humanism; and intimacy.

Aesthetics

In 1884 in his essay 'What is an emotion?' the philosopher and psychologist William James described 'the aesthetic sphere of the mind' as the mind's 'longings, pleasures and pains, and its emotions' (James 1884: 188). Had he written such a description a century earlier he might have claimed that the aesthetic sphere of the mind was the arena of the mind's passions; a century before that he wouldn't have used the term aesthetic but might have written about the soul's passions. The terminology changes and with it the kinds of questions and answers that can be directed at human affairs changes too. Yet there are also longstanding concerns that range across the centuries that can rightly be called aesthetic concerns even before that term was being used to designate them. These are the concerns with human activity and human 'nature' that take as their object the forces at work in the world and across our bodies that seem least amenable to analysis by the procedures of reason and logic.

I have already (in the preface) made a claim for the relevance of aesthetics for ordinary life, and in the next chapter I will go into some detail about the various strands of aesthetic thought that seem most relevant to the study of ordinary, everyday life. For now I just want to point to four qualities of aesthetic thinking that will inform the book as a whole. The first is that, for aesthetics, emotions come from without not from within. Rather than assuming that our profound emotional life bubbles up from our 'inner-selves', aesthetics posits emotions and affects as social, collective and exterior. Yet they are experienced as deeply personal. In this sense the terms 'subjectivity' and 'objectivity', as terms describing experience, are simply unfit for purpose. Of course they were never descriptive terms, but philosophical abstractions that have their proper place in the discussion of epistemology. Yet they do also gesture towards the feeling of experience even if they are inadequate descriptions of it. For instance, weeping while a particularly sentimental movie is playing feels more subjective than collecting your receipts and invoices for a tax claim. Yet the very fact that we cry in response to the television should alert us to the way that emotional life circulates, not from within, but from without, as a response to a public culture determinedly in the thrall of a concern with 'personal life'.

For Immanuel Kant, certain forms of experience and judgement point to the objectivity of subjectivity. This argument is premised on a sense of the universality of certain qualities in the world and in certain forms of attention that take the human subject away from material concerns and concerns of the self. But we do not need to agree with this argument in all its detail to share a sense that what is felt most personally, and what is so hard to share, has a form of objective actuality. For now it is just worth pointing out, first, that if we were 'locked in' to an interiority that is non-social we would be unlikely to have any emotional, passionate life at all. It is by being social beings, by having exteriority rather than interiority, that we feel emotions. Passionate life is learnt through the outward orientations of sympathy and empathy, not by plumbing the depths of 'interior life'.

Second, if it is true that aesthetics emerges as a theorising of the passions, then this theorising doesn't take the passions as passive states of being but as modes of action and orientation. If passions are not always actions themselves they are prequels to actions. The passions (fear, grief, sadness, joy, wonder and so on) are orientations, forms of attunement to the world. They are modes and moods that explicitly describe our attachments and detachments; they name our drawing-towards and drawing-away-from, our attractions, detractions and indifferences. Aesthetics, as a theorising of passion, is concerned with pleasure and pain, virtue and vice: 'passions ... are generally understood to be thoughts or states of the soul which represent things as good or evil for us, and therefore seen as objects of inclination or aversion' (Susan James 1997: 4). What pleases and displeases inaugurates action: we pursue pleasure, turn away from pain. If we are to lead a 'virtuous life' we need to pursue the good and avert the evil.

It was the link between 'feeling' and 'doing' that was central to classical aesthetics and meant that 'taste' (the orientation of our appetites) was never going to designate a purely incidental social arena. Taste mattered because our pleasure and inclination could so easily direct us towards the 'bad', the unworthy, the evil. Aesthetics, in some senses, was always likely to be a utopian arena where people could imagine a world where virtue and plea-sure were united. In the real world, however the discrimination of objects of the passions could be resolutely conservative and bent on preserving the authority of the property-owning classes. So while the entanglement of passions, actions, virtue is problematic, its registering of aesthetic life as something more than a responsive contemplation towards the world, as something that engages us in action, is a central aspect of its productivity for an aesthetics of the ordinary.

Third, aesthetics is an ambitious attempt to approach the human creature as a physiological, psychological and ethical being, through being attuned to sensations, the senses, perception, sentiments and so on. In having a sense of the disparate complexity of creaturely life, aesthetics has a real sense of the confusions of ordinary life as we navigate and register the sensual materiality of the exterior world, drawing it towards us, inclining ourselves towards or away from the world, knowing it from 'below' (from the sensate body) as well as with the discriminating mind. Aesthetics is always an ambition that will remain unfulfilled and unfinished, but it is an ambition that is crucial for engaging in the study of ordinary life.

Fourth, and in the wake of the previous three points, aesthetics turns towards 'style' as something deeply social and significant. Over the last twenty or so years, print and broadcast journalists and entertainers, as well as critical academics, have associated the word 'style' with 'lifestyle' and established the latter as a consumer, 'off-the-peg', choice. Aesthetics reunites lifestyle with something, that while it may be hedged in from all sides by commercial forces, is not simply reducible to it. In his book *The Comfort of Things* the cultural anthropologist Daniel Miller presents thirty portraits of individuals and their relationship to the things they possess (and, as he will suggest, possess them). He writes that:

> There is an overall logic to the pattern of these relationships to both persons and things, for which I use the term 'aesthetic'. By choosing this term I don't mean anything technical or artistic, and certainly nothing pretentious. It simply helps convey something of the overall desire for harmony, order and balance that may be discerned in certain cases – and also dissonance, contradiction and irony in others.
>
> (Miller 2008: 5)

Miller uses the term 'aesthetic' to describe his informants' intimate material worlds, and my guess is that this is partly to mark his distance from the way that the term 'style' has been denigrated as a superficial aspect of our involvement with material culture.

Writing in 1968, Henri Lefebvre recognised the problem and potential of thinking about 'style' in relation to everyday life. His argument is familiar: commercialisation has emptied out the link between style and sociality and put in its place a range of superficial choices:

> With the Incas, the Aztecs, in Greece or in Rome, every detail (gestures, words, tools, utensils, costumes, etc.) bears the imprint of a *style*; nothing had as yet become prosaic, not even the quotidian; the prose

and poetry of life were still identical. Our own everyday life is typical for its yearning and quest for a style that obstinately eludes it; today there is no style, notwithstanding the attempts to achieve one by resurrecting former styles or by settling among their ruins and memories – so much so that *style* and *culture* can now be distinguished and opposed.

(Lefebvre 1984 [1968]: 29)

But here Lefebvre is remarking on the difficulty of associating his contemporary world with a single unified style. It doesn't follow, however, that the lack of a unified 'national' style results in the hollowing out of our specific lifestyles.

Six years earlier Lefebvre wrote about the way that Jean-Paul Sartre and Simone de Beauvoir's relationship was conducted as an 'experiment in transparent relationships and a mutual recognition in freedom, but also in separation'. For Lefebvre 'the essential thing is lifestyle' (Lefebvre 1995 [1962]: 358). Style is no longer the unified aesthetic of social life, but its dispersal doesn't mean that the patterns of one's life have been drained of sensual sociality. Our life practices (our ways of loving, cooking, inhabiting and so on) are not just 'consumer choices' but sensual and ethical responses to a world that makes its own demands on us. We might sometimes hanker after more luxury, but also find pleasure in frugality; we might struggle to pay the rent, but take pride in looking 'well turned out'. The sensual orchestrations and material ecologies that we can control and produce matter precisely because of the limited agency we have in the aesthetic ecology of the larger world.

Humanism

In France, in the 1960s, the foundations of structuralism and poststructuralism were built on a determined refusal of humanism. The luminaries of what became the bedrock of much theoretical work in the humanities and in certain realms of the social sciences declared the death of 'man' as a theoretical entity. For the Marxist philosopher Louis Althusser the idea of humanism could never be anything other than ideological. He argued that in 1845 Marx performed a decisive break (an epistemological break) with humanist philosophy and thereby rendered historical materialism a scientific venture. The humanist Marx gave way to the scientific Marx, and the fundamental character of this rupture was to refit himself as an 'anti-humanist':

One can and must speak openly of *Marx's theoretical anti-humanism*, and see in this *theoretical anti-humanism* the absolute (negative) precondition of the (positive) knowledge of the human world itself, and of its practical transformation. It is impossible to *know* anything about men except on the absolute precondition that the philosophical (theoretical) myth of man is reduced to ashes.

(Althusser 1963: 229)

Humanism, according to Althusser, by taking 'man' as both the subject and object of knowledge, would always be caught in the grip of idealism, because it had to posit an essential human self that it would then set about explaining:

> The earlier idealist ('bourgeois') philosophy depended in all its domains and arguments (its 'theory of knowledge', its conception of history, its political economy, its ethics, its aesthetics, etc.) on a problematic of *human nature* (or the essence of man). For centuries, this problematic had been transparency itself, and no one had thought of questioning it even in its internal modifications.
>
> (Althusser 1963: 227)

The argument was that even if 'human nature' was the object of investigation (and thereby available for competing descriptions) it was always established as a known entity in advance of such investigation.

Three years later Michel Foucault published *Les Mots et les choses* (first translated into English in 1970 as *The Order of Things: An Archaeology of the Human Sciences*). Foucault's book was an encyclopaedic study of the fate of the study of human culture throughout the seventeenth to nineteenth centuries, linking the human subject to a variety of institutional and social arrangements of knowledge. For Foucault such arrangements were the result of accretions and sedimentations resulting in something as seemingly stable as 'the human' but no more stable (in theory) than previous stabilities that now seemed to belong to religion, myth or magic:

> If those arrangements were to disappear as they appeared, if some event of which we can at the moment do no more than sense the possibility – without knowing either what its form will be or what it promises – were to cause them to crumble, as the ground of Classical thought did, at the end of the eighteenth century, then one can certainly wager that man would be erased, like a face drawn in sand at the edge of the sea.
>
> (Foucault 1974 [1966]: 387)

For Foucault, in a bid to erase 'man' from the study of culture, replacements to 'human nature' would be found in such terms as 'discourse', 'power' and 'apparatus' (*dispositif*).

We can work backwards and forwards from this point in the 1960s to make a number of claims for humanism that don't necessarily discredit anti-humanism, but certainly suggest that anti-humanists are often over-stating their case. For one thing, while the earlier 'humanist' Marx wrote about the alienation of man from man, and from his or her species-being, there is no indication of Marx knowing in advance what that species-being consisted of. In fact it would be impossible to know in advance of the endless possibility of humankind's potential as it gets realised and transformed as the material conditions of historically changing life. Thus human species-being is a heuristic device for an experimental approach to life that is dedicated to the process of species-becoming rather than to the fulfilment of a foregone destiny.

The same could be said for philosophers like David Hume writing in the eighteenth century. Hume's humanism, on one level, can hardly be in doubt. His first major study was explicitly titled A *Treatise of Human Nature* (1739–40). Yet for Hume starting out to study human nature didn't necessitate the sort of self-identical intentional subject that some anti-humanists would point to as being the major heresy for anyone wanting to demonstrate his or her theoretical sophistication. For Hume the human is often a fiction that pastes over our or his understanding of human subjectivity as a dispersal of sensations and perceptions, momentarily held together by something as undulating and hard to maintain as pride. Again so-called humanism begins to look much more like an experiment aimed at destabilising as much as stabilising any essential notion of what it is to be human.

Today the 'human being' is on the theoretical and social agenda, not because it would allow us to return to settled values, but precisely because of the insistent instability of the term 'human'. It is not hard to find reasons for this. At a time in planetary history where scientists can replicate human 'essences' under laboratory conditions; where the extinction of human life can be imagined as a real possibility in the wake of possible ecological catastrophes; where our daily life entangles us more and more with machines as much as with other humans – it would be inattentive to imagine that 'being human' wouldn't be on the agenda. While such social forces have produced a barrage of reaffirmations of the importance and centrality of a known quantity 'humanness', there has been a whole range of writing keener to launch their inquiries with an investigative air, to pursue a more modest, less humancentric version of humanism. The planet we share with animals, with the disparate populations of the globe, with machines, with practices that gobble-up the resources required to sustain life, is looking more and more fragile. It would be arrogance itself to claim that such a moment would benefit from the simple assertion of humanism as unproblematic.

Roger Smith's *Being Human: Historical Knowledge and the Creation of Human Nature*, makes the seemingly tautological point that there is no knowledge of what it is to be human outside the various attempts to know what being human is: 'historical knowledge of belief about what is human is knowledge of being human' and this is because 'writing about being human ... therefore constructs what it is to be human' (Smith 2007: 14). In a certain light this might be called an anti-humanist version of humanism, or a form of inquiry into what 'being human' is that has digested the lessons of anti-humanism but still sees the urgency of pursuing the question of what it is to be human, and sees that the most productive route to addressing that question is to open it up to the various historical approaches that have sought to answer it. This is the sort of humanism I'm keen to adopt here: one that seeks to address the question of human nature, but one that doesn't want to call time on history, one that refuses to seek the answers simply in, what at the moment passes for, 'best' knowledge.

Intimacy

There is a sense that a phrase like 'the intimacy of everyday life' is tautological: after all the everyday is full of intimate knowledges precisely because the everyday is the arena of the world most closely met. Intimacy connotes proximity, familiarity and habit. At one level intimacy suggests our bodies: our most intimate arena. How and what we eat, how we wash and what we smell like, the care we take of our bodies and those that are our dependents (babies, sick relatives and friends) are intimate concerns. Those that are closest to us (good friends and family) are our intimates. The knowledge we have of the places we live and work, the tools and equipment we most often use, are intimate knowledges.

In this book I am using the term intimate to point to two aspects of life. The first is that arena of life that is materially closest to us: this is to put forward an argument that proximity matters. Here then 'intimacy' suggests a form of attention that looks at the proximetrics of everyday life; the material world of work, for instance, seen in the form of micro-geography might include office furniture, factory humour, coffee and tea breaks, for instance. Ordinary life is life that is inhabited by fleshly beings, not by positions in the corporate hierarchy. Or rather 'positions in the corporate hierarchy' are lived out by fleshly beings in ordinary life. This is a more neutral sense of the term intimacy.

The other sense of intimacy has connotations of emotional, sexual and psychological closeness. This intimacy has traditionally desired secrecy: the trustworthiness of friends, the discretion of lovers, the enshrined secrecy of the confessional, of the doctor's surgery and the psychiatrist's couch. Yet across the centuries our intimate lives have been an object of management and intervention by governmental and commercial agents. What you do in the 'privacy of your own home' is also subject to moral and political approbation and censure. But if bureaucracy extends into the private enclaves of our intimate world and we can seek succour and solace in the publically professional spaces of medicine and religion, can we maintain a clear separation between the public and the private spheres? And if not what happens to an understanding of everyday life in response to a theoretical and material collapse of these spheres?

A phrase like 'public intimacy', which might initially register as either an oxymoron or else as a euphemism for outdoor sex, can now be used to describe a set of conditions that blur the boundaries of public and private.[4] Symptoms of the suggested collapse of the private/public spheres might be quickly signposted by pointing to the aspects of intimate private life that routinely take place in cyberspace (social networking sites such as Facebook, for instance); the amount of airtime and column inches given over to celebrity life in all its intimate details (indeed intimate details are all that is required, any consideration of the value of a celebrity in terms of professional skills is either of marginal interest or totally off-target); the massive growth of 'reality' formats on television that thrive on capturing the contestants as intimately as possible; and the quasi intimate chumminess that is adopted by politicians, presenters, disc jockeys, news readers and the like.

The media theorist Anna McCarthy, for instance, suggests that if critical studies are to take the massive expansion of reality television as more than a space for interpretive panache, then they will have to acknowledge the aspect of trauma involved in it as well as the aesthetics of neo-liberal governance that it manifests. In discussing the range of reality formats that are in circulation and by attending to the mode that sees its project as altruistic, McCarthy suggests that reality TV works as a form of governance and that 'as a form of governance, these programs are notable in their disciplinary reliance not on the inculcation of virtue but rather on shame and scolding'. Reality TV works to 'retool contempt and other deeply intimate affects into vehicles for lessons in social responsibility' (McCarthy 2007: 18). As an everyday pedagogy, reality TV mobilises the intensity of such passions as shame and contempt for its intimate cultural politics.

But if reality TV and social networking sites are relatively new, 'intimate cultural politics' is not. Eva Illouz's book *Cold Intimacies: The Making of Emotional Capitalism* seeks to give a longer history of the mobilisation of intimacy, a history that takes us back before the neo-liberal reformatting of politics as a form of public intimacy. Illouz's position is useful here as she acknowledges that as soon as you start looking at the politics and culture of intimacy, a sharp separation between public and private breaks down: 'when we view emotions as principal characters in the story of capitalism and modernity, the conventional division between an a-emotional public sphere and the private sphere saturated with emotions begins to dissolve' (Illouz 2007: 4). But this is not just the production of the veneer of 'caring capitalism', it is instrumental as a form of economics too:

> Emotional capitalism is a culture in which emotional and economic discourses and practices mutually shape each other, thus producing what I view as a broad, sweeping movement in which affect is made an essential aspect of economic behaviour and in which emotional life – especially

that of the middle classes – follows the logic of economic relations and exchange.

(Illouz 2007: 5)

Illouz's assessment of modern forms of capitalism as producing a 'cold intimacy' is premised on her investigation of the way that a therapeutic culture has been mobilised by management self-help books and the like.[5]

The relationship between economics and affect is nothing new. In the eighteenth century the philosopher Adam Smith made their conjuncture central to his understanding of human civilisation. His book *The Theory of Moral Sentiments* (1759) was a precursor to his more famous volumes of the *Wealth of Nations*. In the book on sentiments Smith lays out a theory of the passions that accords with an economic view of virtue. Prudence and sympathy will lay the foundations for a benevolent economic practice, and as such will tie the public-facing sense of virtue to the practices and performance of an intimate and private ethical sense.

The structure of the book

This book seeks to explore the ordinary aspects of aesthetics, humanism and intimacy as they overlap in ways that are often mutually reinforcing but also in ways that produce leakage, contradictions and discord. Often these themes will run implicitly through the chapters rather than receive explicit attention. My intention is not to produce abstract discussions of these themes but to see them as crucial for understanding the material actuality of everyday life as it is lived out in work environments, among the paraphernalia of domestic life, and in our sensual commerce with the world. Most of the chapters veer between theoretical discussion and concrete description, with some chapters staying much longer in one camp than the other.

In the next chapter ('Everyday aesthetics') I lay out more fully the sort of philosophical and theoretical inquiries that can be a rich resource for developing an aesthetics of ordinary life. As I have suggested already, aesthetics is often a bridging conversation between forms of feeling, emotion and sentiment and the complex materiality of the world. By attending to the ways that the sensual world presses upon us, soliciting responses and reactions, and by taking seriously the moods, experiences and energies of the perceiving subject, aesthetics is ideally placed to address life lived ordinarily. Aesthetics, at its best, attends to public feelings that are experienced intimately: it posits our most subjective experiences as social. At its worst, though, aesthetics is snobbish 'taste' dressed up as emancipation. More problematically the best and worst of aesthetics are so intricately embroiled that to separate them is often a violation of the original thought.

In this chapter I give an account of the main tenets of classical aesthetic thought in Britain (concentrating primarily on Hume, Burke and Shaftesbury).

While I recognise the dangers of cherry-picking across such a range of work to find morsels to fit an argument, my aim, as always, is to generate an aesthetics of the ordinary; and if this, at times, means skimping on a more nuanced account of the complexity of individual philosophers then that is the price I pay.[6] The chapter goes on to look at aesthetic work in the late nineteenth and twentieth centuries and particularly the work of John Dewey and, to a lesser extent, Wilhelm Dilthey. The chapter ends by exploring Jacques Rancière's recent aesthetic writing, claiming that Rancière's work links back to the ambition of classical aesthetic thought, but also takes us forward through his attention to the political ecology of technology, representation, perception and sensual distribution.

In chapter three ('Familiar things') I try to get 'in-the-midst-of-things'. While ink has been spilt trying to untangle 'objects' and 'things', here I follow the Chilean poet Pablo Neruda's injunction to study things 'at rest'. Neruda suggests that 'things' are inundated from within and from without, and I put this to the test by offering an 'inundated' account of a chair that I first sat on as an eleven year old. But if this is a subjective account of a chair, I would also claim it as a socio-naturalist account too. The chapter poses a dialogue with Michel Serres' suggestion that rather than dividing the world into subjects and objects we treat many different kinds of object as 'quasi objects' and many kinds of subject as 'quasi subjects'. Theoretically this connects to the work of Bruno Latour and others who have envisaged a techno-social project of tracing dynamic networks across human and non-human actors. But this also connects in a small way with David Hume's suggestion that the human subject is a fiction and that there is no subject, but a scattering of perceptions that finds 'subjectivity' out there in among the thingly world of possessions, of nature, of people.

In chapter four ('Doing time: work life') I look at the world of work and how it shapes notions of time, temporality and temporal experience. Boredom, waiting, anticipating and routine – rhythms that are often established through specific work cultures – produce an experience of time, while simultaneously robbing us of a sense of an evenly unfolding experience of time. Work often produces a sense of time that is at once structured and emptied. This chapter focuses on two women's accounts of work. The first is a detailed account of housework and through this I try to show the connections that are evident between temporal experience and emotional, affective life. Emotion colours time; intensifying it, elongating it, syncopating it, truncating it and filling it. We all know that time flies when you are having fun, but what happens to time if resentment is the dominant mood? The second account follows a journalist who interviews men and women involved in highly routinised forms of labour. She finds it hard to get much information about the working life of typists and ends up getting a job filling out membership forms for the kennel club of America. In her account of routine typing the rhythms of patterned work are seen as both highly seductive and exhausting (in many respects the exhaustion is the prerequisite for the seduction). But within her account the sensual and social landscape of the typing pool is a constant material presence that extends routine work beyond being merely an accommodation with the instrumentalism of capital.

In chapter five ('Absentminded media') I look at the roles of media in everyday life. Part of this chapter revisits earlier media theory in the form of the work of Siegfried Kracauer and Walter Benjamin and their use of the term 'distraction'. Distraction is a condensed term bringing together a sense of dispersal, diffusion and drift with a more evaluative sense of misdirection. After all to be diverted and misdirected by a distracting media is only worth mentioning if what you are being diverted from is deemed important in some way (the political aspect of diversion is nearly always to the fore in this understanding of distraction). Like many others I see distraction as crucial for attending to everyday media. But whereas distraction is often taken as a sort of low-level concentration, or lack of concentration, I follow Benjamin here in seeing distraction as intricately tied up with absorption (rather than the inverse of absorption).

This chapter also casts us back into the drift of the ordinary by attending to the dispersal of attention across a variety of media forms, particularly television and radio (though scouring the internet, sites like YouTube in particular follow similar characteristics). Casual radio listening and TV watching provide better examples of dispersed absorption than watching a film or playing a computer game, precisely because these latter forms often solicit a directed and singular form of attention. The sense of distracted attention, that is often encouraged by the media forms that the twentieth century has supplied, link us back to the aesthetic theory of the eighteenth century where the receptive forms of perception were ascribed to those states of mind that were seen as most vacant.

In chapter six ('Senses of the ordinary') the question of habit and routine comes to the fore in the domestic realm. Here I invoke the literal sense of confusion to describe experiences which meld together sensual and mental experiences. What is happening when you are doing something but not concentrating on it? The body knows what it is doing; it is feeling its way around kitchens, undoing jars, stirring bubbling rice, smelling the aromas, tasting the seasoning. The sensual field of co-mingled bodies and things is an arena where habit allows the body to have the cognitive upper hand. Here care is given and love is practised; frustration is enacted and violence is erupting. This chapter looks in detail at an example of aggressive food consumption in the practice of eating ultra-hot (spicy hot) curries in Britain (a practice that may well be in decline but was a popular aspect of young male Anglo-Celtic culture in the 1970s and 1980s). Here food offers a specific example of the deeply intimate encounter with public affects, and collective passions. Food is always simultaneously both supremely intimate and intensely social as it connects us to the culture of agro-business and global food markets, and to the body's most immediate aversions and inclinations. But while the practice of aggressive eating is clearly problematic I argue that food eating is a crucial element of actual multicultural environments and is a continual process of adopting and adapting.

In the final chapter ('Towards a political aesthetics of everyday life') I remind myself that ordinary, everyday life is a consistent theme of state politics: it is used in a number of forms, but is primarily used as a vehicle of protection against all kinds of real-and-fantastical threats. Ordinary national life is what xenophobic politics insists must be protected from cultural migrations that might alter its traditions and dilute its character; ordinary family life, for paternalistic culture, must be protected from sexual dissidents, from predatory culture, from the unknowable outside. Ordinary life is the arena of fear and threat as much as it is of reassurance and safety. In other words it is a highly charged political arena.

Political aesthetic inquiry into the ordinary has a responsibility to try and understand the way that the opaque and oblique machinations of global politics (economic, environmental and cultural) punctuate and syncopate the rhythms of ordinary life. Yet perhaps the bigger obligation is to understand and champion forms of ordinary culture that are generous and world-enlarging but that also maintain the securities of habitual life that are a necessity for any ordinary life.

Notes

1 For an investigative account of shopping that has a wonderfully everyday sense of itself see Meagan Morris 'Things to do with Shopping Centers' in Morris 1998.
2 This, incidentally, turned out to be the case.
3 The literature on modernity is too vast to note here, but see, for example Jervis 1998, and Schwartz 1999, and the edited collection Charney and Schwartz 1996, for useful guides.
4 See for instance Bruno 2007 and the edited collection Berlant 2000.
5 For an account of the links between intimacy and economics in personal life see Zelizer 2005.
6 Work in cultural studies has sometimes exhibited an unhealthy jackdaw approach to theory, which has on occasion meant seriously distorting theoretical approaches. In this book I try to balance a careful account of aesthetic theory with maintaining the focus on substantiating 'everyday-life aesthetics'.

Chapter 2

Everyday aesthetics

To enter the world of philosophical aesthetics, particularly in the period of the British Enlightenment, is to be plunged into a world that is riven with incompatible values, gendered assumptions and class antagonisms. There is no possibility of assuaging these conflicts or pacifying them. Nor is there much point in scouring this discursive terrain with the 'cleaning power' of twenty-first-century values and concerns (it is just too easy to point fingers at elitism). My aim in this chapter is to offer a very selective account of aesthetic theory (from the early eighteenth century to the present day) in an attempt to articulate a set of concerns and approaches that can help me have some purchase on the more opaque aspects of daily life. In this my approach is shamelessly partial and opportunistic: I want to scavenge among some of the monuments of aesthetic thinking looking for shards of insight that can lay the foundations for an approach to everyday life. I'm looking for theoretical opportunities and philosophical happenstance out of which to pursue an approach to everyday life that can maintain an attention towards the wonderfully disparate (but also troublesome and deflating) textures, rhythms and affects of the ordinary.

It is true, of course, that aesthetics is overly enamoured of the beautiful and by art, yet in its approach to social life as a sensorial realm its essential proclivities are directed towards the ordinary. This chapter aims at encouraging these proclivities. But first it is worth acknowledging that aesthetic thinking, at least in its Enlightenment period, is filled with the kind of patrician assertions that can make twenty-first-century readers wince or giggle. This is Edmund Burke laying out his store of what counts as the constitutive elements of beauty:

> First, to be comparatively small. Secondly, to be smooth. Thirdly, to have a variety in the direction of the parts; but fourthly, to have those parts not angular, but melted as it were into each other. Fifthly, to be of a delicate frame, without any remarkable appearance of strength. Sixthly, to have its colours clear and bright; but not strong and glaring. Seventhly, or if it should have any glaring colour, to have it diversified

with others. These are, I believe, the properties on which beauty depends; properties that operate by nature, and are less liable to be altered by caprice, or confounded by a diversity of tastes, than any others.

(Burke 1998 [1759]: 107)

The only thing I could imagine that would fit all this would be a multi-coloured cloud or more realistically a posy of flowers (though it is more likely that what Burke had in mind was a particular form of the female body). To be so assertive about smoothness, and to award it universal value, is to count all those who might prefer roughness as misguided and deficient in their discernment.

If this was all there was to aesthetics we may as well bid farewell to it immediately: clearly it would be of marginal interest in the study of every-day life. But of course there is more to aesthetics, and more to Burke, than this. In this chapter I want to work across three different formulations of aesthetics. The first is Enlightenment aesthetics (though proto-aesthetics might be the more accurate or pedantic term). In the eighteenth century, especially in Britain, taste and discernment are part of a general investigation of human, creaturely life. They take their place in an account of human life animated by the energy of the passions. For a panoply of writers (and there is little sense of a unified discourse here) the question of what it is to be human is also a question of how to live. If human beings are continually responsive to a range of passions that could include ambition, shame, wonder, greed and indifference, then the point of aesthetics was simulta-neously to describe this and to adjudicate on what passions we should surrender to, what passions need to be tempered, and what passions threaten to undo us entirely. The quest that aesthetics names is one aimed at both describing the 'lowly' realm of sensorial perception and directing sensitivity towards virtuous goals (the improvement of sensitivity). What is central here is the way that so many Enlightenment writers give an account of intimate feelings as emanating from the pell-mell of social intercourse. So while the passions might well be experienced 'subjectively' they are in a very real sense objective in that they 'belong' as much to the objective world as they do to the experiencing individual.

The second formation takes us to North America and primarily to the work of the pragmatist John Dewey. Dewey's work draws explicitly on the work of William James and implicitly on the writing of the German philo-sopher Wilhelm Dilthey. This is a tradition of writing that takes its central object to be the examination of the nature of experience. Crucial to this tradition (or at least to both Dilthey and Dewey) is the division of experience into a number of interrelated qualities. Experience, in the English language, is often seen to include both the sense of experience as the ongoing, moment-to-moment, sensate registering of creaturely life (this is the world of sentient experience, of sensations being registered by perceiving subjects) and the notion of accumulated empirical knowledge (for example, when we say something like 'she is an experienced carpenter'). In this chapter sentience and accumulated knowledge are given a third articulation: this is the sense of experience as 'lived through', experience that is eventful for the subject without being retrospectively acknowledged as such through processes of reflection. In German the term *Erlebnis* has been used by philosophers (particularly Dilthey) to describe the sorts of experience that are self-establishing moments while also being prereflexive. Such experience is immediate and foundational, but is also historically determined as perception and expression collide in the 'having' of an experience.

The third and final section of this chapter is concerned with the recent work of philosopher and historian Jacques Rancière. Rancière's contribution to aesthetics mixes art historical sketches (painted with a considerably broad brush) with a political disposition that goes beyond an assessment of either the politics commitments of artists or the political effects of art. For Rancière both art and politics participate in what he calls the distribution of the sensible (*le partage du sensible*). The distribution or parcelling-out of the sensible is what organises a historically specific orchestration of what is seen or felt as notable, perceivable, valuable, noticeable and so on. While it is an awareness of the ranking of the social and natural world, it is an awareness that is lived bodily, consciously and unconsciously, and responsively. It is the form of attention that orientates people towards the sensorial world but doesn't ultimately determine their place within it. Crucially it isn't established once and for all, and in this way both aesthetic and political acts (which certainly aren't limited to those specialists we call artists and politicians) redistribute the sensible in ways that alter sensorial perception.

Giving inordinate attention to the ordinary (and Rancière sees this as a foundational move in most of the artistic movements that have emerged since the end of the eighteenth century) is to participate in the distribution and redistribution of the sensible. For Rancière such attention always has a pedagogic aspect to it, but one not 'handed out' by knowledgeable school teachers and university professors. The pedagogy of the ordinary, then, implicates us all as active participants in its portioning and partitioning. We are both subjected to a specific distribution of the sensible and active in apportioning sensorial actuality.

What links the three parts of this chapter is an insistent questioning of the human subject as originator of feelings, emotions and affects. Here aesthetics both names the subject as the site where worldly sensations take on shape and form (in experience, in perception, in affect) and names the subject that responds to the sensate world and acts by affecting others and by distributing the sensible. In essence aesthetics names the exteriority of 'interior' life and the sociality of passions as they circulate in ways that are interpersonal and transpersonal. This is a material world made up of seemingly immaterial forces (such as ambition, pity and pride). If aesthetics has come to name the ordinary and extraordinary productions and experiences associated with art (or the arts), it also, more fundamentally, names a world of rising and diminishing intensities of affect that congregate and dissipate in society.

Enlightenment aesthetics

When Alexander Gottlieb Baumgarten first extensively mobilised the term aesthetics in his work of 1750, *Aesthetica* (unfinished and written in Latin) he was clear that the goal of aesthetics was never simply explanatory and descriptive. So while aesthetics was going to be the 'science of sensual cognition' (Baumgarten cited in Hammermeister 2002: 7) it was also dedicated to the transformation of 'sensitive knowledge': 'the aim of aesthetics as a discipline is the development and improvement of the sensitive knowledge' (Baumgarten cited in Gross 2002: 410). At one and the same time Baumgarten approaches a realm of life while moving away from it. On one level this is because he distrusts sensual cognition as scientific knowledge: 'impressions received from the senses, fantasies, emotional disturbances, etc. are unworthy of philosophers and beneath the scope of their consideration' (Baumgarten 1750: 490). Yet while this might seem to discourage investigation into the day-to-day experiences of routine creaturely life Baumgarten provides some of the key elements for grasping it. Perhaps his most useful contribution for the production of an ordinary aesthetics is his insistence that the realms of sensual knowledge cannot be characterised by the kinds of value that might be associated with reason. So while we might judge ideas in terms of their clarity, or their simplicity, the world of sensual cognition is more adequately characterised by complexity, confusion and diffusion: 'sensitive knowledge is complex representation below the threshold where the analytical separation of discrete elements of that representation becomes possible' (Baumgarten cited in Gross 2002: 410). The aesthetic realm of life isn't going to be easily analysed by the same tools that are appropriate for analysis in the natural sciences or logic.

While Baumgarten was writing his version of aesthetics in Germany (Frankfurt) a number of 'British' writers (many of whom were working in Scotland and Ireland) had already concocted an approach to the sensorial world that is similarly marked by a desire to 'improve' sensitivity while also providing innovative accounts of the realm of sentiment, sensation and the passions. The work that makes up this body of thought is extensive, but any account that tried to do justice to it would need to mention: the third Earl of Shaftesbury's *Characteristicks of Men, Manners, Opinions, Times, with a Collection of Letters* (first published in 1711); Francis Hutcheson's *An Inquiry into the Original of Our Ideas of Beauty and Virtue* from 1725; Edmund Burke's *A Philosophical Enquiry into the Origin of our Ideas of the Sublime and Beautiful* of 1759; Adam Smith's *The Theory of Moral Sentiments* also of 1759; and Archibald Alison's *Essays on the Nature and Principles of Taste* from 1790. David Hume's essay 'Of the Standard of Taste', from 1757, also belongs to this tradition; and, more importantly, Hume's *A Treatise of Human Nature* (published in 1739 and 1740) needs to be seen as a central component of Enlightenment aesthetic thinking more generally, concerned as it is with mapping sensorial and passionate life.[1]

While many of these writers differ in fundamental ways (some are religious thinkers while others tend towards a form of implicit atheism) there are overriding concerns that shape aesthetic thinking in Britain at this time. Less a shared set of assumptions then, than a shared sense of a problematic to investigate. Enlightenment aesthetics, before it is concerned with taste, for instance, inquires into the conditions of humanness in a world ordered and disordered by interests, appetites and passions. If a human being was fundamentally creaturely, prone to pursuing his or her own pleasures, beholden to their appetites and motivated by their self-interest, then what would this mean for civil society? One answer had already been forthcoming from the seventeenth century and this was Thomas Hobbes' *Leviathan* from 1651. *Leviathan* maps out the social structures for a society where self-interest (the pursuit of self-preservation and the lust for glory) are only held in check by a form of governance of extreme elaboration. The aestheticians of the eighteenth century wanted, on the whole, to explain how humankind was not reducible to self-interest, but had a capacity for a larger range of interests and feelings (which might include, among many possibilities, sympathetic responses to the plight of others). Those that argued for the basic self-interest of human activity and action often clung (of necessity) to a morality that could only function in terms of censure and asceticism. To argue that virtue could be part of nature was, ultimately, to see pleasure as a possible source of good, rather than as an indication that the appetites had been given free reign. At issue then was not just what a human being was but also the possible value of pleasure itself, and an understanding of a virtuous self that is governed by fine feelings, rather than by fancy or appetite.

But while the stakes of aesthetic thinking were directed towards fundamental philosophical questions (the possibilities of virtue, the nature of the self) these writers were also preoccupied with describing a world empirically given. It is the concern with a world that meets a body, with a life populated by perceptions and sensations, that characterises Enlightenment aesthetics. The materialism of the passions is evident across this discursive terrain. Passions activate not just the imagination but also the responsive body. One easy example of this is to look at a passion like fear: 'The Passion of Fear ... determines the Spirits to the Muscles of the Knees, which are instantly ready to perform their Motion; by taking up the Legs with incomparable Celerity, in order to remove the Body out of harm's way' (Shaftesbury 1710: 294). But while fear and desire might be seen to act on the mindful-body in consort with the imagination, the same can also be said about other passions such as envy, wonder, shame, pride and so on. It is this material, sensual world of the body and of the lively energies that circulate between and across people, and that animate the thingly world, that come first in this work. Taste and discernment presuppose the passions and the materialism of our responses to the world. And it is this orientation that holds out so much potential for everyday aesthetics. To pursue this further I am going to discuss aesthetics under three propositions: that aesthetics is a theory of the human self; that aesthetics is a theory of the passions; and that aesthetics is a theory of virtue.

Aesthetics as a theory of the human self

The Enlightenment aesthetics that I'm interested in here is, to a greater or lesser extent, empirical. It is concerned with forms of knowledge that are gathered by sentient creatures reaching out and pulling back from the world.[2] If empiricism proposes that knowledge is gathered by the senses then the question that remains is: what is the condition of that 'self' who possesses sense and gathers knowledge? We could say, then, that Enlightenment aesthetics necessarily posits an 'empirical self'. All sentient humans might flinch when they come in contact with burning wood, but how do we imagine an empirical self in a world animated by passions, perceptions and appetites? Empiricism as a science of knowledge has a number of problems to confront. If the world can only be known via the experiences of sentient creatures then what would give this knowledge validity? If empiricism is to bank on a knowledge generated by a perceiving subject then is that knowledge fundamentally individualistic, and if so, how authoritative could it be? Does empiricism need to suppose that all human creatures are basically the same or could it function assuming that what is known by me is not necessarily known by you? More worryingly, how could it proceed as a reputable philosophical approach if it recognised that not only do individual humans experience the world differently but that a single human might experience the same world differently depending on their changing condition and disposition.[3]

Empiricism responds to such problems by grasping them as central to the actual possibility of knowing the world. The mindful and creaturely body is empiricism's first and only analytic instrument. It is, however, not merely an instrument that passively records the world around it: the productivity of this instrument is guaranteed by precisely that which might lead you to wonder about its reliability. The ability of the mindful, creaturely body to intricately know the world is shown by its capacity to react and adjust, rather than by its constancy. Just as litmus paper changes colour at the merest hint of alkali or acidic solutions, or as mercury in a barometer expands and contracts in relation to atmospheric pressure, so the human being is constantly changing in relation to its sensorial and passionate context: your anger produces fear or shame or anger in me, and my angry-self perceives the world differently from my shamed-self. This, for instance, is the third Earl of Shaftesbury describing the endlessly adjusting subject in a world animated by passion. He writes of how love of praise (vanity) alters a person's interest (their orientation) towards the world, and consequently their perception of it:

> The same must happen in respect to Anger, Ambition, Love, Desire, and the Passions from whence I frame the different Notion I have of Interest. For as these Passions veer, my Interest veers, my Steerage varys; and I make alternately, now this, now that, to be my Course and Harbour. The Man in Anger, has a different Happiness from the Man in Love. And the Man lately become covetous, has a different Notion of Satisfaction from what he had before, when he was liberal. Even the Man of Humour, has another Thought of Interest and Advantage than the Man out of Humour, or in the least disturb'd.
>
> (Shaftesbury 1710: 296–97)

The empirical self of Enlightenment aesthetics is hardly a model of consistency. Yet rather than this undermining knowledge of the world it becomes part of the precondition for what will turn out to be a form of sympathetic empiricism (as opposed to a solipsistic empiricism, if there could be such a thing).

If, when I'm cross and irritable (or 'out of humour' to use the coinage of the eighteenth century) I am, to all intents and purposes, a different self than when I'm happy and patient, then this does not mean that we should think of empiricism as beset by subjectivism. 'Subjectivity' and 'objectivity' don't fit the empirical mindset because empiricism doesn't imagine a self-authoring subject that might be beholden to overly subjective experience. The object world, or the world at large, that someone like Shaftesbury is interested in is a world that could be described as intimate and emotional. In a sense the objective world for Shaftesbury is left looking quite similar to the sort of world that might be described as subjective. In contrast the more internal world, which is constantly adjusting to the circulation of intense forces of feelings, is both one where you could find a means of resisting the endless see-saw of social-emotional life, and where the social takes hold. In the same essay Shaftesbury continues:

> The Examination, therefore, of my Humours, and the Inquiry after my Passions, must necessarily draw along with it the Search and Scrutiny of my Opinions, and the sincere Consideration of my Scope and End. And thus the Study of human Affection cannot fail of leading me towards the Knowledge of human Nature, and of My-self.
>
> (Shaftesbury 1710: 297)

Passionate life might constantly transform the human self, but it also provides an opportunity for learning about the actuality of human nature and about the self as an adjusting organism, often governed by appetites but not ultimately determined by them.[4]

The empirical self in Enlightenment aesthetics takes many forms. Shaftesbury's self is one that 'belongs' to a constantly adjusting organism but also one that struggles to temper the excessive vagaries of passionate life. The epistemological enemy of empiricism in Shaftesbury is not subjectivity but 'fancy': 'For if Fancy be left Judg of any thing, she must be Judg of all. Every-thing is right, if anything be so, because I *fansy it*' (322).[5] Fancy is the empirical self bereft of discernment, unable to register the social-sensual world because he or she is too beholden to self-interests (to ambition, to vanity, to their appetites). Fancy is the name of the asocial self, locked into a solipsistic universe, desensitised to the passions circulating without. For Shaftesbury, sensitivity (which, paradoxically, is both learnt and innate) is not an inward looking accomplishment but a worldly and social form of empiricism. The empirical self for Shaftesbury is a production within a larger empirical universe in which the subject is an instrument measuring and adjusting, while also adjudicating and readjusting.

Writing slightly later than Shaftesbury, David Hume provides a radical reinterpretation of the empirical self. If Shaftesbury's self is one that has to steer an endlessly adjusting organism, then Hume's self is ultimately 'fictitious' (Hume 1985 [1739–40]: 306). For Hume the human 'subject' is the meeting place of sensations and passions that are herded together (but not held together) by the body's cognitive and corporeal capacities. The various modes and states of the empirical self:

> are nothing but a bundle of different perceptions, which succeed each other with an inconceivable rapidity, and are in a perpetual flux and movement. Our eyes cannot turn in their sockets without varying our perceptions. Our thought is still more variable than our sight, and all our other senses and faculties contribute to this change; nor is there any single power of the soul, which remains unalterably the same, perhaps for one moment. The mind is a kind of theatre, where several perceptions successively make their appearance; pass, repass, glide away, and mingle in an infinite variety of postures and situations.
>
> (Hume 1985 [1739–40]: 300–01)

If there is a 'self' here that offers any possibility of coherence and sustained discernment it is certainly nothing that you would ascribe the word 'identity' to.[6] For Hume the self or the soul is a loose confederacy of different elements knitted together by dependency, rivalry and reciprocation:

I cannot compare the soul more properly to any thing than to a republic or commonwealth, in which the several members are united by the reciprocal ties of government and subordination, and give rise to other persons, who propagate the same republic in the incessant changes of its parts.

(1985 [1739–40]: 309)

Hume's subject is a disparate coalition of the faculties. Hume, then, might seem to offer us a subject that is a non-self which acts like a rudderless craft blown hither and thither by the winds of passion. Such a state of affairs would not be too far away from a self that is ruled by fancy. Like Shaftesbury, Hume has to establish forms of management that could steer this dispersed vessel on something other than a wayward path. For Hume this management takes two forms: one is the practice of tasteful discernment that holds the passions in check by moderating them; the other is through the passions themselves, and primarily through the passion of pride.

Aesthetics as a theory of the passions

Before we get back to Hume and pride it is worth momentarily recognising how the passions are imagined in relation to the task that aesthetics is most commonly thought to pursue.[7] For Edmund Burke one of the most trenchant aims of A Philosophical Enquiry into the Origin of our Ideas of the Sublime and Beautiful was to contribute towards 'an exact theory of our passions' (1998 [1759]: 1). The method was empirical and required: 'a diligent examination of our passions in our own breasts'; an investigation of the characteristics and qualities of things that incite passions; and 'a sober and attentive investigation of the laws of nature, by which those properties are capable of affecting the body, and thus of exciting our passions' (1). What may seem on the face of it to be a fairly ad hoc account of the sublime and beautiful sees its task as trying to understand the nature of the passions as they animate human bodies. What could be passed off as an exercise in inculcating taste, conceives of itself as a treatise on the natural and social interactions between world and body as both are energised and governed by passions.

The passions are essential for aesthetics because, paradoxically, they link artistic material to the creaturely world, as well as separating a world of rehearsed passions from the world of actuality. Thus Burke can recognise that there are lots of passions that we enjoy as an artistic performance (the tragic, the horrific, for instance, or fear) that we would hate if they were part of actuality. But he also recognised at the same time that passions, irrespective of their condition as actual or performed, intimately connect us to social emotions: 'for terror is a passion which always produces delight when it does not press too close, and pity is a passion accompanied with pleasure, because it arises from love and social affection' (Burke 1998 [1759]: 42).[8] The passions then are crucial for aesthetics because, for writers like Burke and Hume, passions are what give social force to communication and artistic performance, and this allows us to reflect on and manage our passions. For Hume, in particular, the passion of pride is central in that it organises the sensorial subject into a perceiving self.

The second book of Hume's *Treatise*, which is called 'Of the Passions', starts out by outlining the importance of pride and humility. For Hume pride is the most important of the passions precisely because it can give shape to the empirical self and thereby give some coherence to the experience of the passions in general. The status of pride (and to a lesser degree humility) is so central to Hume's account of the passions that one commentator refers to pride as a 'meta-passion'.[9] Pride knits together the disparate perceptions and affects that the individual undergoes and marshals them around a narrative of self:

> nature has given to the organs of the human mind, a certain disposition fitted to produce a peculiar impression or emotion, which we call *pride*: To this emotion she has assign'd a certain idea, *viz.* that of *self*, which it never fails to produce.
>
> (Hume 1985 [1739–40]: 338)

Pride and humility make the self in the name of what today would more likely be called ego. Pride and humility mark subjects' sense of self-worth both in their own eyes and in the eyes of a community. At times it is hard to see the causal relationship between pride and self. In the order in which Hume writes it would seem that it is pride as a social passion that produces the self, yet he also seems to suggest that it is self that allows pride and humility to be experienced: 'when self enters not into the consideration, there is no room either for pride or humility' (1985 [1739–40]: 329). Nor is the relationship between humility and pride particularly clear: if pride knits the self together, would this mean that humility pulls it apart? Or, perhaps more likely, are pride and humility equally strong in constituting and vivifying the self, while the other passions are devoid of self-making abilities? This might follow from ordinary experience. Pride puffs us up, makes us 'glow with pride'; humility and its cognates (shame, for instance) make us 'self-conscious' in our excruciating embarrassment, draw attention to our self-failings. Fear, for instance, in the face of a roaring lion, neither makes nor unmakes the self (that would be the lion's job); rather it produces non-self experiences, even if we 'fear for ourselves'. Yet there are self-undoing aspects to shame and, probably, self-constituting aspects to other passions (envy, for instance, or jealousy).

Pride suggests that the empirical self is reformatted by passion to the point where the fiction of the self at least has a coherent (though perhaps not reliable) narrator. But does this suggest that the self that discerns, that experiences the world through the prism of self-esteem and its opposite, is self-interested? One of the tasks that Hume performs by privileging pride and humility as the central passion is that it forces a relationship between self and social collectivity. Initially Hume's account of pride seems entirely bound up with property ownership, to the point where unless you had a nice house it would be hard to see how you might be proud in Hume's world. Yet pride is not only about self-interest. Pride for Hume is where social approbation and disapproval are acted out across the individual's body and soul.[10] For Hume you can't have pride in what has been deemed socially unworthy. In this sense of course, humility and humiliation are even more evident of the social nature of the passions.[11] Yet I am less interested here in whether shame and pride are the primary passions or whether they are the only passions that are constitutive of a sense of self, than I am in looking at the form and movement of passions in relation to self. This might best be referred to as 'aesthetic ecology', in as much as it is concerned with the relationship between organisms and the environment, and here pride and humility have something more general to say about the dynamic circulation of passions and the empirical self.[12]

Hume suggests that houses and possessions allow you to experience pride.[13] Yet, like the other passions, pride and humility are not once-and-for-all conditions. Hume's work on possessions can be read as an attempt to stabilise what seem to be inherently unstable states. You say my singing-voice is nice but how long can I thrive on the energy of this compliment; how much pride can I muster from it and how long will it last? Clearly this is the condition of all the passions: I am filled with wonder when I first see a new city, but after a few years of living there the city is perceived through a veil of worn familiarity. And it is this aspect of the passions – their incessant intensifying and dissipating – that brings the passions onto the stage of the ordinary.

The first book of Hume's *Treatise* has an astonishing ending that offers a snapshot of how passion and self connect and disconnect with daily life. As a conclusion to book one ('Of the Understanding') Hume tells us, at considerable length, that his condition is 'wretched':

> I am first affrighted and confounded with that forelorn solitude, in which I am plac'd in my philosophy, and fancy myself some strange uncouth monster, who not being able to mingle and unite in society, has been expell'd all human commerce, and left utterly abandon'd and disconsolate.

(1985 [1739–40]: 311–12)

In some ways it is a classic rhetorical ploy telling you, the reader, how much it has cost the writer to journey into such deep and uncharted philosophical waters. It is also recognition that Hume's findings are not 'easy': not only does their scepticism dissolve the presence of divine power, they also undermine the idea of personal identity located in either a secular or a divine soul. In this sense the desolate isolation he feels is an anticipation of the possible reception that the book might garner.

But first and foremost it is an act of self-humiliation: of seeing his words as monstrous and uncouth, as a foul and impolite thought. It thereby anticipates the beginning of the next book ('Of the Passions') which begins by alerting us to the importance of pride and humility for producing a 'self'. To a degree it works to balance an account of humility and pride that over-privileges pride. But if we weren't prepared for Hume's despair, more surprising still is a passage which follows which witnesses the dissolution of Hume's desolation:

> Most fortunately it happens, that since reason is incapable of dispelling these clouds, nature herself suffices to that purpose, and cures me of this philosophical melancholy and delirium, either by relaxing this bent of mind, or by some avocation, and lively impression of my senses, which obliterate all these chimeras. I dine, I play a game of back-gammon, I converse, and am merry with my friends; and when after three or four hour's amusement, I wou'd return to these speculations, they appear so cold, and strain'd, and ridiculous, that I cannot find in my heart to enter into them any farther.
>
> (1985 [1739–40]: 316)

Despair disappears as Hume eats, plays backgammon and chats. It is a moment of bathos: one minute he is dying of shame, then next happily chatting to friends. It is a point that many people caught in cycles of psychic pain would find trite, but it is a point that has more general significance for an ecology of everyday affects: intensities dissipate, passions dissolve, emotional concentrations scatter. Hume doesn't so much make the point as perform it.

This suggests that the aesthetic investigation of the empirical self, however much it may be constituted through the work of pride, is always in a relationship of centripetal and centrifugal forces: coming together and falling apart, rising and falling, solidifying and melting. If the everyday can be considered an ecology where passions circulate in a perpetual state of intensification and entropic decline, the empirical self (and not just Hume's version of it) is essentially in a state of flux. This posits the human as an organism constantly adjusting to its passionate environment, with a self that is constantly appearing and disappearing, crystallising and dissolving.

Aesthetics as a theory of virtue

Throughout this section I have been rehearsing a point that is central to the book as whole: our feelings, emotions and passions that seem so 'private' and 'internal' are, in actuality, social-material forces that circulate externally. These forces are constitutive of experience and of experiences that are felt to be 'internal'. It is the world that has got under our skin and has stirred us to the core. The question, though, is by what mechanisms could passion work to animate our soul and motivate our actions? How do these passionate intensities get from 'out there' to 'in here'? Once the argument that humans are only motivated by self-preservation and by glory is dispatched something needs to put in its place that can account for the circulation of feelings that are more indirect than fear, desire and hatred. What for instance could be said about the passions of pity or envy? Pity, it turns out, leads us most directly towards the decisive mechanism for the circulation of the indirect passions, especially those that might seem to encourage 'finer feelings':

> 'Twill be easy to explain the passion of *pity*, from the precedent reasoning concerning *sympathy*. We have a lively idea of every thing related to us. All human creatures are related to us by resemblance. Their persons, therefore, their interests, their passions, their pains and pleasures must strike upon us in a lively manner, and produce an emotion similar to the original one; since a lively idea is easily converted to an impression. If this be true in general, it must be more so of affliction and sorrow. These have always a stronger and more lasting influence than any pleasure or enjoyment.
>
> (Hume 1985 [1739–40]: 418)

The empirical self, we must remember, is first and foremost an instrument, and this instrument's sensitivity in registering or knowing the passionate world is dependent on its ability to be transformed. The world as a series of passionate intensities 'strike upon us in a lively manner', and in doing so passions move from one empirical self to another (though there is no reason to assume that non-human intensities couldn't also work in the same way). This is the empirical self as an adjusting organism, as both emitter and receiver of circulating intensities (of high and low frequencies).

Sympathy, while it may afford pity, has to be thought of as a social mechanism rather than as a quality.[14] A sympathetic relationship might be fashioned in relation to joy, wonder, fear and so on, not simply in relation to a tragedy that has befallen another.[15] A sympathetic connection can be made in the name of greed and monstrosity. Sympathy, of itself, is neither virtuous nor villainous: it requires training. And it is here that taste becomes the crucial moderator for an organism that might be too easily struck 'in a lively manner'. In an essay called 'Of the Delicacy of Taste and

Passion' Hume warns against being over-delicate in matters of worldly passion. By this he means that being too 'responsive', too sensitive, to the vagaries of the passions will not just heighten pleasure, but will also heighten pain. To react to each and every emission of passion is to be blown hither and thither, and to be beholden to a world beyond your control.

Yet while delicacy of passion can be a dangerous thing, delicacy of taste can manage worldly sensitivity, directing it towards virtuous ends, moderating the hold that the passionate world might have over us:

> I am persuaded that nothing is so proper to cure us of this delicacy of passion, as the cultivating of that higher and more refined taste, which enables us to judge of the characters of men, of the compositions of genius, and of the productions of the nobler arts.
>
> (Hume 1777: 11)

Hume posits taste as the social training ground for moderation and virtuousness. But taste is an unstable and contested terrain:

> Among a thousand different opinions which different men may enter- tain of the same subject, there is one, and but one, that is just and true: and the only difficulty is to fix and ascertain it. On the contrary, a thousand different sentiments, excited by the same object, are all right; because no sentiment represents what is really in the object. ... Beauty is no quality in things themselves: it exists merely in the mind which contemplates them; and each mind perceives a different beauty.
>
> (Hume 1757: 136–37)

On the one hand, then, the very forum that could guarantee a certain degree of control over passionate life is itself radically unstable. On the other hand just because sentiments are unstable doesn't mean that the object world isn't, for all that, organised around qualities that produce these sentiments:

> Though it be certain that beauty and deformity, more than sweet and bitter, are not qualities of objects, but belong entirely to the sentiment, internal and external, it must be allowed, that there are certain qualities in objects which are fitted by nature to produce those particular feelings.
>
> (Hume 1757: 141)

Hume's philosophy of taste is caught in the empiricist trap of having to posit a world of secure values that might be found 'out there' in the object world. In the end such a position is secured only by the most conventional and ideological assertions. For Hume 'good taste' (or sensitive taste) is secured through critical elites and national traditions:

> Wherever you can ascertain a delicacy of taste, it is sure to meet with approbation; and the best way of ascertaining it is, to appeal to those models and principles which have been established by the uniform consent and experience of nations and ages.
>
> (Hume 1757: 143)

It is also asserted by the 'innate' superiority that 'men of taste' decree: 'The coarsest daubing contains a certain lustre of colours and exactness of imitation, which are so far beauties, and would affect the mind of a peasant or Indian with the highest admiration' (Hume 1757: 144). Taste, then, is most immediately a lesson in convention and obedience, and it is a lesson that is structured by imperial and aristocratic structures. There is little point in trying to recover a progressive cultural politics from taste training.[16] Yet as a way of directing sympathy it is worth making one last point.

Sympathy, directed out towards the passionate and objective world, is not, for eighteenth-century aesthetics, a form of identification. While Hume suggests that sympathy requires 'resemblance' he is clear that this resemblance is at the level of species rather than social group. In as much as sympathy is an opening out towards the qualities of the world then 'identity' would be a hindrance rather than a help. And it is here that Enlightenment aesthetics poses a form of attention that will be crucial for an understanding of the aesthetic ecology of the ordinary. The sympathetic orientation to the passionate world activates the interests of the subject. But as we have seen with Shaftesbury 'interest' is clearly not homogenous. If self-interest posits one extreme of the orientation of the subject disinterest posits the other. When Kant published his *Critique of Judgement* in 1790 disinterested contemplation became the cornerstone for aesthetic thinking. Historians of philosophy have argued that 'disinterested' contemplation can already be seen in the tradition of British empiricist aesthetics from earlier in the century.[17] This argument doesn't need rehearsing here. More crucially I want to draw attention to the way that interests are more finely modulated. Kant uses disinterest to argue that aesthetic judgements result in a form of subjective objectivity. But in as much as the British empirical tradition describes a much more dynamic ecology where the self (and the self-interest, or self-concern) is in a perpetual state of flux, what is worth suggesting is that interest is itself multiple and that it isn't either selfish or selfless, but moves across a continuum of outward orientation and inward orientation.

In this way 'interest' is never characterised by its presence or absence but by the various qualities it possesses. A form of attention that might be non-self-interested might exhibit other interests (after all sympathetic attention is itself a form of interest). For the study of everyday life what might be more useful than Kant's disinterested contemplation is the form of non-self-interest that you find in a writer like Archibald Alison writing at the end of the century and very much in the tradition of Hume. Here interest and attention is of a low intensity and follows the rhythm of the drift. Alison is writing about a form of attention that is amenable to taste, but it is also descriptive of the sorts of 'disinterested' interest that might be characteristic of the everyday:

> That state of mind, every man must have felt, is most favourable to the emotions of taste, in which the imagination is free and unembarrassed, or, in which the attention is so little occupied by any private or particular object of thought, as to leave us open to all the impressions, which the objects that are before us can produce. It is upon the vacant and unemployed, accordingly, that the objects of taste make the strongest impression.
>
> (Alison 1815 [1790]: 10–11)

Here interest is not negligible but is directed outwards. It is also a form of interest unencumbered by the passions of pride and humility (the phrase unembarrassed suggests as much). Here the self is in abeyance as the passionate world offers the strongest impressions. In the eighteenth century there was virtue to be found here, as the self dissolved into something else, something that might be, from the position of empiricism, only speculated about. If it was beauty it was also what Hume referred to, obliquely, as 'je-ne-scai-quoi'. They might call it beauty; we might call it 'the ordinary'.

Enlightenment aesthetics and ordinary life

As a way of concluding this section it is worth getting a clear sense, not of what was essential to Hume or to Shaftesbury or to any other eighteenth-century thinking, but of recognising what there is within this vast terrain of words that connects with the everyday world of diverse and routine experience.[18] To my mind, the greatest contribution that empiricist aesthetics makes to the study of the ordinary is the dynamic sense it gives to the public intimacies and feelings that circulate across and between individuals. Human creaturely existence is lived-out communally even when (or perhaps especially when) the values being pursued are set to encourage critical elites to imagine that they have the sensitivity to produce standards and values that could only further the cultural superiority of aristocratic taste. This is, of course, to oversimplify the results of aesthetic empiricism. The point, for me, is that before aesthetic empiricism could produce sensitive, virtuous and discerning subjects with taste and empathy, it had to describe a social ecology of unstable feelings, an ecology where the passions circulated as a condition of necessarily provisional self-making.

To me this is what the everyday feels like. It is not endlessly governed by identity; rather self-identity (whether proud or shamed, governed by appetites or by sensitivity) comes and goes, moves into focus and becomes opaque, rises in intensity and dissipates surreptitiously. At times you can almost feel the prickly force of envy or disdain at work in a room full of people, or the bubbly power of exuberance and joy. But at other times flatness and dispersal seem to characterise the everyday; a seeping languid vacancy. But this is not a vacancy of world-orientated interest, just a vacancy of self. Perhaps most often the passions (as low-intensity hum, or full-beam glare) exist in confused state, indecipherable as clarified emotions. Similarly, most of the time the self seems to be there and not-there, an ego in abeyance but still, potentially, there nonetheless. Here the word 'intensity' seems to overstate what is often a sympathetic pull towards calmness and indifference.

If the ordinary constitutes a world where most of the time 'there is nothing to write home about' it is partly because of the messy saturation of affects of energies and their dissipation that would make it so hard to know where to start. The word 'ecology', as I've suggested, seems useful here to describe a field of affects and intensities that is peppered with non-affect, flatness dissipation and non-self-ness. It is a creaturely world energised by passions (which includes the passion of indifference). Since the eighteenth century the world of performed passions has changed considerably. In many ways the most insistent aspect of life that has received aesthetic attention since that period has been the ordinary. We will see in the third part how central this attention has been for an aesthetics of everyday life. Now we need to turn to John Dewey to get a sense of the peculiar details of the ordinary as they are played out in experience.

John Dewey and the grain of experience

Aesthetic theory, perhaps more so than any other arena of theoretical writing, is concerned with experience. More particularly, though, it is concerned with the distinctive qualities and peculiarities of experience; with the grain of experience. Of course, the sorts of experience it tends to be interested in routinely pit the everyday world of experience against the aesthetic realm. My gambit here is to claim that by exploring the nature of experience, even if the focus is on a realm of experience defined by its distance from the ordinary, aesthetic theory can contribute to an under-standing of everyday life. John Dewey's 1934 book on aesthetics, Art as Experience, is, I think, exemplary in this regard.

Dewey makes everyday experience one of the central components in a book that is also intent on relegating the everyday to the non-aesthetic. The path that Dewey wants to take requires that he negotiate two propositions: that the realm of aesthetics originates in ordinary life, but that aesthetic experience transforms and supersedes its origins. For Dewey this super-session occurs both in ordinary life (when experience resolves itself into an 'authentic' experience) and in the work of art (or in activities that have an aesthetic or artistic aspect). At its heart Dewey's aesthetic theory rests on the notion of 'unity' that is both there in ordinary life (at decisive moments) while being fundamentally distinct from the disunity of the dispersed on-going-ness of ordinary experience.

John Dewey was a philosophical pragmatist who carried on the North American empiricist tradition of William James and Ralph Waldo Emerson, and his philosophy of art has to be seen in this light.[19] Empiricism meant that experience was primary; pragmatism meant that philosophy had to be measured as a form of social practice.[20] Dewey insisted that philosophy should be constantly tested, and his test put the notion of ordinary life at its centre:

> a first-rate test of the value of any philosophy ... is offered us: Does it end in conclusions which, when they are referred back to ordinary life-experiences and their predicaments, render them more significant, more luminous to us, and make our dealings with them more fruitful? Or does it terminate in rendering the things of ordinary experience more opaque than they were before, and depriving them of having in 'reality' even the significance they had previously seemed to have? Does it yield enrichment and increase of power of ordinary things which the results of physical science afford when applied in every-day affairs? Or does it become a mystery that these ordinary things should be what they are; and are philosophical concepts left to dwell in separation in some technical realm of their own?
>
> (Dewey 1958 [1929]: 7)

It is worth bearing in mind this test of the ordinary as we navigate the terrain of Dewey's aesthetics.

Dispersal and unification

Art as Experience begins by stating that its 'task is to restore continuity between the refined and intensified forms of experience that are works of art and the everyday events, doings, and sufferings that are universally recognized to constitute experience' (Dewey 1980 [1934]: 3).[21] By locating the realm of aesthetics in ordinary, experiential life Dewey's philosophy is dedicated to the perceiving and producing subject as a human 'creaturely' being. To situate aesthetics in ordinary life, and the ordinary life of crea-turely beings, Dewey's book works to avoid a number of pitfalls that he sees as severely damaging to aesthetic thought and to the understanding of artworks. First of all it avoids the deadening removal of artworks from their lively social context; a removal which brushes them away into the houses of the wealthy, into the discourse of connoisseurship, and into museums where the main function is to become 'specimens of fine art and nothing else' (9).[22] Second, it avoids having to choose between positing art as primarily a sensual response to the world or primarily an intellectual response.[23] Third, and as part of what is clearly a gestalt approach, it allows Dewey to connect aspects that seem to belong to artworks (for instance the dynamism of a painterly surface, with its areas of low intensity and high intensity) to the rhythmic energies of life. Throughout the book Dewey is at pains to offer us a version of the human subject that is both biological and social. Indeed it is precisely because the human 'lively' creature is constantly fashioned by an environment that it has to adjust to that the biological creature is also social. Like the Enlightenment philosophers mentioned above this posits emotional life, for instance, not in a subjective interior, but in a creaturely commerce with the world around it. Aesthetic experience might be intimate but it is certainly not a private matter: 'The first great consideration is that life goes on in an environment; not merely *in* it but because of it, through interaction with it. No creature lives merely under its skin' (13).[24]

But if the first task is to reconnect the artwork to the world of ordinary experience, 'by going back to experience of the common or mill run of things to discover the esthetic quality such experience possesses' (11), it soon becomes clear that to do this means having to exercise a sense of discrimination about what is going to count as aesthetic within the everyday. And it is here, in allocating what will and what won't count as aesthetic experience, that Dewey fashions his philosophy of art. Initially this means connecting aesthetics to activities that have the properties of cultivation, contemplation and play:

> The sources of art in human experience will be learned by him who sees how the tense grace of the ball-player infects the onlooking crowd; who notes the delight of the housewife in tending her plants, and the intent interest of her goodman in tending the patch of green in front of the house; and zest of the spectator in poking the wood burning on the hearth and in watching the darting flames and crumbling coals.
>
> (5)

While these are everyday activities (with their casually gendered distribution of pleasure) this is not the main emphasis for Dewey's definition of aesthetics.

We might well learn aesthetic appreciation by the flowerbed or by the fireside, but the real aesthetic experience will hit us when our ordinary experience fulfils itself in a unified and self-sufficient moment. For Dewey this moment can be seen as when 'an experience' stands out from the crowd of ordinary experience. This isn't to jump wholeheartedly from the ordinary to the extraordinary (from routine to catastrophe, say) but it does require experience to resolve the ordinary into its quintessence: to find the extra-ordinary ordinary, so to say. Routine experiences of eating, or of weather, for instance, find their aesthetic moment by becoming fulfilled as an experience that is both discrete and resolved:

> There is that meal in a Paris restaurant of which one says 'that was an experience'. It stands out as an enduring memorial to what food may be. Then there is that storm one went through in crossing the Atlantic – the storm that seemed in its fury, as it was experienced, to sum up in itself all that a storm can be, complete in itself, standing out because marked out from what went before and what came after.
>
> (36)

While weather and eating clearly belong to the everyday, routine world, the experiential significance of them only emerges for Dewey when the possibilities of food and weather are played out to fulfilment. The aesthetic realm may be made up of everyday-like material, but the everyday needs to be resolved so that art can function 'to shape it into a satisfyingly integrated whole' (Shusterman 1992: 53).

The result of all this though is a finely wrought distinction between those aspects of daily life that will constitute something like aesthetic value and that which is mere routine. Unity is the overarching figural value that Dewey accords aesthetics, to the point where the two are mutually constitutive: there is no aesthetic quality unless there is unity; where there is unity there will always be aesthetics.[25] But demarcating aesthetics in this way not only isolates the inchoate and disunity of ordinary experience (which might very well be its characteristic quality), it establishes the 'slackness' of everyday, unexceptional experience as *the* enemy of aesthetics: 'The enemies of the esthetic are neither the practical nor the intellectual. They are the humdrum; slackness of loose ends; submission to convention in practice and intellectual procedure' (40).

The aesthetics of lived experience

By distinguishing 'an experience' from what he calls humdrum experience Dewey might in effect be delivering a deadly blow to my attempts to construct an everyday aesthetics. We could simply turn away from Dewey claiming that he really only figures the ordinary to show how art both transforms it and improves it, but leaves it remaindered in the process. Yet there is an aspect of Dewey's approach to experience that can be used to adjust his allocation of aesthetic experience and which allows us to read certain passages within *Art as Experience* as positioning humdrum experience as aesthetic (or potentially aesthetic) experience.

Wilhelm Dilthey's work on experience is crucial here. While Dewey doesn't reference Dilthey there are clear correspondences between the two thinkers.[26] One of the consequences of Dilthey's work was to encourage German speakers to consider the different words used for experience: in German there are two words for experience – *Erfahrung* and *Erlebnis*. The distinction between the two terms corresponds roughly to the English-language distinction between experience of something ('she was an experienced carpenter', 'in my experience it always rains in Bristol') and the idea of experience as the actual condition of being a sentient, perceiving being. The former suggests the notion of experience at one remove, a stock-taking of accumulated experiences (*Erfahrung*), while the latter suggest the on-goingness of experience (*Erlebnis*). For this reason the translators of Dilthey often translate *Erlebnis* by the slightly cumbersome and tautological phrase 'lived experience'. For Dilthey (writing in about 1905) *Erlebnis* is experience without distance:

> Consciousness of experience is one with its content just as subjectivity is one with its subject; the experience is not an object that confronts the person who has it, its existence for me cannot be distinguished from *what* is presented to me. Here there are no different points in space from which to observe what is there. Different points of view from which to conceive it can only arise afterwards in reflection and do not affect its character as an experience.
>
> (Dilthey 1976: 184)

Erlebnis is experience at the moment in which it is lived. Such a categorisation of experience, distinct from experience as accumulated knowledge, or second-order accounts of experience, is clearly crucial to an understanding of ordinary life.

But Dilthey understands *Erlebnis* not simply as sentient experience, but as the base for individual self-understanding and self-contemplation (*Selbstbesinnung*) and in this way it is precisely because *Erlebnisse* can be singled out from the continuum of everyday life that they also transcend the everyday:

> That which in the stream of time forms a unity in the present because it has a unitary meaning is the smallest entity which we can designate as an experience. Going further, one may call each encompassing unit of parts of life bound together through a common meaning for the course of life an 'experience' – even when several parts are separated from each other by interrupting events.
>
> (Dilthey cited in Palmer 1969: 107)

It is precisely the unifying notion of an experience that connects Dilthey to Dewey and it is the separation of 'an experience' from the humdrum on-going-ness of experience that makes it meaningful for individuals.

The sense of experiences as not only meaningful in and of themselves, but also as foundational to a sense of self, is similar to the way that Dewey posits 'an experience' as the bedrock for aesthetics and for the production of art:

> *Erlebnisse* for Dilthey are those experiences around which an individual life organizes itself, the crucial experiences that orient a person's self-conception and hence life-conduct. An *Erlebnis* in this sense is expressed in English in terms of 'having an experience', in terms of going through a trauma or adventure that is, on the one hand, totally separated from the normal course of one's life and, on the other, peculiarly suited to revealing or changing the meaning of one's life as a whole.
>
> (Warnke 1987: 28)

But if experience is the material out of which a life is fashioned, this experience is also profoundly historical. What we can experience is also determined by the cultural forms that allow it to find expression in both ordinary life and in artforms. So experience may lead to expression (artistic or more generally 'cultural') but expression is also what informs experience and what makes it register 'as experience' (rather than as incoherence, for instance).

Thus experience is not some unmediated contact with the real, but must include the very cultural material of representation as it is lived out, in performances, in action, in everyday life. For the anthropologists Victor Turner and Edward Bruner, in a collection of essays called *The Anthropology of Experience*, it was this aspect of experience that drew them to both Dilthey and Dewey and to see the important connections between the two thinkers. Edward Bruner makes the point that:

> There are no raw encounters or naive experiences since persons ... always enter society in the middle. At any given time there are prior texts and expressive conventions, and they are always in flux. We can only begin with the last picture show, the last performance. Once the performance is completed, however, the most recent expression sinks into the past and becomes prior to the performance that follows. This is straight Dilthey. Life consists of retellings.
>
> (Bruner 1986: 12)

In this way aesthetics (as an arena where experience and expression necessarily meet) becomes the living cultural expression of experience that is also constitutive of experience. For this the relationship between experience and expression must be two-way. For Dilthey aesthetic expression is not something that we use to give form to experience after the event, it is coterminous with experience; it is, so to speak, the expressive forms found in experience. This means that experience is the living-out of expressive possibilities in the actual lived experience of significant moments.

And this is where it is worth returning to Dewey. Significantly and perhaps surprisingly Dewey's descriptions of significant aesthetic experiences remain almost silent. Rather than try and describe them he simply points to them and uses the 'pointing' language of deixis to figure them.[27] Thus there is no attempt made to describe the sort of experience that might take place while undergoing a particularly fierce storm or eating a gorgeous meal, it is enough to point to them: '*that* meal, *that* storm' (37). More surprising still though is that when he comes to describe the 'enemy of esthetics' – the humdrum – he seems to use a fiercely descriptive language that really struggles to register the specific grain of ordinary experience:

> Oftentimes, however, the experience had is inchoate. Things are experienced but not in such a way that they are composed into an experience. There is distraction and dispersion; what we observe and what we think, what we desire and what we get, are at odds with each other. We put our hands to the plow and turn back; we start and then we stop, not because the experience has reached the end for the sake of which it was initiated but because of extraneous interruptions or of inner lethargy.
>
> (35)

Inchoate experience is unfinished experience; it is experience that is constantly beginning again, full of repetitions, red herrings, distractions and unfulfilled wishes.

Against the stand-out moments that constitute 'this' or 'that' experience, the routines of everyday life operate as a morass of only partial significance and incompleteness. And in as much as routine experience is often unresolved, open to contingency and peculiarly formless it simply counts itself out of full aesthetic consideration:

> Things happen, but they are neither definitely included nor decisively excluded; we drift. We yield according to external pressure, or evade and compromise. There are beginnings and cessations, but no genuine initiations and concludings. One thing replaces another, but does not absorb it and carry it on. There is experience, but so slack and discursive that it is not *an* experience. Needless to say, such experiences are anesthetic.
>
> (40)

And yet here, precisely at the moment when Dewey is busy excluding the kind of experiences that seem characteristically routine, just at the moment when he demands that we reserve aesthetics for those experiences that are more fully formed, he himself seems to find a way of producing an aesthetics of ordinary routine life. I can't think of many better descriptions of the experience of everyday routine-ness than those offered by Dewey. The idea of slack experience seems eminently suited to the diffuse consciousness of routine. Similarly the idea of 'drift', the picking up and letting go of concentration, works to point to the strange character of routine, humdrum life. Dewey beautifully articulates the impossibility of finding an origin to routine: the way routine and habit creep up on you, the way you can never locate the moment when an activity became routine. It should also be noted that 'slackness' and 'drift' are themselves descriptions of forms, albeit more formless forms than those more self-contained entities that Dewey wants to privilege.

It is this sense of the opening up of humdrum experience to aesthetic expression which will also constitute new forms of experience that is being performed by Dewey, against his own intentions but in a way that partially proves his thesis. Dewey produces an aesthetics of the humdrum because he turns it into 'an experience' by giving expression to the particular qualities that make the humdrum distinctive and allow it to stand out from the sorts of more defined experiences he points to. It is also a main accomplishment of the literature and culture more generally that has focused on 'ordinary life' and would include forms of realism and what has been called modernism (the literature of Virginia Woolf or James Joyce, for instance) and it is this which takes us to the philosophical writing of Jacques Rancière.

Jacques Rancière and the distribution of the sensible

In my attempt at whittling a quotidian aesthetics out of the forest of philosophical aesthetics it is worth paying particular attention to the work of the French philosopher and historian Jacques Rancière. In recent years Rancière has directed his provocative research towards the field of art and aesthetics and has become the 'theorist of choice' for many contemporary artists.[28] From one angle the trajectory of Rancière's work looks like it passes from politics to aesthetics: his intellectual career began as a graduate student where he contributed to Louis Althusser's influential rereading of Marx's *Capital*; he was active in the revolutionary firmament of 1968 and its aftermath; he conducted extensive archival work on nineteenth-century proletarian associations; he has written extensively on emancipation and equality; and now works mainly on film, art and aesthetics.[29] The diversity can seem unsettling for those looking for a system of thought, yet there are clear continuities across this work and a clear sense both that the writing on political culture was already aesthetic in emphasis and that the work directly concerned with aesthetics continues to 'do' politics (or to do what Rancière would term metapolitics).

Rancière is perhaps the contemporary writer most alive to the productive and necessary confusion between aesthetics as a general field describing the realm of sensate perception, and the more limited meaning relevant to the field of art that has taken shape in the West in the last two hundred or so years.[30] And it is in this confusion (a confusion that infuses both the general and limited economy of aesthetics) that we can find the materials to help us build a quotidian aesthetics. In his more limited economy of aesthetics Rancière will show that the art of the last two centuries (including romanticism, realism, impressionism, symbolism, abstraction and so on) constitutes an 'aesthetic regime' that is constantly inaugurated by a recognition of the ordinary and which was the necessary prerequisite for the emergence of such modern forms as photography and cinema. In his more general economy of aesthetics such a regime has much wider repercussions, redistributing the field of perception and signification in everyday life. This more general economy of aesthetics as 'the distribution of the sensible' (the parcelling out of spaces, times and forms for specific activities and expressions and understanding) is Rancière's insistent object: it is a dynamic arena constantly managed by the policing activities of forces bent on maintaining what and who will be visible and invisible and constantly disrupted by aesthetic and political acts that will redistribute the field of social perception.

To get a sense of the potential of Rancière's approach it is necessary to rehearse his description of the social and to listen to the way he reaccentuates a variety of terms in ways that can seem counter-intuitive (police, politics, aesthetics, subjectification and so on). It is also necessary to get a sense of the context of his often antagonistic writing: his privileging of dissensus and disagreement in the face of consensus and communication; his refusal to treat politics as a form of statecraft; his insistence on the temporal mingling of artistic regimes set against narrative schemas of modernism, avant-gardism and postmodernism. But amid this complex architecture it is also worth noting how much his work coincides with earlier work undertaken by writers like Raymond Williams and art historians dedicated to a social history of art.

Yet before all that I want to provide a snapshot of the sort of constellations Rancière produces and the way that they might inflect an 'aesthetics of the ordinary'. In his recently published *Aesthetics and its Discontents* (2009) he once again details the emergence of what he calls the 'aesthetic regime of art': the form of art emerging at the end of the eighteenth century that fundamentally reorganises the sensorial realm. His example comes from the writer Stendhal. Looking back on his late eighteenth-century childhood in provincial France Stendhal recounted that the noises that marked his childhood were 'ringing church bells, a water pump, a neighbour's flute' (Rancière 2009a: 4). Stendhal would, of course, go on to be one of the major authors of literary realism. For Rancière the aesthetic regime of art is founded on an indifference to a hierarchy of significance (the water pump is as glorious as the cathedral organ) and on a concomitant sensual pedagogy (the material recognition of the water pump as a potentially glorious noise). Thus the literary registering of the everyday constitutes a 'new writing made up of sensory micro-events, that new privilege of the minute, of the instantaneous and the discontinuous' (Rancière 2009a: 10), which is coterminous with a 'new education of the senses informed by the insignificant noises and events of ordinary life' (6). The republican ethos of Stendhal's French childhood provides the sensorial education that will allow the erstwhile insignificant sounds of water pumps to become significant, and this education will be an aesthetic one, enacted by a range of different elements including literature.

For Rancière art is always social in as much as it always describes a sensorial realm and is always 'constituting forms of common life' (2009a: 26). Stendhal's writing not only demarcates an orchestration of sensual life, whereby what had been considered insignificant becomes newly significant, it allows new collective and democratic experiences to come into being on the grounds that older forms of significance have been disorganised and superseded. That such an approach to aesthetics will have profound consequences for the understanding of ordinary, everyday life should be obvious. Rancière offers a way of accounting for the new visibility and vividness of ordinary life in the last two hundred years. Rather than see this visibility emerging in the wake of new conditions of social life (increased urbanisation, newly regulated industrial labour and so on) he sees it taking place in the wake of aesthetic and political disruptions performed in the name of democracy. As we will see there are as many problems with such a position as there are theoretical opportunities for delineating the foundations for a quotidian aesthetics. Rancière's work doesn't come ready-packaged for my purpose and I will need to reinflect some of his central insights for this book. No doubt such alterations will end up denuding his thought of some of its essential critical ingredients, but my task requires that my first priority is towards the project of constructing an everyday aesthetics.

The aesthetics of the social

Rancière's doctoral thesis was published in France in 1981 as *La nuit des prolétaires* (translated and published in English in 1989 as *The Nights of Labor: The Workers' Dream in Nineteenth-Century France*). In it he follows the lives of worker-poets and worker-philosophers in the 1830s and 1840s, many of whom are converts to the utopian socialism of Saint-Simon. The lacemakers, seamstresses, cabinetmakers, joiners, printers and floor-layers, that Rancière introduces us to, do not unite in fraternal solidarity demanding the recognition of the 'dignity of labour'. Far from it, they know that hard manual labour robs them of what they most want: freedom. Instead of desiring better conditions, they desire the languid existence of bourgeois leisure: time to think, time to write. So they graft during the day, and live their bohemian lives at night.

For Rancière it is a significant discovery: the history of workers doesn't correspond to the historical mission laid out by doctrinaire Marxists. More crucially it lays the foundations for Rancière's political aesthetics. *The Nights of Labor* is faced with an orthodox distribution of time, money, rest and leisure, where 'good workers' (seen by both the left and the right) exert themselves on the work of others during the day and replenish themselves by sleep during the night. To know your place as a worker is also to know your partition of time: a time for work, a time for rest. By stealing back the hours of night for another form of existence, the worker-poets don't simply intervene in the production of poetry, they intervene in the distribution of allotted time. And this intervention, for Rancière, is the condition of politics:

> Politics occurs when those who 'have no' time take the time necessary to front up as inhabitants of a common space and demonstrate that their mouths really do emit speech capable of making pronouncements on the common which cannot be reduced to voices signalling pain.
>
> (2009a: 24)

These worker-poets who are reusing the nights that are meant for proletarian sleep, who are making themselves at home in a medium that is not theirs (poetry, philosophy) and dreaming of a life that they weren't born to, are performing politics.[31]

Against the dominant usage of the term politics that would see it as a theory of parties and policies, Rancière trenchantly allows it only one meaning: the enacting of a disruption in the parcelling out of allocated space, time and sense. The workers' dreams make no sense in the prescribed landscape of *proper* social relations. Rancière will describe his subsequent inquiries as emanating from this capturing of night by the worker-poets: 'substituting a topography of the *re*distribution of the possible and a multiplicity of lines of temporality for the order of time prescribing the impossible has been a red thread in the process of my research' (Rancière 2005: 23). The possible is the workers' dream deemed as impossible by a temporal ordering that would offer workers no time and no dreams. It is only by behaving improperly, by disrespecting propriety, that a new distribution of the sensible is possible.

Central to this is a description of the social that is fundamentally aesthetic. Rancière, as we have already seen, terms it 'the distribution of the sensible':

> the system of *a priori* forms determining what presents itself to sense experience. It is a delimitation of spaces and times, of the visible and

the invisible, of speech and noise, that simultaneously determines the place and stakes of politics as a form of experience.

(2004: 13)

The smooth running of the inequalities of a distribution of the sensible is maintained by 'police'. Again it is an idiosyncratic usage of an ordinary term: Rancière is not referring to cops (though at times they have their part to play in maintaining such a distribution):

The police is thus first an order of bodies that defines the allocation of ways of doing, ways of being, and ways of saying and sees that those bodies are assigned by name to a particular place and task; it is an order of the visible and sayable that sees that a particular activity is visible and another is not, that this speech is understood as discourse and another as noise.

(Rancière 1999: 29)

Policing is the activity that might designate the complaints of a woman in the nineteenth century as 'hysterical' (as producing noise rather than speech) when she signals dissatisfaction with the legal arrangements of marriage (that institute obedience to her husband as her primary role in marriage).

But we know from the worker-poets and all the women who refuse matrimony, that all is not in order in the distribution of the sensible. Acts of politics and acts of art disrupt and reorder the social sensorium, making new experiences possible, making new voices heard as speech, altering the horizons of visibility. Dislocations in the distribution of the sensible occur when attention is drawn (again and again) to something that had previously been deemed unworthy of attention, or when someone who was deemed as having 'nothing to say', speaks in a way that solicits an audience and community of listeners (however small). Rancière's political aesthetics is less interested in the kind of edifices that might be built in the name of proletarian poetry (for instance), than in that initial rip in the distribution of sense. It is the moment of negativity that counts: in the rip all sorts of things are possible.

The rip ushers in emancipation, democracy, equality as its infinite potential. When Stendhal hears the noise of the water pump as significant he is not simply adding 'water pumps' to the list of things worth listening to. The redistribution of the sensible inaugurates (continuously) the possibility of everything and anything being significant: if the noise of water pumps can be significant why not the squelch of mud or the hacking cough of a miner?[32] The negativity of the rip is what produces new forms of experience and new subjects of experience. Thus the redistribution of the sensible doesn't consolidate an identity already in existence: it is a moment of fundamental disidentification that Rancière terms 'subjectification':

Any subjectification is a disidentification, removal from the naturalness of a place, the opening up of a subject space where anyone can be counted since it is the space where those of no account are counted, where a connection is made between having a part and having no part.

(Rancière 1999: 36)

Subjectification, then, is fundamentally a new democratic experience built on the possibilities opened up because old identities have been called into question.[33] The potential of redistribution is not then the legitimation of an already established identity, but the throwing off of an identity that might associate women's speech with hysteria (for instance).

An inherent splendour to the insignificant

Artworks are the privileged example of the way that the sensible is redistributed and this is partly due to the way that they function as *metapolitical* forms. Artworks and politics (in Rancière's sense of this term) are joined by their relationship to a distribution and redistribution of the sensible.[34] But while a political act might confront the police with the speech of a previously discounted group, art functions at one remove from this, preparing the ground for new experiences, and opening up spaces for new subjectifications. Art in the era of the aesthetic regime of art is always political but its politics is often one that acts as a pedagogic invitation.

The designation of the art of the last two hundred years as occurring under the 'aesthetic regime of art' has important implications for an everyday aesthetics, but it also works to alter the periodisation that operates in the field of cultural history as it has been influentially practised. Thus Rancière's goal in naming the last two centuries of art as 'aesthetic' is partly to refuse the logic that would claim that a realist tendency in art was replaced by a modernist one and this was subsequently replaced by a postmodernist tendency. Rancière's regimes of art tell a much longer history and one that doesn't participate in a linear narrative: for instance the aesthetic regime reworks history, while previous regimes continue to be practised alongside a contemporary regime.[35] The term modernism, which has a tendency to privilege the non-mimetic practice of visual art, for instance, becomes dysfunctional in Rancière's parcelling out of artistic practices and periods. Rather than abstraction heralding a new kind of art, one autonomous from the world of representation, for instance, abstraction was only possible when the distribution of the sensible was disorganised by a more fundamental redistribution:

for abstract painting to appear, it is first necessary that the subject matter of painting be considered a matter of indifference. This began with the idea that painting a cook with her kitchen utensils was as noble as painting a general on a battlefield.

(Rancière 2004: 54)

The aesthetic regime introduces an equality and democracy to what is pictured that allows both painting of cooks and painterly abstraction.

It is not insignificant that Rancière's work performs what it theorises: reading his accounts of politics and art is to be faced with a constant redistribution of times and places, of the meaning of words, and allotment of significance. If the aesthetic regime of art works to dedifferentiate an abstract painting from a naturalistic rendering of a scene of ordinary life, it does so by designating both as ordinary. Abstract paintings function to constitute 'forms of common life' by their invitation to a community of painters and onlookers that anything is a possible subject of art. And this, in a different way, is also true of the painting of a cook. What both share is their negative response to a regime of art where everything had its place in a pecking order of value:

> What is the kernel of the aesthetic revolution? First of all, negatively, it means the ruin of any art defined as a set of systematisable practices with clear rules. It means the ruin of any art where art's dignity is defined by the dignity of its subjects – in the end, the ruin of the whole hierarchical conception of art which places tragedy above comedy and history painting above genre painting, etc. To begin with, then, the aesthetic revolution is the idea that everything is material for art, so that art is no longer governed by its subject, by what it speaks of; art can show and speak of everything in the same manner. In this sense, the aesthetic revolution is an extension to infinity of the realm of language, of poetry.
>
> (Rancière 2003: 205)

For visual art the significant moment is when genre art (still lives, paintings of peasants working the land, domestic scenes and so on) was given the kind of attention that had previously been reserved for history paintings (religious scenes, great battles and so on).[36] For any reader familiar with the Anglophone tradition of the social history of art this will hardly come as news, and Rancière's account of the history of visual culture often reads like a schematic rendition of what is elsewhere taken as current orthodoxy.[37]

Yet it is Rancière's insistence that the aesthetic regime of art institutes the opening up of art onto the everyday and the ordinary, and that it does this not just through its subject matter but by its ability to produce a world held in common, that makes it theoretically useful for this book. Similarly it is the very fact that Rancière holds onto the value of art in relation to the everyday not as a representation but as a sensorial pedagogy that gives it such potential for a quotidian aesthetics. The aesthetic regime of art works on our senses, on the sensate world that we perceive and experience, and in doing so gives new significance to the ordinary, as well as fundamentally transforming our experience of the ordinary. Thus Rancière's work is never simply art history (or literary history) because its task is always to see the metapolitical pedagogy at work in any artform.

Such an approach also reworks the idea of medium and technology.[38] By foregrounding the crucial but ludicrously simple idea that 'for art to exist, what is required is a specific gaze and form of thought to identify it' (2009a: 6) he alerts us to the extra-artistic sensorium of the social that is both shaped by art and is the necessary requirement for art. As such it is the dynamism of the distribution of the sensible that is the final determinant of both art and our experiences of the ordinary, and it reshuffles the deck of determinism by allocating the role to the task of recognition. And it is by seeing a form of life (the everyday) as significant that the recognition permitted by a distribution of the sensible determines the blossoming of such everyday forms of art as cinema and photography:

> According to the logic of the esthetic regime of art, in order for photography or the cinema to belong to art, their subjects first had to belong to art. Everything that could be taken in by a glance had to have been already susceptible to being something artistic; the insignificant had in itself to be potentially art. The rupture of the system of representation was first brought about by what was so ineptly called 'realism'; this 'realism' held that not only was everything that was represented equal, but also that there was an inherent splendour to the insignificant.
>
> (Rancière 2000a: 253)

Rancière's insistence that the aesthetic regime of art, which seems to encompass so much of the visual and literary culture of the nineteenth and twentieth centuries, is premised on a recognition of the 'inherent splendour of the insignificant' and opens up a new role for aesthetics in the study of everyday life.

Cinema, photography, literature and visual art will at times act as active witnesses in what follows. But it isn't just as witnesses that such work interacts with the everyday. The splendour of the insignificant (which becomes significant precisely to the degree that its splendour is recognised), enacted by any number of literary and filmic texts, is also a training ground, sensitising us to the textures and tempos of the daily. Artworks, then, are part of the general economy of aesthetics in their pedagogic role of alerting us to different kinds of alertness.

The orchestration of passions

Rancière's primary concern is with emancipation: his is a perspective that highlights the disruptive moments when speaking out-of-turn and out-of-place alters the normative landscape of assigned sense. In this way Rancière is mainly concerned with language, speech and visibility. As a political aesthetics of the everyday it is of inestimable value, because it allows us to attend to the consequences of the becoming-noticed of the unnoticed of everyday life. The daily lives of the discounted and unaccounted constitute the subterranean ground of the ordinary. Their becoming-visible in literature, in political actions, in cultural forums, are the stakes that an aesthetic politics of everyday life will eventually rest on.

As other commentators have argued, Rancière's work is partly understandable as a politics of recognition, where the emphasis is on charting the success and failure of how the unrecognised become historical subjects by speaking in such a way and in such a context that their speech is recognised as 'sensible' (rather than as 'noise'). While Rancière finds many of his examples in nineteenth-century France, twentieth-century North America provides other vivid moments: second wave feminism, the Stonewall riots, the Montgomery bus boycott and so on. Rancière's work allows such moments to be read against the dominant interpretation of identity politics. Rather than seeing the Stonewall riots, for instance, as a moment when homosexual identity in the USA coalesced into something assertive and consolidated, Rancière's position would suggest that it could more productively be seen as a moment of subjectification, a moment of profound disidentification, a refusal to be treated as 'a homosexual' (with all that that then implied).

For my purpose, though, the landscape that Rancière charts is already too dramatic, too hilly. The heroic moments of refusal, of disidentification point to important theorisations of how new experience emerges. It is, significantly, a humanist approach where changes to the social sensorium are decidedly human endeavours. There is, to my mind, nothing much wrong with this. Yet the sense that the distribution of the sensible is animated just by artists and activists, while held in check by police activity, is simply too abrupt for my purpose. 'The distribution of the sensible' is an endlessly suggestive phrase for thinking about the aesthetics of the everyday, but it is limited (for the purpose of this book) by being tied to a politics of recognition. The sensible, in all its sensual possibilities, is not limited to the way it legitimates speech acts. The sensible is reordered in all sorts of ways all the time and a good deal of this can't be accounted for by the dynamism of police and politics, nor is it explainable only in terms of human endeavour. The wide accessibility of central heating, domestic electricity, carpets and radio in the mid-twentieth century fundamentally reordered the social sensorium of most people's lives. It altered their sense of being at home, of being connected to a wider world, of what comfort meant and so on. To read it as either an act of politics or police would be to fail to see this reordering altogether. Similarly the changes in the last ten or so years in the status and sense of waste products (packaging, bottles, outmoded commodities and other 'trash') has fundamentally altered as climate change becomes a more and more pressing reality. Much of the encouragement to treat waste differently has been directed by the state, yet does this mean that the sensual alterations of waste have been meted out in the name of police?

Rancière's cultural history is at once sweeping and vague. It continues in the tradition of some of the best social historical work, even though it keeps its distance from such a tradition. His sense of 'regimes of art', for instance, is not a world away from the sort of reparcelling of periods that Raymond Williams announced by the phrase 'structures of feeling'. And it has some of the same results that Williams' work achieved (for instance, Williams refused the medium specificity of film, seeing it as a continuation of dramatic forms). But Rancière is not an art historian or a literary historian, and by his own account he is not a political philosopher (political philosophy is simply a contradiction in terms in his system of thought). He is, then, perhaps best thought of as an aesthetician. And it is this role that he seems most ready to inhabit. It is as an aesthetician that he is most useful for constructing an everyday aesthetics.

Coda: towards a quotidian aesthetics

This chapter has presented a constellation of aestheticians in the attempt to find opportunities for theorising a quotidian aesthetics. In the rest of the book I want to build on these initial findings and to scaffold on to them a number of other quasi-aesthetic investigations orientated to specific regions of the everyday: thingly life; the experience of time and work; media; and domesticity, routine and habit. Taking stock of what this chapter has covered and the path it has taken there are themes that criss-cross the work I've been looking at. Subjectivity and identity, for instance, become fragile and provisional phenomena for an ordinary aesthetics and have to be set against a much more dynamic landscape of drifting energies and sudden eruptions of passion, politics and experience. For an ordinary aesthetics art is no longer a privileged site, but nor can it be filed away in the drawers of sociologists of art who might see it as contributing to a world of distinctions. Art, as Raymond Williams knew, is lively sensual material that both shapes and articulates intimate worldly experience. The landscapes of ordinary lives are not rendered aesthetic by the practice of art, they are already aesthetic as they are lived in a world sensually and sensorially shaped by a whole panoply of form that includes artistic materials. Perhaps most fundamentally an aesthetics of the ordinary would suggest that ordinary life engages us in a sensual pedagogy (a shaping of perceptions, of sentiments, of discernment) that is constitutive of our sociality. This idea will become clearer and more concrete, I hope, as the book progresses and as the subject of habit in everyday life is developed. In the next chapter I want to follow the idea of sensual pedagogy by looking at some familiar things.

Notes

1 I will be paying particularly close attention to the writing of David Hume as his work is the most philosophically expansive and, for me, has the most potential for connecting to ordinary culture.
2 The work of John Locke is foundational for British Empiricism:

> Our Observations employ'd either about *external, sensible Objects; or about the internal Operations of our Minds, perceived and reflected on by our selves, is that, which supplies our Understandings with all the materials of thinking.* These two are the Fountains of Knowledge, from whence all the *Ideas* we have, or can naturally have, do spring.
>
> (Locke 2008 [1690]: 54 – italics in the original)

3 This, for instance, is Francis Hutcheson:

> A Change in our Organs will necessarily occasion a Change in the Intenseness of the Perception at least; nay sometimes will occasion a quite contrary Perception: Thus a warm Hand shall feel that Water cold, which a cold hand shall feel warm.
>
> (Hutcheson 2008 [1725]: 21)

4

> These Passions, according as they have the Ascendency in me, and differ in proportion with one another, affect my Character, and make me different with respect to my-self and others. I must therefore, of necessity find Redress and Improvement in this case, by reflecting justly on the manner of my own Motion, as guided by Affections which depend so much on Apprehension and Conceit.
>
> (Shaftesbury 1710: 294–95)

5

> Every Man indeed who is not absolutely beside himself, must of necessity hold his Fancys under some kind of Discipline and Management. The *stricter* this Discipline is, the more the Man is rational and in his Wits. The *looser* it is, the more fantastical he must be, and nearer to the Madman's State. This is a Business which can never stand still. I must always be *Winner* or *Loser* at the Game. Either I work upon my *Fancys*, or They on *Me*. If *I* give Quarter, *They* won't.
>
> (Shaftesbury 1710: 323)

6 'For when we attribute identity, in an improper sense, to variable or interrupted objects, our mistake is not confin'd to the expressions, but is commonly attended

with a fiction, either of something invariable and uninterrupted, or of something mysterious and inexplicable, or at least with a propensity to such fictions' (Hume 1985 [1739–40]: 303).

7 As I mentioned in the preface the passions are most commonly thought of as emotional states. The passions, as they were written about prior to the end of the eighteenth century, would have included phenomena that would today be thought of as emotional (fear, sadness and so on). It should be noted, however, that the passions would also have named a good deal that would be hard to include under this title. Burke, for instance, includes 'sympathy, imitation and ambition' within the passions. The passions are a much larger category than the emotions and include mechanisms for the dissemination of states of mind (sympathy, imitation) as well as a number of states of mind that don't feature in more contemporary accounts of emotions (ambition, wonder, glory, etc.). For an account of the passions see Dixon 2003; Fisher 2002; James 1997; Meyer 2000; Solomon 1993.

8 As Adela Pinch notes: 'whether one is responding to a person or to a representation of a person suffering, seems, in many cases, ultimately not to make any difference to the emotional experience itself' (Pinch 1996: 45).

9 'Pride is a meta-passion that organizes relations between emotions and individuals' (Pinch 1996: 24). For further discussion on Hume in relation to pride and humility see: Gross 2006; McIntyre 1989; Pinch 1996; and Rorty 1982.

10 The sociality of pride is described in Jane McIntyre's commentary on Hume: 'a good or a bad reputation is therefore itself a source of pride or humility. Furthermore, we depend on the love and approval of others to second our own view of ourselves and shore up our frail self-esteem' (McIntyre 1989: 552). See also Gross 2006 chapter four.

11 The social affects of humiliation are most clearly revealed in recent writing around the theme of shame: see for example Munt 2007; Probyn 2005; Sedgwick 2003.

12 In Matthew Fuller's book *Media Ecologies* he writes that he uses the term ecology as 'the most expressive [term] language currently has to indicate the massive and dynamic interrelation of processes and objects, being and things, patterns and matter' (Fuller 2005: 2).

13 Hume is a writer who is philosophically radical and culturally conservative (his emphasis on property is only one aspect of the latter). For an account that pays much more heed to Hume as a conformist see Eagleton 1990.

14 For a more general account of sympathy as a moral sense in the decades prior to Hume's *Treatise* see Turco 1999.

15 When Amélie Oksenberg Rorty notes that 'sympathy only provides the conditions for morality; it cannot assure it' (1982: 170) she is recognising that sympathy is a relationship between passions, and between passionate organisms, rather than a relationship of moral succour.

16 Though it might well be worth noting that if taste is reliant on the mechanism of sympathy then there is a political form to this that is certainly *not* reducible to the inculcation of traditional values. Sympathetic passionate communication stands as an alternative to Hobbes' understanding of humans as motivated by the direct passions associated with glory and self-preservation:

> When fear and anger are the prime examples of invading passions then we are 'overcome' by love, pity or compassion. In such a system, it is rationality that assures justice. But when the primary examples of the passions include sentiments acquired by sympathetic vibrations to others like ourselves –

when we sorrow because others sorrow – the virtue of justice can become the *sense* of justice, its operations assured by benevolent social passions rather than by rationality.

(Rorty 1982: 159)

17 A sense of the arguments and interpretations of disinterestedness can be found by consulting the following: Rind 2002; Stolnitz 1961; Townsend 1982 and 1987.

18 Were we in the position to question these authors about their ultimate intention for the sort of aesthetic empiricism that they were concocting it would seem feasible that they might have claimed that the civilising project of producing discerning, virtuous and sensitive citizens was uppermost in their minds. Given the times they might have invoked the glory of God as an ultimate purpose. What they might have said to themselves, of course, is anyone's guess.

19 For an account of Dewey in relation to pragmatism see West 1989; for Dewey's aesthetics see Shusterman 1992.

20 For Dewey's contribution to a philosophy of experience see Jay 2005.

21 From now on in this section I will reference *Art as Experience* by page number only.

22 He continues by stating that:

> Objects that were in the past valid and significant because of their place in the life of a community now function in isolation from the conditions of their origin. By that fact they are also set apart from common experience, and serve as insignia of taste and certificates of special culture.
>
> (9)

23 'Oppositions of mind and body, soul and matter, spirit and flesh all have their origin, fundamentally, in fear of what life may bring forth. They are marks of contraction and withdrawal' (22).

24 Dewey makes a similar point about emotions: 'emotions are attached to events and objects in their movement. They are not, save in pathological instances, private' (42).

25 For instance: 'no experience of whatever sort is a unity unless it has esthetic quality' (40).

26 This was vividly pointed out in a selection of anthropological essays put together by Victor Turner and Edward Bruner (1986).

27 Deictic expressions use shifters (words that have no object but designate objects only in their specific performance): thus 'yesterday' could refer to any day but if I'm talking to you on a particular day the shifter 'yesterday' secures its object. Similarly words such as 'this' or 'that' are exemplary deictic signifiers.

28 For instance the international art journal *Artforum* dedicated a special issue to Rancière in March 2007.

29 Rancière provides an outline of his career in 'From Politics to Aesthetics?'(2005) and 'A Few Remarks on the Method of Jacques Rancière' (2009b).

30 'On the one hand, it [aesthetics] names a specific regime of identification of art, historically determined. On the other hand, it names a dimension of human experience in general' (Rancière 2009b: 121).

31

> Political activity is whatever shifts a body from the place assigned to it or changes a place's destination. It makes visible what had no business

being seen, and makes heard a discourse where once there was only place for noise; it makes understood as discourse what was once only heard as noise.

(Rancière 1999: 30)

32 While it may seem like an oxymoron, the idea of a 'continual inauguration' needs to be seen against the backdrop of police activity (that might reinstitute an initial distribution of the sensible) and that any redistribution of the sensible is the result of 'a thousand creeping encroachments' (Rancière 2000b: 19).

33 'By *subjectification* I mean the production through a series of actions of a body and a capacity for enunciation not previously identifiable within a given field of experience, whose identification is thus part of the reconfiguration of the field of experience' (Rancière 1999: 35).

34

The relationship between aesthetics and politics consists ... in the way in which the practices and forms of visibility of art themselves intervene in the distribution of the sensible and its reconfiguration, in which they distribute spaces and times, subjects and objects, the common and the singular.

(2009a: 25)

35 Thus: 'the temporality specific to the aesthetic regime of the arts is a co-presence of heterogeneous temporalities' (Rancière 2004: 26); while 'at a given point in time, several regimes coexist and intermingle in the works themselves' (50).

36

The destruction of the representative regime in painting started at the beginning of the nineteenth century, with the revocation of the hierarchy of genres, with the rehabilitation of "genre painting" – the representation of ordinary people engaged in ordinary activities, which used to be contrasted with the dignity of history painting as comedy to tragedy.

(Rancière 2007: 76)

37 For John Dewey, writing before the parcelling out of art historical periods into pre-modernist, modernist and post-modernist, 'the novel has been the great instrument of effecting change in prose literature. It shifted the centre of attention from the court to the bourgeoisie, then to the "poor" and the labourer, and then to the common person irrespective of station' (Dewey 1980 [1934]: 189).

38 'A medium cannot be reduced to a specific materiality and a specific technical apparatus. A medium also means a milieu or a sensorium, a configuration of space and time, of sensory forms and modes of perception' (Rancière 2008: 185).

Chapter 3

Familiar things

As human beings we attach ourselves to the thingly world: our ordinary lives are lived out in the midst of things. We often surround ourselves with keepsakes and mementos; we arrange our intimate spaces with furniture, tools and utensils; we simultaneously hide and reveal our naked bodies with clothes. For their part things turn towards us: they call us, sidle up to us. Tools subtly weathered by daily human contact demand to be held and used. Soles of shoes scuffed smooth like pebbles seem to yearn for our feet. Tables scratched and scorched by the paraphernalia of cooking tell us their secret histories. Beds, chairs and clothes accommodate us: most of the time they receive our 'daily inattention'. We don't notice them, but we do interact with them. What are the circumstances of a favourite armchair when we seem to be so unconcerned by it, while it perfectly performs its role of comfortably supporting us precisely so we don't have to 'give it notice'? Is noticing or not noticing significant for the intimacy of our relationship with some of our most familiar things? Does the old adage 'familiarity breeds contempt' really apply when we consider the preciousness of a family photograph that we see each day but rarely pay any heed to?

Things act on us (affect us, entice us, accompany us, extend us, assist us) and we act on things (make them, break them, adjust them, accredit them with meaning, join them together, discard them). There seems to be a symbiotic relationship between them and us; a mutually constituting interaction between people and things. The osmosis between the thingly and the creaturely would suggest that we shouldn't start out by privileging the one over the other. Yet how easy is it to cast off creaturely privileges of automatically granting authority to us over them? What could it mean to aspire to some equality between us and them when the 'them' in question remain so stubbornly mute, so obdurately insentient? A variety of intellectual traditions (from zoology to Marxism) routinely warns us against the twin dangers of reification (the thing-ifying of cultural processes) and the anthropomorphising of non-humans (the treatment of animals and objects as human-like), yet in ordinary life we routinely commit such theoretical misdemeanors.[1] Perhaps if some equality or accord is to be found between things and human creatures, then rather than trying to avoid the 'magical' thinking of anthropomorphism and reification (and the prohibition on these forms of attention seems to implicitly prescribe an unbridgeable divide between the human and the non-human), it might be better to practise them more diligently, and perhaps more excessively.[2] Rather than seeing this as willful theoretical perversity I think that it could mean taking the everyday seriously.

What follows is an account of various objects and thingly situations.[3] I start out by noticing a chair that most of the time (and especially when I'm sitting in it) I fail to notice. The thingly world, I argue, is neither most usefully explained through the optic of cultural symbolism (what the chair stands for, what cultural values it embodies) nor through the sense that an 'owner' makes objects significant by investing them (and infesting them) with their own meanings. Both side, too easily, with the world of 'us' leaving 'them' held captive by a world of meanings that to some degree are neither here nor there from the chair's point of view. Symbolism and investment will be part of the story, but I hope too that my chair, from its own thingly perspective, will get something of a look in. To do this I will need to follow digressions and detours (theoretical and anecdotal) and allow other objects (toys, pebbles and door-closers) to hold my attention. But it is to the chair that I will ultimately return.

Inundations

In 1935 the Chilean poet Pablo Neruda wrote 'Towards an Impure Poetry'. It was a manifesto of sorts. The tract is an implicit attack on the sort of surrealism that had been taken up by poets across Latin America and which sought to render life mystical and exotic in a way that, to Neruda's way of thinking, was allergic to the ordinary and thingly qualities of everyday life. Neruda's manifesto demanded:

> a poetry impure as the clothing we wear, or our bodies, soup-stained, soiled with our shameful behavior, our wrinkles and vigils and dreams, observations and prophecies, declarations of loathing and love, idylls and beasts, the shocks of encounter, political loyalties, denials and doubts, affirmations and taxes.
>
> (Neruda 1994a: 39)

He warns that 'those who shun the "bad taste" of things will fall flat on the ice'. His would be a poetry 'worn with the hand's obligations, as by acids, steeped in sweat and in smoke, smelling of lilies and urine, spattered diversely by the trades that we live by, inside the law or beyond it' (39). In among these avant-garde demands for the ordinary (demands that will be repeated by artists in search of the real across the century) he also offers a method for connecting to the ordinary, thingly actuality of objects:[4]

At certain hours of the day or of the night, it is very convenient to watch intensely how things rest ... Those worn-out surfaces, the scratches that hands have left on things, the often tragic and always charged atmosphere of things, they all produce a pull towards the reality of the world. We sense the blurred impurity of human beings in those things, the classification, the use, and the waste of materials, the imprints from fingers and toes, the eternity of a human atmosphere that inundates things from outside and from inside.

(Neruda cited in Gumbrecht 2006: 312)[5]

To watch an object 'rest' is to notice it not 'working' while also recognising that it has work to do. It is at once to recognise its properties, its potential, its sense of self.

I'm drawn to this sense of inundation, of atmospheres inundating things from outside and inside (whether human or not). Inundation suggests the scale and insistence of the qualities flowing from the chair, as well as those that bleed into the chair from outside. Inundations also suggest qualities that may or may not have meaning (a chenille cardigan, for instance, might have a meaning but it also has tactile qualities that aren't easily reducible to ideation and signification). The sense of 'blurred impurity' that Neruda writes about seems to double the complexity of the traffic between the creaturely and the non-creaturely: impurity is to already blur the boundaries between the false abstractions of pure and discrete entities.

So this is my chair at rest (Figure 3.1). It is relaxing at the moment. Time off, for a while, before it has to cope with the distribution of my weight, before it has to work supporting me in a semi-reclined position. The chair was one of a pair, but the sibling is long gone. The stretched rubber that provided the bouncy support for the loose cushion perished and split. The foam within the cushion wasn't looking too good either; it had started to fossilise and crumble. I dare not wonder how long this chair will last. One of the benefits of its design is that when it does collapse it is not an entirely unpleasant sensation: you haven't far to fall, in fact you're almost there already. Sitting in the chair is sitting in a chair that feels half collapsed.

What do these inundations of atmosphere that Neruda speaks of amount to? Or rather, where do we locate them and how do we describe them? Can we say that when the chair absorbs them (if this is what it does) then it acts something like a sponge absorbing water? Does it retain these atmospheres? Does the chair produce its own inundations; an object spawning inorganic, genetic-like matter? Does the chair possess its own species-being, so to say, its own generic dispositions? Or, as Neruda's quotation also suggests, perhaps the chair has been marked, its witnessing activity there to be read on its surface: the peat-coloured fabric stained with decades of spillages; the hard, painted wood scratched and chipped through myriad clashes with a world even more unyielding. We need, I think, to work backwards, to

Figure 3.1 My chair at rest

get some sense of the chair's particularity through the anecdotes (some 'belonging' to me, some the chair's and some shared) that comprise its social and cultural life story.

I can remember my Dad putting the chair together when it arrived in the early 1970s. It was the first item of flat-pack furniture to arrive in my Mum and Dad's house – my teenage home. It came from Habitat or 'shabby-tat' as it came to be known. Looking through the Habitat archive I discovered that the designation of 'flat-pack' to this system of furniture is an anachronism: while items were indeed 'packed flat' they were called, at the time, KD funiture. KD meant they were knocked-down (built then un-built, knocked-up then knocked-down) and it was up to you to get them knocked-up again.[6] The knocking-up of this particular chair involved huge amounts of frustration and ensuing angry mutterings. The chair's basic architecture was easy to assemble: it required ten bolts to screw the five pieces together. The problem – the thorn in my Dad's side – was the obstinate rubber-mini-trampoline support. This seemed to require the strength of Atlas to assemble – it was totally ungiving and unforgiving. You slotted one of the corner metal triangles of the rubber mat to one of the chair's hooks and then pulled and puffed as you tried to get any of the others to attach. To manage to get two triangles and hooks to attach to each other seemed overly hopeful; to get all four to join in seemed highly improbable. It looked like my Dad was not cut out for such shows of brute strength. It must have happened though, but I've forgotten the ending, just retained the bubbling intensity of its difficult assembly.

Incidentally KD wasn't the only coding that Habitat employed: items could also be QA, which meant quick assembly. As a company directive from 21 August 1970 states:

> This is the first time ever, anywhere in England, that a chain of retail stores is offering a large range of KD furniture packed flat in 'carry homeable' cartons, for customers to satisfy instantly that 'can't wait to get it home feeling'. Habitat makes that 'can't wait to get it home feeling' a reality.
>
> (V & A archive)

You take the KD furniture home (or get it delivered) and then it's just a matter of a bit of QA. Clearly this chair veered more towards KD than QA. Impatience and patience, desire and delay, were built into KD furniture: the instant gratification of walking away with your chair was mismatched to the frustration of working out how to assemble it, and the difficulty of knowing how to achieve its finished form. The immediacy of desire, which KD furniture was meant to satisfy, was stymied by an array of items that seemed so steadfast in their desire to remain disassembled.

I think it was about 1971 or 1972 when the chairs arrived. I was 10 or 11. My Mum and Dad can locate the date, sort of, but can't remember much else about buying the pair of chairs, apart from that they think they saw them in the Habitat in Cheltenham and that they were delivered by post. They might have had a look in the Cheltenham Habitat shop, sat on a few chairs and ordered them from there. Alternatively they might have used the new Habitat service, Habitat by Post, which was introduced in late 1969. The new postal service marks a swing in Habitat's story that directly relates to my chair: to show this I need to tell you a little bit about Habitat.[7]

I'll be brief. The first thing to note is that Habitat originally set itself up (in the Fulham Road, in the Brompton Cross area of London, in 1964) as a boutique lifestyle shop. Terence Conran, the managing director, claimed that: 'we see ourselves as the Mary Quant of the furnishing world' (V & A archive).[8] Conran was already a successful designer and manufacturer of designer furniture and when Habitat opened there were already plans that the shop would be the first in a chain of about sixteen spreading across the country. When the Fulham Road shop opened it was much more than an outlet for Conran designs. The shop itself was a semi-brutalist interior: 'open plan showroom lit by stage spotlights, rough white walls [as well as unpainted brick walls], bare steel girders and cool black and white floor tiles' (Habitat press statement, 11 May 1964, V & A archive). You could buy toys, hi-fi equipment, as well as herbs, cooking utensils, cookbooks, kitchen furniture, bedding, chairs, sofas and so on. As Conran claimed: 'We aim to provide the complete look in furnishing, a kind of high-style household kit at the lowest possible cost which can all be seen under one roof' (*House Beautiful*, non-dated: 56, V & A archive). Habitat is an assembled 'life-image' as a form of boutique shopping that was new to the retail market.[9] Here's Conran again in 1964:

> we are determined that each item in Habitat will be a 'find' in itself. Customers will find the best designs in everything at Habitat from simple carving knives to comfortable chesterfields and we can prove that they need not cost the earth either.
>
> (V & A archive)

Habitat, then, was an edited version of the shopping experience: items had been selected from a range of manufacturers and shopping outlets as a kind of filtered department store. Whereas a large department store might have to cater for a range of tastes, here everything was already sieved – all you were left with was 'style', taste for a certain aesthetic.

The press, particularly the new Sunday colour supplements, picked up on this immediately, declaring Habitat to be part of an anti-plastic, back to basics style (which in one sense it was).[10] Other journalists were less impressed, declaring the shop a sort of one-stop 'instant good taste' emporium. The first Habitat in Fulham Road was managed by the ex-model and wonderfully named Pagan Taylor. When discussing the notion of 'instant good taste' she would claim 'I don't like the phrase but I suppose it is roughly descriptive of what Habitat aims to do' (V & A archive). So while you might buy a butcher's apron and chopping board, you would also buy herbs to season your food, and cookbooks telling you how to cook, and a chicken brick for that authentic Mediterranean experience.[11] Tables had lighting that suited them, wallpaper that blended in and storage units for orchestrating all your nick-nacks (all available from Habitat, of course). In 1974 Terence Conran brought everything together in *The House Book*, where style and practical considerations were firmly knitted together. Actually the book didn't look too different from the annual Habitat catalogue which not only showed you what you could buy, but offered vivid tableaux of how the world of Habitat should be lived. Habitat produced a world of Habitaters. As the *Guardian* icily declared:

In any big city, on Saturdays, you find them, living like peasants, exchanging rustic jokes. While he (ham-fisted handyman) puts up his pinewood units with melamine working tops and lots of drawers for clobber, she brings back a rough rush game bag, full of shopping and donning butcher's apron, makes a weekend rural lunch: huge hearty stew with hot crusty rolls and creamy mounds of butter (made by wooden butter-pat): then the thinnest crispiest pancakes from a heavy cast-iron crepe pan and coffee drunk in red enamelled jolly workmen's mugs.

These are Conran people. Or imitation Conran.

(Fiona MacCarthy, the *Guardian*, 5 October 1966,
page numbers missing, V & A archive)

These 'imitation Conran people' were, to some extent at least, the shock troops of gentrification, buying large tumble-down Georgian and Victorian houses in working-class areas, stripping them back to reveal 'their original features' (as the estate agents would have to learn to say) and furnishing them with second-hand pine kitchen tables (the ones that had been junked because of their association with servant furniture) and creating little nooks to stack the requisite jars of Provençal herbs.

There is a lot more that could be said here about Habitat in its first years, but I mustn't lose sight of my chair and its inundations, of which this is a fainter trace than some others. By 1971–72 Habitat was a different beast than it had been in 1964. Its boutique exclusivity had been dissipated in a whole host of ways: the 'Habitat by Post' service was one; the opening of various other outlets, including the Ikea-like depot in Norfolk was another. By 1971 Habitat was no longer solely owned by Conran but was a company jointly owned by the high-street stationers Ryman as well as by Conran Ltd (later Conran would buy back the Ryman shares and try to reinstate the original boutique vision of Habitat). From the late 1960s through most of the 1970s Habitat was at its most non-exclusive. In 1969 Ryman-Conran bought the company Lupton Morton, which, tellingly, Terence Conran described as the 'Marks and Spencer of the furniture world' (V&A archive), that is, exactly unlike the Mary Quant world of the initial vision.

And this is where my chair comes back again. The chair is a peat and white Campus chair made by Lupton Morton as part of their latest range of affordable modern furniture that coincided with the moment of being taken over by Ryman-Conran. It is a cheaper version of the more designer modern styles being produced by more up-market retailers. As the name 'Campus' suggests the furniture seemed to be aimed at the parents of school-age and university and polytechnic-age kids. It offered desks that could be used as dressing tables and chairs, tables and wardrobes as relatively cheap KD furniture.[12] It was an available version of designer mass-modernism. You could sit in it and feel part of a switched-on, cool, designery world but at a price that could be afforded by the more general middle and lower-middle classes.

And this is something worth staying with. If the initial vision of Habitat suggested a certain commitment to a whole-way-of-taste (pine tables, Provençal herbs, hi-fi, white wall and chicken brick) this more 'Marks and Spencer-ry' Habitat addressed a customer with fewer commitments to systematic taste regimes. At times our Campus chairs jostled for space with darker, heavier inherited furniture; at other times they were consigned to children's bedrooms, to sit marooned among Biba posters and David Cassidy mementos, as if they had been sent to bed early without their tea. It was the juxtaposition as much as anything that seemed to illuminate these two chairs; their presence as a new thing, a thing that was vividly new because it was in among old things, or things that even if they were new still looked old. And my chair, my Campus chair, made this physically evident. For a very short 11 year old, sitting in such a low-slung chair, the view I got was the underneath of things: the underneath of old tables that might be smooth and polished on top but from underneath looked dusty, wooden and generally thrown together, with little sprinklings of glue, random wooden pegs and nail heads. It turned the chair into a little island of the modern in among all the pressing presence of the 'ghosts of the past'.

But, of course, this is more than a story of the old-fashioned versus the newly modern; it is also a story about values, desires and dreams. Sitting there looking at the obviously hand-bodged underside of furniture, I felt marginally part of a less-up-tight, a less 'hands-on-laps' world. Here was an initial training in a more supine world, a step towards floor cushions and dope (not that I knew about dope when the chairs arrived). It was a more relaxed, sexy, improvisational, informal world – that sat, literally of course, in stark contrast to sitting up straight at table.

One or two years after the chairs arrived, my cousin Chris sat in one of them as I showed him my latest acquisition: the album *Tubular Bells* by Mike Oldfield.[13] Chris sat in the chair and listened to the whole of the first side of the record through headphones and declared it, with all the solemnity that a seventeen-year-old boy with a junior moustache can muster, a 'great record'. Chris was one of my ways into the world of prog-rock (the other was my sister, but she tended towards the glam end, and had a catholic interest in soul music too) and looking at his attentiveness to the music I recognised the chair as connected to another set of taste choices far away from chicken bricks and Provençal herbs.

The familiar things we live with may or may not have the sort of entangled interplay of desire and memory that I've been describing here, but if they do then they require a good deal of time for both the accumulating and revealing of these entanglements. Looking at my chair as a black and white photograph there is little to distinguish it from a hundred other chairs. There is nothing exceptional about it. Its visceral and mnemonic thing-ness requires a telling that takes time because its thing-ness took time to form. Serial television shows offer another way of catching the density that some familiar things can be made to show.[14] A chair that has knocked around a bit picks up a history of use that inundates it with a 'personal' life story. My Campus chair eventually found its way into my adult home and is one of the few possessions that have made their way from childhood to adulthood. My partner and I used it for middle-of-the-night bottle feeding when our children were little (its low-lying disposition provided just the right body angle for safely combining dozing and feeding). Removing the square cushion exposed the stretched rubber base that proved so irritatingly difficult for my Dad, and provided a trampoline for them when they were slightly bigger. If you look closely at the peat-brown fabric you can probably still see slight stains of milky residues.

But if 'my' chair (and ownership of things is problematic) is made up of both anecdotes and remembrances that belong to the chair and to me, then isn't there a danger of over-particularising this chair? After all most of the time I simply sit in the chair or bump into it when I'm at my most clumsy. This chair is a host of different things at the same time: an obdurate object that takes up space and occasionally trips me up; a designed 'thing' that acts on me; a functional object that allows me to be suspended just above the floor; a sentimental object that pieces together my childhood and adulthood; a piece of 1970s furniture; an overly familiar thing that I don't often notice; and so on. Its familiarity took some time to produce, but not too long (something 'new' can become 'part of the furniture' fairly swiftly): the sentimental object took much longer.[15] Familiarity is a process of becoming habitual and I'll have a lot more to say about habit and routine in following chapters. For now though it is worth asking the question of how an ordinary thing might become (for us) a more general thing. How do we get the ordinary, the overly familiar, to show itself in a light that allows the ordinary to register the social in a way that isn't endlessly particularised?

The particular is, of course, entangled with the social in imminent ways: the feeling of a world-to-come that was more informal, more improvisational, is an embodied sociality of my Campus chair. It suggested a way of responding to the world that wasn't locked into a self already fashioned (for me it had a world-opening aspect). One way, then, of edging beyond the particular towards the general is to suggest that objects can be treated as symptoms for something wider, more diffuse. Jacques Rancière, for instance, suggests that we practise symptomology with familiar things:

> 'Prosaic' objects become signs of history, which have to be deciphered. So the poet becomes not only a naturalist or an archaeologist, excavating the fossils and unpacking their poetic potential. He also becomes a kind of symptomatologist, delving into the dark underside or the

unconscious of a society to decipher the messages engraved in the very flesh of ordinary things.

(Rancière 2002: 145)

Symptomology would be a way of recognising the more worldly properties of the chair (and thereby the aesthetic world-ing that the chair performs). It would connect it not just with people and their intentions but also with other things. Symptomology would require treating this chair as a thing among things, rather than as an isolated object. But there might be a danger in Rancière's suggestion too, in that things could become mere ciphers for something else. Alongside symptomology there may be a host of other forms of attention that will help disclose the ordinary thing-ness of objects in all their familiarity and in all their lively sociality.

In the midst of things

In his book *Minima Moralia: Reflections from Damaged Life*, Theodor Adorno contemplates a variety of new techno-mechanical things, in particular 'automatic' door-closers and the catches and handles on windows, cars and refrigerators. It is an example of a materialist symptomology that is both vividly suggestive and purposefully problematic:

> Technology is making gestures precise and brutal, and with them men. It expels from movements all hesitation, deliberation, civility. It subjects them to the implacable, as it were ahistorical demands of objects. Thus the ability is lost, for example, to close a door quietly and discreetly, yet firmly. Those of cars and refrigerators have to be slammed, others have the tendency to snap shut by themselves, imposing on those entering the bad manners of not looking behind them, not shielding the interior of the house which receives them. The new human type cannot be properly understood without awareness of what he is continuously exposed to from the world of things about him, even in his most secret innervations. What does it mean for the subject that there are no more casement windows to open, but only sliding frames to shove, no gentle latches but turnable handles, no forecourt, no doorstep before the street, no wall around the garden? And which driver is not tempted, merely by the power of his engine, to wipe out the vermin of the street, pedestrians, children and cyclists?

(Adorno 1989 [1951]: 40)

Such an instrumental assessment of a new mechanical order is, of course, an exaggeration of the things scrutinised. But Adorno is not offering a sober dialectical account of the thing-world that was emerging, primarily in North America, at the end of the Second World War. His task is to speak from the perspective of 'damaged life', offering a wilfully negative critique of ordinary subjective life caught in the midst of things orchestrated by the demands of instrumental reason. His questions ask what things want and how they might produce us as subjects.

Adorno's understanding of the pedagogy of things (the way they 'make', 'expel', 'tempt') is drawn, to some degree, from the work of his friend Walter Benjamin. Benjamin's account of the emergence of modernity (which preoccupied him from the 1920s until his untimely death in 1940) is consistently concerned with the emergence of new sensoria. Benjamin's work describes a world of people and things where the distribution of the sensual and sensorial is cast in a new industrial morality. The world that Benjamin describes is focused on glass architecture, on trains, on shopping and on traffic, but also on such 'small technologies' as matches and the click of a camera button. For Benjamin there is a relay between factories and funfairs, busy roads and international exhibitions.[16] What the emergence of modernity constituted was a new sensorium adjusted to more abrupt movements, to machines that click and whirr, to forms of motion that need slighter movement but quicker reflexes. To isolate one element as pedagogic in itself would be to fail to see the way that the techno-mechanical world in consort constituted a training ground for the social sensorium.

Benjamin is often concerned with 'habit-things': things, like manufacturing tools on an assembly line, that are used over and over again and gradually demand new dispositions from the body's sensorium.[17] In this Benjamin follows Georg Simmel in describing a world where humans have adapted themselves to the thing-world. Not only have they learnt how to cross busy roads (through the redistribution of nervous energy) they have also internalised a world of more instrumental commerce and communication. Yet for Benjamin there is a more positive dialectic here, that isn't made explicit in Adorno: while the new machines shape us in their own image (so to speak) they also make available forms of attention, ways of orientating ourselves, that actually produce the conditions necessary for engaging with the new sensorial world. (I will have much more to say about Benjamin's dialectic of attention in chapter five.)

While Adorno sees only negativity in the habit training performed by new things (by habit-things), the implicit role he accords them is not essentially different from a range of other accounts of techno-mechanical things that don't share Adorno's sense of modern life as catastrophe. While Adorno doesn't share Marshall McLuhan's upbeat sense of modern communications as resulting in a 'global village', his account of technical objects does implicitly accord with McLuhan's understanding that the materiality of objects extends the human sensorium (McLuhan 1997 [1964]). But it has been the work of science and technology studies over the last twenty odd years that allows us to really fill out Adorno's sketch of the morality and effect of things.

Bruno Latour's contribution to the study of ordinary objects has introduced a form of thingly attention that is at once exhaustively materialist and
(partly as a result of this) unswervingly surreal. By looking so closely at
things, and by following things rather more than human intentionality,
Latour has provided accounts of our mundane, thingly world that resolutely
defamiliarise routine things. In his essay 'Where Are the Missing Masses?
The Sociology of a Few Mundane Artifacts', Latour sets out the polemic of
his case:

> To balance our accounts of society, we simply have to turn our exclusive
> attention away from humans and look also at nonhumans. Here they
> are, the hidden and despised social masses who make up our morality.
> They knock at the door of sociology, requesting a place in the accounts
> of society as stubbornly as the human masses did in the nineteenth
> century. What our ancestors, the founders of sociology, did a century
> ago to house the human masses in the fabric of social theory, we
> should do now to find a place in a new social theory for the nonhuman
> masses that beg us for understanding.
>
> (Latour 1992: 227)

The argument that sociology fails to understand society because it is blind
to the presence of non-human objects is premised on the recognition that
things are social agents too. For Latour social things are actants in the
production, transformation and reproduction of social worlds.[18]

By promoting things to the role of social agent Latour opens up a perspective
that allows ordinary things, whose tasks may seem fairly undistinguished, to
take on a much more extensive position in society. His example is, like
Adorno's, the device that automatically closes the door after you walk
through it. These gadgets are called 'grooms' (or butlers) as an acknowl-
edgement of the job that they do, and the human agent that they replace (in
posh hotels you might find people whose sole job is to open doors for you
and shut them after you pass). But Latour's attention is not simply on this
neat mechanism that is destined to an eternity of perpetual door-closing,
nor is he as concerned with Adorno about the 'bad manners' that might
result from a culture where you don't have to think about closing the door
after you. Latour sees the 'groom' as a technology that is itself part of an
assemblage of devices that perform a number of tasks just so humans don't
have to.

The technological assemblage that the groom is part of would include
walls, doors and hinges. Faced with a wall the problem that objects and
humans face is how they might allow people to pass from inside to outside
and back again and how they might do this without letting heat out (for
instance), and without undue expenditure of time, energy and resources.
Each addition to the assemblage is necessary to allow the wall to function as

something more than an impenetrable barrier or, just as unsatisfactorily, a wall with an unprotectable hole in it:

> The problem is that if you make holes in walls, anything and anyone can get in and out ... . So architects invented this hybrid: a wall hole, often called a *door*, which although common enough has always struck me as a miracle of technology. The cleverness of the invention hinges upon the hinge-pin: instead of driving a hole through walls with a sledgehammer or a pick, you simply push the door ... ; furthermore – and here is the real trick – once you have passed through the door, you do not have to find a trowel and cement to rebuild the wall you have just destroyed: you simply push the door gently back.
>
> (Latour 1992: 228)

Once the hinged door has been fabricated, though, the unreliability of human agents is evident: will you remember to close the door after you have entered a building or a room? Will you slam it into the face of the person walking behind you? The 'groom' is not simply an addition to the hinged-door assemblage, it is an insistently 'moral' actant in its role, because its task means that you are no longer obliged to be a polite door closer, or to think of others walking behind you, or worry about keeping the door closed in case of fires.[19]

Latour's approach is ruthlessly anthropomorphic: to recognise the groom as an actant means it is necessary to see it as a delegate for human actions and that it has human qualities and human attributes. But as importantly (and vitally for Adorno) these non-human actants shape and reshape humanness:

> *Anthropos* and *morphos* together mean either that which *has* human shape or that which *gives shape* to humans. The groom is indeed anthropomorphic, in three senses: first, it has been made by humans; second, it substitutes for the actions of people and is a delegate that permanently occupies the position of a human; and third, it shapes human action by prescribing back what sort of people should pass through the door.
>
> (Latour 1992: 235)

Things as actants are delegates of human actions. For instance a chair is delegated to hold a person in a crouching position without that person having to squat.[20] It is a substitute for (in this case) a person's own technological capacities (to balance on your haunches). But it is also a shaping device that prescribes certain ways of sitting and is fairly strict in who it will disallow (for instance my mother can't sit in 'my' Campus chair as she finds it almost impossible to get out of again).[21]

Latour is, as you might have already guessed, pretty enamoured of gadgets and while he recognises that delegation has its negative effects he doesn't dwell on this in this essay. Adorno does. Of course it is explicit in how Latour approaches objects that, just as they might become effective delegates for human actions, they also redistribute competences. The door groom becomes a great door closer so I don't have to be. Devices redistribute abilities and competences. Think of how computer technologies have changed so many areas of work. In architecture and graphic design, for instance, the physical processes of drawing and 'cutting and sticking' have been absorbed into computer programs. Graphic designers have been enabled by software production; but in a fundamental way they have also become 'disenabled' in as much as younger generations have lost a whole range of skills that were once central field skills.

In pedagogic terms when technologies (and chairs and doors are both technologies) redistribute competences then learning and unlearning are always on the cards.[22] In a recent book that deploys aspects of Latour's work the point is made with regard to paint technologies: due to 'advances' in paint performance older painting skills are no longer required: 'today, amateur decorators can choose fast-drying, non-drip, water-based paints that "know" how to go on to a door: with these technologies in place, even novices can produce an acceptable finish' (Shove et al. 2007: 55). Skills of painting have been taken up by the paint: 'aspects of the competence needed to paint the door have been redistributed between persons and technology, the paint having effectively absorbed capacities previously embodied in the individual wielding the brush' (55–56). The result of a redistribution of competences is inevitably deskilling, forgetting and unlearning.

The example of the automatic door-closer, an example that unites Latour and Adorno, redistributes competences, but it also redistributes manners and social dispositions. For Adorno all the devices that he mentions result in an unlearning of what could be called a care for others. For Latour, in less judgmental prose, the groom acts to make up for the unreliable aspect of human agents. Design solutions are there because the alternative is inefficient. In the case of the groom the alternative is to discipline humans into being reliable door closers (or safety belt wearers, for example): 'either to discipline the people or to *substitute* for the unreliable humans a *delegated nonhuman character* whose only function is to open and close the door' (Latour 1992: 231). For both Latour and Adorno objects are agents with an ethos: objects demand that we 'do this, do that, behave this way, don't go that way, [you] may do so, be allowed to go there' (232).

There is in Adorno's sketch a sense of the modern object world working in concert to produce what the poet Robert Lowell described as a 'savage servility' (Lowell 1974: 97); an aggressive disposition that was also compliant and fundamentally conservative (and the example of Nazism is never far from the surface in Adorno's writing). Adorno's symptomology is more extensive (but also looser, vaguer) than is possible through Latour's concentration on specific assemblages of things and humans. It designates a thingly world that produces subjects in its own image. Thingly instruments are, literally, instrumental, producing, for Adorno, an ethos of self-centered ungraciousness and ill-mannered disdain for others. There is no sense that any one item could produce such an ethos alone. In this way automatic door-closers align themselves with fridge doors and car motors. Each thing is a thing among things.

My Campus chair is a chair among chairs, a thing in the midst of other things. It is a slouchy, floor-descending chair. Its closest cousins are beanbags, scatter cushions and coloured light bulbs. No doubt Adorno could have (if he had lived that long) cast a mordant eye over such objects and diagnosed the ethological tendencies of such things. He might have claimed them as furnishing a dream state where the horrors of the contemporary world are swapped for a somnambulist's retreat to the embryonic interior. He may have seen the informality designed into such objects as ameliorating stricter and harsher formalities achieved in the social world at large.[23] In a more optimistic turn he might also have recognised the casualness of such objects as containing the seeds of a sociality yet to come: one not riven by the uprightness of status. And yet, out there in the thingly world, my chair can't choose its companions, it has to make do with the family it is given – old tables, upright chairs and so on. In ordinary life symptomology has to be cut with the actuality of a more piecemeal and ramshackle existence. Symptomology is essential for understanding the proclivities and proscriptions of objects, and for recognising the ethological tendencies of things, yet it has little to say about the obdurate and sentimental presence of them.

In the thrall of things

Sherry Turkle calls them 'evocative objects'; Donald Winnicott called some of them 'transitional objects'; anthropologists and psychoanalysts have referred to them as totems and fetishes. One of the most famous examples of such an object is the sledge in Orson Welles' film *Citizen Kane* (1941). The film is the story of a wealthy and powerful newspaper proprietor who cashes in friendship and journalistic integrity for circulation figures of his newspaper. His dying word (and it is the first word you hear in the film) is 'Rosebud'. What follows in the movie is the story of Kane's life and an attempt to find out who or what 'Rosebud' is. Rosebud, it turns out, isn't a loved or hated person or anything of monetary value, but an ordinary child's sledge:

> Actually, as it turns out, 'Rosebud' is the trade name of a cheap little sled on which Kane was playing on the day he was taken away from his home and mother. In his subconscious it represented the simplicity, the comfort, above all the lack of responsibility in his home, and also it stood for his mother's love which Kane never lost.
>
> (Welles cited in Mulvey 1992: 82)

By choosing a child's toy as the mystery that the film unravels, *Citizen Kane* recognises an aspect of things that, potentially, take us from childhood towards death. Such totemic objects can be both lively and deathly at one and the same time; and this is their mystery and allure. If this sounds over-dramatic, perhaps we can reframe this assertion by saying that some objects have the capacity to represent powerful qualities beyond their prescriptions and affordances, while also, and as a necessary complement to this, insisting on *our* own thingly, inorganic status (the very fact that we are matter too).[24]

Psychoanalysis (and Orson Welles' description of 'Rosebud' is, of course, indebted to psychoanalysis) has a sense of this dual, and seemingly contra-dictory, aspect of things. Psychoanalysis is by definition a human-centred approach to understanding the world (though the 'human' that it posits is not a seamless or coherent whole), nevertheless it does have a lot to say about objects. Melanie Klein, for instance, established a post-Freudian approach to psychoanalysis that understood the infant's orientation to the intimate world and the people in it, as negotiated through 'part-objects' (for instance the mother's breasts), objects that can become 'good' or 'bad' in relation to the child's desires and frustrations.[25] In Freud's classic work on sexuality, objects can become stand-ins for the traumatic and imagined event of sexual differentiation. This is exemplified in Freud's account of fetishism when the male child turns away from the shocking sight of his mother's sexual difference and fixates on a nearby object that will take the place of the missing penis (Freud 1927).[26] Whether or not we believe in the predominance of sexual energy as the animating force attaching people to other people as well as to ideas and things, psychoanalysis offers a way of describing how things matter to people in profoundly affective ways. Its description of our commerce with objects can offer an account of how an object can become 'charged' with something more than an ascription of our interest.

Much of what psychoanalysis tells us about how these objects become significant and 'charged' is explained by the process of cathexis. Cathexis is the transfer of energy from a person to another person, or thing or idea. It is what can make an idea 'loaded', or can make someone phobic about certain objects and phenomena. Cathexis is an 'economic concept' whereby 'a certain amount of psychical energy is attached to an idea or to a group of ideas, to a part of the body, [or] to an object' (Laplanche and Pontalis 1983 [1967]: 62). For Freud one way of describing this psychic energy was as 'the quota of affect' or the 'sum of excitation', and while he struggled to treat it as a neurological process (whereby energy is discharged and redistributed from instinct to object, for instance) it is probably most easily understood as a materialist analogy of the way that we attach ourselves to things and the way that they become invested with a degree of emotional intensity. We love objects such as teddy-bears and sentimental heirlooms, not just because they have comforting associations but because we have enlivened them with a degree of energy. Of course the difficulty with cathexis is that the energy hasn't actually moved from bodily excitation to the toy lying inert on the floor. Cathexis may describe the orientation and the aim of our affections but the energy is attached to the representation or the idea of the thing, rather than the thing itself. Of course to the person who loves the object it may seem that the thing possesses unique power; to the stranger it is often just another soft toy or glass ashtray.[27] The role of the object is designated (however unconsciously) by the subject who is attaching themselves to it. Attachment and investment go one way: objects don't choose us, we choose them. Psychoanalysis, then, has a tendency to see the object becoming a thing-that-matters by a process of unconscious transference of affections and energy. This is what Orson Welles is claiming for the sledge in *Citizen Kane*: Kane's mother leaves and Kane's sledge becomes invested with the energy of this traumatic moment and the love that can no longer 'find' its object.

Perhaps the most commonly cathected inorganic object is the child's 'special' toy or 'blanky'. The child's comforter is termed a transitional object by the psychoanalyst D. W. Winnicott. Winnicott's work follows on from the tradition pioneered by Melanie Klein (Winnicott was supervised in his clinical training by Klein between 1935 and 1941) which is primarily

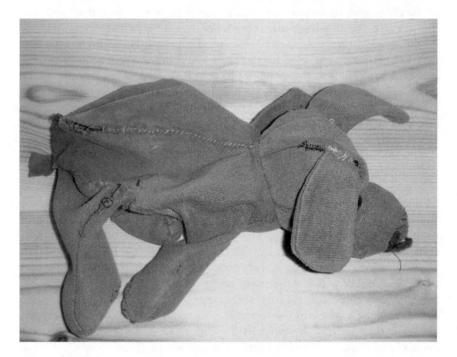

Figure 3.2 A special toy

concerned with the way babies become mature subjects. Central to this tradition is a concern with the world and the bodies within it (including the child's) as a series of connected and disconnected objects. One of the major contributions that Winnicott was to make was to look at the way that subjects, infant babies through to adults, negotiate their affective environment and extend themselves from a world of control outwards towards a larger sense of the environment.

Like Klein, Winnicott saw the world of the infant as an experience of part-objects (in particular the mother's breasts) that become a site for a range of affective experiences (aggression, love, anxiety, etc.). According to Winnicott the child initially experiences the world and the people in it in a fragmentary way (though there is no indication that the baby would have consciousness of this fragmentation as such) and this continues when the child (from as early as four months) starts having an intense relationship with the object world and with what Winnicott calls its first 'not-me' possession (a toy, a bit of blanket, etc.). This is an object 'that becomes vitally important to the infant for use at a time of going to sleep, and is a defence against anxiety' (Winnicott 1951: 4). Such objects are 'transitional objects' for Winnicott and they fulfill a number of tasks:

> The first possession is related backwards in time to autoerotic phenomena and fist- and thumb-sucking, and also forwards to the first soft animal or doll and to hard toys. It is related to the external object (mother's breast) and to internal objects (magically introjected breast), but is distinct from each. Transitional objects and transitional phenomena belong to the realm of illusion which is at the basis of initiation of experience.
>
> (Winnicott 1951: 16)

Transitional objects are objects cathected with a 'quota of affect' that ties the object to the drives or instincts (libidinal drives but also, and importantly, the instinct to satisfy hunger). As well as a defensive object, transitional objects (as the name suggests) help to extend the child's world as it separates from its intense attachment to a primary carer out towards the world of the 'not-me'.[28]

Tracy Gleason gives a wonderful description of her little sister's 'stuffed bunny' named 'Murray'. Gleason describes how her sister, Shayna, picked Murray from an array of stuffed bunnies that had been given to her and used 'him' as a constant companion through her early years. As Shayna gets older Murray follows her development in a sort of parallel world, where he lives a mirrored existence, attending school, learning to read and write, making friends with other bunnies and so on. All this takes place in Bunnyland: 'a utopia of peace and prosperity, with festivals every Sunday and on alternate Wednesdays' (Gleason 2007: 174). Murray constantly adapts to the new situations of Shayna's life. As Sherry Turkle notes, in a gloss on Gleason's description of Murray:

> Winnicott writes that the transitional object mediates between the child's sense of connection to the body of the mother and a growing recognition that he or she is a separate being. When Shayna starts preschool and its rules insist that Murray cannot accompany her, she is challenged to invent ways of bringing him along. Her solution is to invest Murray with new powers. He develops the ability to read Shayna's mind and intuit her every emotion. In doing so, Murray makes it possible for separation to be not-quite separation. Transitional objects let us take things in stages.
>
> (Turkle 2007: 314)

For both Turkle and Gleason, Murray is an affective invention of Shayna, and one that is so powerful that it affects those who live with her and who love her. Shayna's attachment to Murray and her ability to conjure a loving world around him affects family members to the extent that they find themselves placing Murray in comfortable positions when they pick him up off the floor, and by generally caring for him.

Yet there is another side to transitional objects that is less immediately evident: they are, and at times insistently so, inorganic matter. No matter how loved the object, no matter how animated such objects can become, they are also (and this is another side to their magic) lifeless. Anyone who has spent much time around children who possess these objects will know how easily, throughout an average day, they can be cast aside, trampled on, unceremoniously kicked away and stuffed behind radiators. (And this is part of the reason that they are always getting lost.) Children do not consistently 'love' their transitional objects; or rather they appear to love the fact that they can be so precious one minute and so lifeless the next. And it is the constant ambivalence between these two states that makes them fascinating for both children and adults:

> Murray shows signs of love and age; his jumpsuit is starting to tear a little over his bum, and his rattle is visible through worn patches and no longer makes any sound. A turn in the washing machine with something red made him decidedly more pink than white. At times when he is tossed aside – in favor of Barbie, say – at these moments, as he lies on the floor with his arms and legs akimbo, the simplicity of his being becomes apparent.
>
> (Gleason 2007: 175)

If Murray as a pupil in Bunnyland is purely Shayna's cathected projection, then Murray as a threadbare assemblage of cloth, stitching, stuffing and rattle is a property belonging entirely to 'Murray'. And it is this side of things, the thingly quality of objects, that might be seen to 'pick' us out and hold us to account.

In 1920 Virginia Woolf published a short story about a professional man (an up-and-coming politician) who is lured into a world of things to the point where he gives up his political career. The story is called 'Solid Objects' and in it the protagonist is drawn in fascination towards some of the most lifeless things imaginable: a sea-smoothed lump of glass; a broken piece of crockery; a 'globular' bit of iron. As the narrator suggests, these things are not worlds away from transitional objects, and the process of valuing them shares something of the child's cathected projection. Thus the protagonist, John, is seen as projecting an anthropomorphic representation onto the thing by exhibiting:

> The impulse which leads a child to pick up one pebble on a path strewn with them, promising it a life of warmth and security upon the nursery mantelpiece, delighting in the sense of power and benignity which such an action confers, and believing that the heart of the stone leaps with joy when it sees itself chosen from a million like it, to enjoy this bliss instead of a life of cold and wet upon the high road. 'It might so easily have been any other of the millions of stones, but it was I, I, I!'
>
> (Woolf 1920: 63)

Woolf's sense of the child imputing liveliness in an inorganic pebble gets us halfway towards the fascination of these objects. Yet there is something macabre about the protagonist's fascination that others, including the reader, recognise. All of these things are weighted, clumpy, unformed and useless.

In a bravura reading of this short story, Bill Brown connects Woolf's tale to a culture of material scarcity as well as state-sponsored demands for people to turn domestic stuff into war-matter (metals for guns, bones and fat for explosives) (Brown 2003a). Here is not the place to rehearse Brown's reading but it is worth heeding his more general project of orientating cultural analysis towards things rather than towards objects.[29] For Brown things as objects come complete with a form of interpretation sitting alongside them (their assumed use, their categorical order); to treat objects as things is first and foremost to refuse this seemingly adequate interpretation. His example is the window: usually we would describe its ability to frame a view or let in light. Occasionally when a dirty window catches the light all we can see is a crust of glass flush with a wall:

> As they circulate through our lives, we look *through* objects (to see what they disclose about history, society, nature, or culture – above all, what they disclose about *us*), but we only catch a glimpse of things. We look through objects because there are codes by which our interpretive

attention makes them meaningful, because there is a discourse of objectivity that allows us to use them as facts. A *thing*, in contrast, can hardly function as a window. We begin to confront the thingness of objects when they stop working for us: when the drill breaks, when the car stalls, when the windows get filthy, when their flow within the circuits of production and distribution, consumption and exhibition, has been arrested, however momentarily. The story of objects asserting themselves as things, then, is the story of a changed relation to the human subject and thus the story of the how the thing really names less an object than a particular subject-object relation.

(Brown 2004: 4)

The useless object becomes a thing, and this is what endlessly fascinates the protagonist in Woolf's story. But while turning objects into things could be a sort of parlour-game, its potential for Brown is much more than a simple estrangement of the usual habits of mind.

Brown's last sentence holds the key. Objects becoming things (which is certainly not something limited to literature, as I hope is already clear) opens up a space for a new relationship between subjects and the worlds they inhabit. And within this space different accounts of our modern world are possible, ones that might allow for more thingly experience, which may well be more collective, and will undoubtedly be less egocentric. A thingly approach to culture would ask:

How it renders a life of things that is tangential to our narratives of modern production, distribution, and consumption; how it can contribute to a materialist phenomenology that does not bracket history, but asks *how*, in history (how, in one cultural formation), human subjects and material objects constitute one another, and *what* remains outside the regularities of that constitution that can disrupt the cultural memory of modernity and modernism.

(Brown 2003a: 402)

For Brown this means that things can offer us counter-histories of modernity, histories less caught in the thrall of the objects' capacities to function as a commodity. For my purpose such an approach would, I think, also have to confront two essential components of culture. The first is that while much has been written about consumption in modern Western culture, little has been made of the end point of the commodity's journey – the dustbin, the landfill site, the incinerator. Consumption is not just about buying and having, it is also about using up and destroying. The second component is the fact of death. It is not difficult to see how one element of 'civilised' culture has been the constant veiling of the fact of death.

The same year that Virginia Woolf published her story 'Solid Objects', Sigmund Freud published the long essay *Beyond the Pleasure Principle*. In it he offers an account of his grandson playing with a cotton-reel attached to a piece of string. The child (who was one and a half at the time) uses the reel to play a game of losing then finding, by throwing the reel out of his cot and intoning an approximation of the German for 'gone' and then pulling the string to get the reel back into the cot and saying 'here' (*da*). In Freud's interpretation the child's activity is a continuation of an aspect of his play that had been noted before: 'This good little boy, however, had an occasional disturbing habit of taking any small objects he could get hold of and throwing them away from him into a corner, under the bed, and so on, so that hunting for his toys and picking them up was often quite a business' (Freud 1920: 284). The use of objects to repetitively enact loss is given as an example of how children incorporate feelings that might be painful into their ordinary life. Indeed it seems that the 'gone' part of the game is much more obsessively played out than the act of finding: 'as a rule one only witnessed its first act, which was repeated untiringly as a game itself, though there is no doubt that the greater pleasure was attached to the second act' (284).

Freud tells the story of his grandson's game as a prelude to his introduction of the notion of the death instinct or death drive. In an economic account of human psychical life it would seem to be a fundamental principle that people are drawn to do things that increase pleasure, lessen pain and release anxious excitation. How then to explain his grandson's activity of ceaselessly enacting departure (his mother's, for instance, or his own disappearance) through play? For Freud it is the repetition that is so striking as well as the pleasure in the return of the object (though as he notes this isn't the main focus of the game).[30] Drawing the cotton-reel back into the cot allows the child to magically turn unpleasure into the pleasure of mastery and control. The argument would go something like this: you might not be able to control the bigger world around you and you will be lost in an ocean of uncertainty as to when love is given and when love is denied, but here in your cot with your reel, at least you are in charge of when the going and the returning take place.

As a prelude to the death drive this little scenario might seem an unlikely antecedent. But it is the compulsive repetitiveness that was important for Freud. The death drive is Freud at his most speculative and it is an aspect of his work that is probably easiest to discredit. For my purposes though I neither want to explore its theoretical dimensions nor poke at its inconsistencies or contradictions. I want to simply and lightly use it for a description of the way that we might be drawn to objects as lifeless things. The death drive, for all its suicidal-sounding orientation, is not an existential category but an economic one. If the pleasure principle suggests an economic model whereby the subject seeks to increase the amount of pleasurable energy and reduce unpleasant energy, the death drive is dedicated to the dissipation of all energy, of heading towards the entropic condition of becoming inanimate. To think of an economic force that moved 'beyond the pleasure principle' meant recognising that 'the most universal endeavour of all living substance' was to 'to return to the quiescence of the inorganic world' (Freud 1920: 336). This is not antithetical to a desire for pleasure; rather it is a radical aspect of it, namely the pleasure of not being a 'self', the pleasure of being a thing. For Freud the condition of all the drives is a return to a former state. And here for the death drive it means returning to a moment before life, where energy levels were obviously set at zero:

> If we are to take it as a truth that knows no exception that everything living dies for *internal* reasons – becomes inorganic once again – then we shall be compelled to say that '*the aim of all life is death*' and, looking backwards, that '*inanimate things existed before living ones*'.
>
> (Freud 1920: 310–11, italics in the original)

Death, in this sense, is not itself traumatic but is 'merely' radical non-being (and its attraction is its non-traumatic aspect: it is non-living, not the awfulness of dying). Depending on your theoretical disposition the death drive will seem either reasonable or ludicrous or somewhere in between. It does however chime with a sense of our jealousy towards things. Freud's grandson chose a cotton-reel, a little wooden object that had served its purpose and was now 'nothing' but a thing.

Nothing resides in this world with such ease as a thing: nothing seems so still and so content as a pebble or a brick or a glass paperweight with a silver-foil flower trapped forever inside it (Figure 3.3). There is a compelling ease to the way that things reside in the world that we (endlessly fidgety) can only marvel at. Like moths to the flame we nervously circle around things, jealous of their calm. Even that most animating of things, a computer, becomes an amorphous conglomeration of lifeless wires and circuits when it is unnetworked and unplugged. Off duty and resting, unperturbed by personal and cultural memory, my Campus chair is insentient and still. I am drawn towards the stillness of things. A chair's enthralling aspect is to draw me towards its lifelessness. It entices me with the promise of its inorganic contentment. A successful chair encourages me to copy its stillness, to move ever closer to the stasis of things. It sends me to sleep.

The paperweight opposite was once my grandfather's: I used to notice it sitting on his desk. Its heaviness was immense for an object not much bigger than a pair of clasped adult hands. Its green glass refracted the world around it and bent it out of shape. The scattering of tiny bubbles seemed to be ironic markers of weightlessness in an object where gravity is magnified. The silver-foil flower, a naïve rendering of an idea of what might pass as

Figure 3.3 Glass paperweight

natural, seems to poke fun at the miniscule life-cycles of most plant life ('plants come and go in the blink of an eye, I am here forever', thinks the paperweight). I'm sure 'my' paperweight will live for eternity. It outlived my grandfather and it will undoubtedly outlive me. Looking at it occasionally reminds me of time spent on best behaviour with a man I barely remember. If pushed I'd have a sense of a presence leaning into me to greet me, smelling of cigar smoke, of his moustache, harsh and otherworldly, brushing my cheek. But it was never just remembrance that attracted me to this thing.

The paperweight picked on me, called me to account as so much flimsy gristle and bone, of flesh and liquid, of mind and mindlessness.

The word 'possession' has an ambiguity: not just the owning of property but also the ghostly presence of another (to be possessed). Things that we possess can also possess us. To be possessed by things (rather than simply possessing them) interrupts the endless cycle of newness and obsolescence. To enter into the lure of a thing's intransigent stasis is to be in part possessed by the thing-ness of things, and to lose the I-ness of self:

> What if the collector's ambitions were in fact driven by some effort not to represent the self or to collect the self, but to dissolve the self into its nonhuman environment, to become an object, a thing among things, in the collection's perfect order? What if that object you long for were simply the object-cause of a more profound desire to achieve some Thing that amounts to subjective oneness with your nonhuman environment? And what if that object were – at the same time – precisely an impediment to that desire, perpetuating the desire simply by being apperceived as nonhuman?
>
> (Brown 2006b: 103)

But if this is to perceive (or apperceive) the world from the point of view of things, does this mean that things (all things) only and forever have one voice, one utterance, and a deathly one at that? And do all things announce the desire for non-being in the same way? Automatic door-closers and fridge handles don't (for me) announce the lightness of non-being in the way that my Campus chair and paperweight do. It is the coupling of dreams and incorporeal, insentient life that is crucial. My Habitat chair couples the reneged promises of the 1970s with the matter-of-factness of light wood, mottled hessian and crumbling sponge. My paperweight knits together the density of morality (my grandfather's and my own) with the ludicrous substantialness of a thing that resides so effortlessly in eternity. Here, death is not trauma or sadness, but the light breezyness of nothingness. Things like this aren't morbid; they constantly knit and unknit the arrogance of self-hood in the same way that Hume's backgammon set could puncture his inflated sense of pride and humility. A jealousy for thingness is not to wish for death, but to wish for a life less beholden to the fragility of a historically situated ego. Familiar things call attention to time and call time on attention. This is the world seen as a snapshot from the perspective of eternity.

Notes

1 Where I live vernacular expression regularly refers to inorganic things as 'he' or 'she' (and the explicit gendering that results needs to be seen as an aspect of the anthropomorphising of things). At the same time children (and some adults)

will often refer to parts of the body (particularly genitalia) as things: 'your bits', 'my thing' and so on. On reification see Lukács 1971 and Bewes 2002, on anthropomorphism see Berger 1977 and Daston and Mitman 2005.

2 As we will see this in itself is not new. Walter Benjamin, for instance, could be seen as someone who uses anthropomorphism to critical effect. It will be harder to argue for the value of reification. My aim is less to justify reification and anthropomorphism as forms of critical practice than to explore their role in ordinary life and in the commerce between things and those that claim to be non-things.

3 The literature on things and objects is vast and covers a range of disciplines from literary history to anthropology. The literature that I found most useful included: Appadurai 1986 and 2006; Attfield 2000; Brown 2003a, 2003b and 2004; de Grazia and Furlough 1996; Kiaer 2005; Miller 2008; Tamen 2001; Thomas 1991; and Turkle 2007.

4 The pop artist Claes Oldenburg called his manifest of 1961 'I am for an Art' and includes lines such as 'I am for an art that takes its form from the lines of life itself, that twists and extends and accumulates and spits and drips, and is heavy and coarse and blunt and sweet and stupid as life itself' (Oldenburg 1961: 728).

5 Gumbrecht's translation uses the term 'inundates' rather than the more usual 'engulfs' for this line. Inundation is to my mind a more useful term as it suggests a continual process rather than a finite condition. For examples of Neruda's thing poetry see, for instance, his *Odes to Common Things* (1994b), a collection of his poetry from the 1950s.

6 Papers, catalogues, clippings and images relating to Habitat are kept at the Victoria and Albert Museum archives in London. Much of the material (press releases, for instance) is anonymous (produced by publicity staff), unpaginated and sometimes undated. Where it is possible I have referenced quotations in the usual way. For other Habitat material I have provided as much information in the text as I can and have signalled that it is from the V & A archives in parenthesis. For an account of self-assembly products see Molotch 2003: 138–42.

7 For more information on Habitat see Phillips 1984 and Conran 2001.

8 Mary Quant was a fashion designer who opened the boutique clothes shop Bazaar in the King's Road in 1955. Quant was the leading designer for a number of looks that became associated with the 1960s (particularly the mini-skirt). See Quant 1967.

9 The closest progenitor for Habitat is the shop Liberty's, though this was modelled on the department store in a way that Habitat wasn't. For a history of Liberty's see Adburgham 1975.

10 From the early 1960s onwards the 'Sunday colour supplements' promoted domestic style (alongside socially and politically orientated reportage) in Britain. *The Sunday Times Magazine* began life in 1962 and the *Observer Colour Magazine* started in 1964 (see Slavin 1987).

11 The chicken brick was a rustic, unglazed ceramic pot, made up of two interlocking ovals. In 1966 it was one of Habitat's best selling items, costing 12/6d (just over 50p GBP in today's money, or about 75c in US dollars at the current exchange rate).

12 Personally I think that the desk/dressing table combination might have been something of a mistake: my sister, who had one in her bedroom, seemed to have school books permanently tattooed with globs of eyeliner and mascara.

13 Mike Oldfield's *Tubular Bells* (1973) launched Richard Branson's Virgin record label. The record is an example of progressive rock (prog-rock, as it was known at the time) and provided the sound track to the film *The Exorcist* (also 1973).

14 The link between television and furniture (and the class taste involved in linking them) is given a useful rendition in the TV series *Friends*. In encountering someone without a television, Joey (the 'friend' with evident working-class roots) asks 'but what do you point your furniture at?' The comedy series *Frasier* also features a significant chair: a yellowy-green barcalounger, see Highmore 2009: 27.

15 The duration of newness is, of course, relative. In households where new things are arriving on a regular basis, newness will last less time than in households where they aren't. Newness is superseded when objects are in a context of things that are newer. The class dimension of this is central, but so too are generational concerns. My 'thoroughly middle-class' parents are of a generation that experienced the Second World War and the austerity that followed. Waste was a sin. The arrival of the Habitat chairs was, at the time, a big deal.

16 For instance, Benjamin would write that 'what the fun fair achieves with its dodgem cars and other similar amusements is nothing but a taste of the drill to which the unskilled labourer is subjected in the factory' (Benjamin 1939: 133).

17 In discussing the writing of Edgar Alan Poe Benjamin writes that 'His pedestrians act as if they had adapted themselves to the machines and could express themselves only automatically' (Benjamin 1939: 133–34).

18 Madeleine Akrich and Latour define an actant as:

> Whatever acts or shifts actions, action itself being defined by a list of performances through trials; from these performances are deduced a set of competences with which the actant is endowed; the fusions point of a metal is a trial through which the strength of an alloy is defined; the bankruptcy of a company is a trail through which the faithfulness of an ally may be defined; an actor is an actant endowed with a character (usually anthropomorphic).
>
> (Akrich and Latour 1992: 259)

19 For Latour 'no human is as relentlessly moral as a machine' (1992: 232).

20 Marcel Mauss recognised this in the 1930s. He starts from a premise that is roughly the obverse of Latour's: if Latour starts out by arguing that devices are similar to humans in the tasks they perform, Mauss begins by recognising that in as much as humans act (for instance, by squatting), then their bodies are their first technology. See Mauss 1934.

21 Latour suggests that non-human devices not only prescribe uses and forms of behaviour but also users. Grooms are usually found on fire doors and have fairly heavy mechanisms – this then would be part of their prescription and 'because of their prescriptions, these doors *discriminate* against very little and very old persons' (Latour 1992: 234).

22 In cultures where sitting in chairs predominates then humans unlearn what is a human capability: to squat for long periods of time (see Mauss 1934).

23 A decade or so after the birth of my Campus chair, during the years of Margaret Thatcher's governments, social security offices (as well as job centres and other related offices) fundamentally altered. The harsh linoleum and hardwood floors became carpeted; the grilled bank of windows through which you would talk to a civil servant was replaced by open-plan desks; the waiting areas began to resemble the foyers of corporate offices. These spaces began to look 'comfortable', 'informal'. What gave the game away was the fact that the new offices always included a cluster of uniformed and austere security guards.

24 In Christianity there is, alongside all manner of transubstantiations, a recognition of inorganic materiality: 'In the sweat of thy face shalt thou eat bread, till thou

return unto the ground; for out of it wast thou taken; for dust thou *art*, and unto dust shalt thou return' (Genesis 3.19).

25 Object relations psychoanalysis is only secondarily interested in inorganic things. For the most part the important term is 'relations', with 'object' referring to the target of a subject's instinct or drives. For an overview of object relations see Gomez 1997.

26 For Freud the fetishised object is often the last object the boy had seen before the sight of sexual difference, hence the occurrence of shoes, stockings and underwear as the objects of male fetishism. In Freud's account of fetishism it is clear that his primary concern is the boy child. For an interesting account of female fetishism see Gamman and Makinen 1994.

27 Importantly there is a third category of people who are affected by their proximity to the charged object, because of their intimacy with the 'owner'. For instance, a carer might feel a good deal of attachment to a child's teddy. Commercial culture has endlessly sought to capitalise on this process, whereby a customer might 'catch' an affective projection made by others. Advertising and promotional culture more generally is endlessly soliciting us to care about products because other, recognisably famous, people seem to.

28 This process of opening out to the world of the 'not-me' is something that I will return to in chapter six, particularly in relation to eating, and I will give a fuller account of it there.

29 Brown's work on things and what he calls, partly ironically, 'thing theory' can be followed by consulting Brown 1996, 1998, 2003a, 2003b, 2004, 2006a and 2006b.

30 In her work on masculine subjectivity the cultural theorist and film analyst Kaja Silverman notes the striking imbalance between the grandson's interest in throwing objects away and the relatively lower interest in recapturing them (at least numerically). Highlighting this aspect of the game allows Silverman to see masochism as a central component of male subjectivity (1980, 1992).

Chapter 4

Doing time

Work-life

So much of work-life can be about waiting: waiting to get going, waiting to clock-off, waiting for a tea break, waiting for a promotion, waiting for redundancy or retirement, waiting for holidays, waiting for the rush to be over, for the queue to shorten, for the crowds to die down, for the boss to leave, for the pay cheque to come through. Waiting to stop work so that you can do other things: soak tired muscles, fall asleep in front of the TV, cook tea, wash children, go to bed, get up again. The cyclical nature of everyday life is often expressed as a deadening cycle of redundant repetition: the Parisian's '*métro, boulot, dodo*' (commute, work, sleep) or the anarchist slogan 'eat, sleep, work, consume, die', formulate a list that is ongoing and never changing (apart from the final cessation of death). Lefebvre's mordant summary of the relationship between work and leisure recognises just how 'vicious' such a cycle can be: 'so we work to earn our leisure, and leisure has only one meaning: to get away from work. A vicious circle' (Lefebvre 1991 [1958]: 40). And of course it is work that is pitched as the primary vicious element in the cycle. The deadening aspect of repetitive work-life is its lack of narrative possibilities and development (no quest, no transcendence): here it is now and forever, always the same.

Such a perception of work-life is hardly unanimous. For some work is a métier, a calling, a vocation, that can produce satisfactions that could never be completely erased by the alienating conditions of modern work-life. Between the factory worker and the company executive a host of incentives can function to make some cycles more exciting or bearable, or more deadeningly inhuman. Their distribution is uneven and unequal, often deployed in a manner designed so that one person's prize is another's punishment (the key to the executive washroom makes the ordinary washroom starker and even more unlovely; the extraordinary gap between the wage of one and the salary of another makes the lower wage appear even meaner). Yet while the wealthy professional might have more of a sense of forward motion than someone working 'the line', even the well heeled and the well remunerated can find the routine aspects of work-life deadening.[1]

Alongside feelings of pride and achievement, the affective rhythms of routine work-life often fall on the side of boredom, fatigue and frustration. In many countries that have seen a shift away from industrial production towards service provision (for instance the USA and UK), assembly-line labour has become less and less visible. Yet while many industrial forms of production have been outsourced to countries where labour is cheaper, 'service' jobs often have a fixed routine to them: the telephone sales operator has a definite script to follow; the packer at a warehouse fulfilling internet orders must meet their quota. The vast assembly-line production plants of the mid-twentieth century may be less evident, but the ordering of time and work that they instituted is still a crucial aspect of work-life.

Crushing slowness and anxious velocities can be used to describe the sense of duration and rhythm pertaining to work routines. The uniform drag of the assembly line, for instance, has the ability to slow down time. Robert Linhart described his experience of working on the Renault assembly line in the 1970s in the following way: 'the formless music of the line, the gliding movement of the unclad gray steel bodies, the routine movements: I can feel myself gradually enveloped and anesthetized. Time stands still' (Linhart 1981: 13–14). Interviewing workers at the end of the 1960s Studs Terkel spoke to Ned Williams who had been working for Ford for twenty-three years, and describes what it is like for an assembly-line worker to 'take your work home with you':

> Sometimes I felt like I was just a robot. You push a button and you go this way. You become a mechanical nut. You get a couple of beers and go to sleep at night. Maybe one, two o'clock in the morning, my wife is saying, 'Come on, come on, leave it.' I'm still workin' that line. Three o'clock in the morning, five o'clock. Tired. I have worked that job all night. Saturday, Sunday, still working. It's just ground into you.
>
> (Terkel 2004 [1972]: 175)

The rhythm of the assembly line has seeped into his muscles and hijacked his dreams.[2] The time of the line has become his general time, infusing its beat into his 'own' time (into time off).

The slow drudgery of some work produces particular stress, while the harried rhythms of other work generate their different tensions and anxieties. Take the publically emotional labour of waiting on tables. The lunchtime and evening services have their rhythmic peaks and troughs.[3] The preparation of a busy lunchtime service often starts with cleaning tables and arranging them according to bookings, laying-up, writing out a 'specials board', with prepping condiments and restocking the bar and the coffee machine, sweeping the floor, getting the menus out and so on. The first customers often start drifting in just before midday with the onslaught of customers arriving between 12.30 and 13.30. The vast majority of 'covers' (or customers) will have a fixed lunch hour and orders need to be taken quickly and efficiently so that tables can be turned round as soon as possible. The shift will have a curve to it: the speeding-up as the first orders are taken and the slowing-down as the last tables are cleared. The gradual diminution of calmness as the frenzied pace of a busy service clicks into gear, and the gradual return to calm as that frenzy dissipates, is a defining trajectory of the public side of the restaurant trade. But the pace of a shift, its acceleration and deceleration, is also animated by the performance of emotional work: the constant smiling and subtle sycophancy that has to be performed as part of the labour. This takes its toll too. The emotional element has an energy and a rhythm all of its own: when customers are happy and food and drink is moving smoothly, emotional energy allows the shift to flow; but when things start going wrong, when the kitchen gets backed up and orders get confused, and when customers are impatient and rude, then the mixture of anger, forgiveness and shame shatters the smooth unrolling of time, and you feel as if you are caught in the stuttering draw of a perpetual humiliating apology.

It is clear that time doesn't simply exist as a uniform pattern that follows the regular beats of a ticking clock. The common saying that 'time flies when you're having fun' recognises that experiential time doesn't follow the standardised time of clocks. More crucially it recognises that affective states (happiness, fear, boredom and so on) have a temporal dimension to them. Our moods and passions affect our experience of time: a child who can't wait for their birthday experiences the days leading up to it in that strange state of interminable excitement where time teases you with its excessive ability to delay. For the person terrified of a visit to the dentist, time moves too quickly. But the sense of fast or slow time doesn't quite describe the permutations of what has happened to time in relation to forms of work-life and their affective dimensions. What happens to our sense of time, for instance, when we are 'bored out of our brains'?[4] What does time feel like when work is accompanied by guilt or anxiety or anger?

If the standardisation of clock time has been one of the achievements of industrial society, so too has the practical denaturalisation of calendar time and clock time through artificial lighting and widespread temperature control (it maybe a late winter afternoon but we will walk around in the glare of fluorescent lighting wearing T-shirts and jeans). Perhaps the greatest division in time can be rendered as a split between public time (the time of clocks, of eight-hour shifts, of hourly news bulletins, of national holidays) and forms of intimate time (the time of the body, of hunger, of stream of consciousness).[5] And it is in work-life where the conflict between public and intimate forms of time is often experienced most starkly.

The conflict between a 'public' parcelling out of time and the felt time of the body and its streaming consciousness is most vividly enacted in the discipline and strict physical supervision of assembly-line factory labour. The act of clocking-in, of being directed by the sounding of bells and buzzers, of following the tempo of the line, contrast with the body's changing energy, with the debilitating tedium of the task, with the excruciating feeling of time not moving. This is a young worker interviewed in the early 1970s; he works in a factory that makes ping-pong sets:

> You wanna know what I do. I'll give you my whole day. Here it is. They ring a buzzer at seven-forty. Seven forty-five they ring another. You clock in after the first buzzer. If you're not in by the second buzzer you're late. And that's the end of your life till break. Around ten o'clock they give you ten minutes' break. ... Lunch is the same deal as the morning. Two buzzers in, two buzzers out and forty minutes between 'em. Then death till three when the canteen [truck] comes back. Then you go out of your head till the last buzzer.
>
> (Garson 1975: 4)

The public time of the factory is homogenous, empty time and it drains the life out of this worker. The time imprisoned by buzzers feels like the cessation of time, it feels like death, and this nullification of time is its affective product, its emotional tone. (We will come back to the ping-pong factory later.)

But in this chapter I will be less concerned with the conflict between the time of the machine and of the time of the body as it is experienced in assembly-line work; instead I want to focus on what at first might seem to be more informal and amorphous work regimes. The work of 'house-keeping', for instance, which is still mostly invisible as a public form of labour, is not regulated by buzzers and klaxons. Nor is it rewarded by piece-work rates of pay (or any pay for that matter). The tempo isn't set in advance and the end of the working day isn't usually marked by a cold beer. And it is precisely the amorphousness of its temporality, and the impossibility of being finished with it, that has characterised its deflating qualities. This is Simone de Beauvoir's classic description of housework:

> Few tasks are more like the torture of Sisyphus than housework, with its endless repetition: the clean becomes soiled, the soiled is made clean, over and over, day after day. ... Eating, sleeping, cleaning – the years no longer rise up towards heaven, they lie spread out ahead, grey and identical. The battle against dust and dirt is never won. Washing, ironing, sweeping, ferreting out fluff from under wardrobes – all this halting of decay is also the denial of life; for time simultaneously creates and destroys, and only its negative aspect concerns the housekeeper.
>
> (de Beauvoir 1997 [1949]: 470)

The very cadence of de Beauvoir's prose seems to underline the temporal argument: time no longer moves forward ('the years no longer rise up towards heaven'), everything is stuck in endless uniformity and repetition.

If the tone of de Beauvoir's writing casts housework into the mythic realm of hellish oppression and interminable misery, other writers have sought to offer alternative understandings of routine domestic life. Daniel Miller (1998), for instance, in his account of domestic shopping routines argues that shopping for many women (based on his ethnographic research) can more adequately be seen as the routine and difficult performance of practices of love and care. His account carefully acknowledges the subordinate position of those women who are the main carers in households, while also allowing their own understanding of what they do as a practice of material and ordinary love to come to the fore. Luce Giard, in her contribution to the second volume of *The Practice of Everyday Life*, similarly combines the recognition of the subaltern status of women with an account of daily domestic cooking that sees it as a repository for an array of techniques and affects that connect women across generations (de Certeau 1998). Hers is an account of routine domestic cooking that conjures up a world of ordinary life that is at once sensual, canny and emotionally rich, but doesn't ignore the distribution of gendered inequality. In what follows I'm particularly interested in the range of affective energies that circulate around routine domestic work within a cultural context where the predominant experience of it is negative. I'm also particularly interested in the way that contradictory feelings coexist, and in the way that emotions affect our experiences of time in ways that conflict with rationalistic measurements of time.

The history of the last century and a half has seen the same sort of rationalistic 'scientific management' that produced the assembly line, deployed in the home: the will to turn housewives into domestic operators, fully integrated with the latest domestic technologies has been a persistent theme of domestic science since the end of the nineteenth century.[6] During this same period there have been more opportunities for women to find white-collar work in arenas that had previously been the preserve of men. The company office, for instance, underwent a form of regendering from about 1870 onwards. At the same time as women entered these hallowed grounds, and as a determining condition of their greater presence there, office work fundamentally altered. If a mid-nineteenth-century clerk had a good sense of how the whole company was run, and might realistically see his role as one leading to higher office, the twentieth-century secretary is the result of a much more elaborate division of labour, one that consequently affected the extent and range of clerical work as well as the value and prospects of the clerical worker.[7] The twentieth-century secretary was located in the personnel office, or in accounts, or the legal department, or in a host of other locations and her sphere of influence and concomitant chances of advancement were exponentially less than the early nineteenth-century scribe. The image of a female work-force in the twentieth century (which, of course, in actuality would include cleaners, engineers, lawyers, politicians, psychiatrists and myriad other roles) is perhaps dominated by the image of the secretary and the typing pool. Or rather, the image of the typing-pool becomes the image of mass feminised labour, of 'white-collar' labour, with all its complex class associations.

By focusing on office work (particularly routinised forms of typewriting) and housework it should be clear that the gendering of time in everyday life is very much at issue in this chapter. Women's time is not here rendered as biologically distinct from men's.[8] But I wouldn't want to argue that temporal differences of gender are simply a condition of a surface organisation of roles, labour and emotion. Rather, the organisation of roles, labour and emotion is fundamental to the 'distribution of the sensible' (see chapter two) and to the cultural ontology of the self. A cultural argument that takes seriously the sex-gender system would see it as a constituting force, producing us as gendered subjects.[9] This isn't either strategic essentialism or cultural relativism writ large; rather it recognises that we are essentially (and by this I mean constitutionally) social and cultural creatures that are born into second-hand worlds that are fundamentally and seemingly exhaustively gendered. In what follows I will concentrate on housework, but I will also finish with a smaller section on typing and the lure of routine.

Housework and emotion time

Housework is a vaguer term than 'cleaning' or 'cooking' or 'childcare': it can include all these elements (and more) and has no specific practices, set of objects or temporal boundary. At what points of the day does house-work begin and end? What forms of routine domestic 'maintenance' would not be included in its amorphous sweep? The time of housework is more or less invisible because it is never ending, because it is often taken care of under solitary circumstances and because it has traditionally been done by women.[10] So much of what it achieves is both necessary and ephemeral, essential to the life of a household, but so quickly needed again. How long does a meal last before the next one must be prepared? How long does a sink stay clean?

In 1983 as part of the revival of Mass-Observation (a project begun in 1937 to gather 'a weather map of popular feeling' [Mass-Observation 1937: 30]) a directive was sent out to five hundred or so diarists to record their domestic life and, more particularly, the routines of housework.[11] The choice of housework as the topic for its autumn directive is hardly arbitrary; while it is true that Mass-Observation has always paid particular attention to private life and domesticity as the central arena of the everyday, this specific orientation towards housework should be seen in the light of feminism's politicising of housework as a public issue in the 1970s. The renewed Mass-Observation project of the early 1980s coincided with a period of intense reflection and politicising of housework that included, as one of many phenomena, the campaign for 'wages for housework'.[12]

Mass-Observation is dedicated to 'recording everyday life in Britain'[13] and in the period of Mass-Observation after 1981 diarists were explicitly asked to write for future historians who would want to understand the lives of ordinary people.[14] By framing the project of writing about ordinary life in this way, correspondents were being asked to provide as much detail about their daily life as they could; who could tell what a future cultural or social historian would be interested in? But while it is primarily an encouragement to produce thickly rendered accounts of the present, and to explain the taken-for-granted aspects of it, writing for the historians of the future also has other temporal affects. Like ordinary diarists, Mass-Observation correspondents probably have a complex sense of audience, which would include an audience projected into the future. For Mass-Observers this is made explicit by being asked to write for a putative and virtual set of future historians and this accounts for something of the temporal atmosphere that often pervades these documents: all this, the correspondents seem to be telling the reader, will have happened a long time ago. Mortality, both the finitude of death and the mourning of passing time, is a subterranean seam that runs through these documents as correspondents consider their (and others') pasts and futures in the context of an ever-changing present. The future-perfect, or future-anterior, is a tense where hope and fear meld with melancholy (all this will have had to have happened; the future I hoped for and feared is now past), and it is a tense that corresponds to an experience of living historical time. Living historical time infuses with daily time in ordinary life, because as well as living 'now' we also live with the possibilities (with the limits and opportunities) that the future is seen as providing (or will have provided). Being able to see the future as significantly different or substantially the same as the present, places the intimate politics of living within the realm of the day-to-day imagining of narrative cohesion, continuity and change.

Rita Felski proffers a heuristic division of time split into three overlapping categories: 'everyday-time', 'life-time' and 'large-scale time'. Everyday-time is time as it is phenomenally experienced. She asks 'is our daily sense of time most strongly influenced by the relentless, impersonal regularities of clocks and timetables, by the frenzied flickering pace of television and media culture, or by the subterranean flow of natural bodily rhythms?' (Felski 2000: 17). The answer for many will be 'all of the above and more'. Everyday-time is the time of day-dreams and punctuality (or the lack of it); of routines of ablution, eating and defecation; of procrastination and hitting deadlines; of sleep and radio alarm clocks. Life-time, for Felski, is time shaped into intimate narrative forms:

It is the process of understanding one's life as a project that encompasses and connects the random segments of daily experience. It is the creation of oneself as an autobiographical subject and the act of reflecting on one's existence and finitude.

(Felski 2000: 17)

This is the time that is most likely to be recorded in diaries and it is the time where the question of whether the years 'rise up towards heaven' or not is most often addressed. The third time category is large-scale time: 'these larger time frames allow us to talk about shared pasts and collective futures and to fashion larger narratives around group identities such as nation, religion, or ethnicity' (Felski 2000: 18). Here personal political imaginings coalesce or conflict with more collective imaginings: a less patriarchal future, a life where routines are valued and rejuvenating, for instance.

While it might be tempting to see these three levels (from everyday-time to large-scale time) as time becoming progressively ordered and public, this doesn't quite fit with actuality. While life-time can be experienced as a linear progressive narrative, it is also often experienced as a sense of competing accounts of what you are and could be; accounts that are also in a constant state of being constantly redrafted and replotted. Similarly large-scale time can also provide living contradictions. Between, for instance, a large-scale sense of political hope and hopelessness, we can forge stories of human progress and catastrophe that seem mutually exclusive but are contradictions lived in a constant state of negotiation. That we live across and between these three levels of time should be easily apparent when we think of how, during the course of a day, we flit between: the random minutiae of the daily; the puffery and self-deprecation of our autobiographical lives; and the competing stories of life projected into a collective future. (Such flitting is also a feature of broadcast media.) But here it is the way that gender and feminism animate these temporalities that is of primary concern.[15]

The 1983 Mass-Observation directive (which was a letter sent out to the correspondents) asked: 'Over one week please keep a "log" of jobs done and time spent cleaning, tidying, shopping and cooking, noting who does these. If, however, there is no *significant* variation between one day and another, then please just log one day.' I want to focus on just one person's response to this directive. The Mass-Observation project contains many extraordinary documents partly because the diarists are encouraged to write extensively in response to the directives that they receive. They can also include drawings, photographs, swatches of wallpaper and curtain material, alongside the relatively long written responses. The response I'm interested in is a fifty-page type-written account of two weeks of domestic life.[16] It is an astonishing document not least because it carries out the job of undertaking a weekly log twice: the first time it is recorded as a descriptive narrative in the life of a household and the labour that is required by the female correspondent to maintain it; the second time the household chores are undertaken by her with a stopwatch and with a desire to be more organised with her time and to delegate chores to other family members. But it is also extraordinary for the varied affective states that it registers, from depression, anger, guilt and frustration, through humorous interludes, to deeply moving transformations and reflections. This Mass-Observation correspondent writes empirically (in the Humean sense) because as well as recording and reflecting on the experience of housework she also experiments with it, transforming and sensitising the very instrument of empirical knowledge (herself). If empiricism takes the human sensorium as the instrument for registering experience (and the knowledge associated with it), then it logically follows that such an instrument can be sensitised and desensitised towards different aspects of the world. Empirical knowledge isn't a once-and-for-all task, but is a process of calibration and recalibration, where the human subject is in a constant state of adjustment, reflection and experiment. Or at least this is what empiricism promises and it is what is delivered in this correspondent's writing.

The correspondent was in her mid-thirties when she wrote the text, living on a smallholding on the edge of a provincial town in Essex. We find out that she dislikes the way she is. She admits to being bad at housework, of not getting up early enough to pack the kids off to school. She loves reading feminist literature but also blames this for her feelings of dissatisfaction:

> The trouble is I don't like the way I am but it obviously doesn't bother me enough to actually change my ways it just means that I have a constant low opinion of myself which I try and cover up by laughing about it. I think it stems from reading too much feminist literature.
>
> (8)

It is not hard to read irony in this last comment: this is someone self-identifying as a feminist who is constantly aware of the patriarchal distribution of domestic tasks, but who also recognises the difficulty and emotional price of living 'the feminist life' within the institution of the family. Her husband, Matt,[17] takes care of some household chores and seems generally sympathetic to her desire to transform their family life.

The log begins some months after the original directive was sent out. It follows the course of the first week with loose descriptive accounts of activities that are written in a way that is as revealing about her lack of commitment to housework as it is successful in itemising the maintenance of the household. Here is the beginning of the first day:

> Matt was up before me, this log was kept just after Christmas [1983], the children were still on holiday and Matt was easing himself gently

back into work again. I don't know what time he left the house, but he brought me up a mug of tea which was cold when I got up about 10.30 am. ... I presume the children got themselves some cereal and a drink whenever they got up.

And here is the end of that same day:

Started ironing and packed up when Matt came in. Made him a cup of coffee and bowl of soup which he washed down with sherry and then fell asleep watching TV with the kids. I wanted to watch the *Arena* series on George Orwell so I was relegated with my bowl of soup and toasted cheese to watch the black and white TV in the bedroom. The mobile fish and chip van didn't arrive as expected so Matt prepared ham, egg and baked beans for the kids and himself.

(1)

Like any snippet of diary we are left with questions and speculations: is it 'special interest' TV that gets relegated to the bedroom or just TV that she wants to watch? Does Matt usually drink sherry or is this left over from Christmas? The ordinary routines and rituals of eating, drinking and watching TV are distributed in uneven and idiosyncratic ways.

The second day of the log is a Saturday and the diary raises the question of whether Matt is behaving as he usually does or if he has cottoned on to the fact that she is itemising household labour:

Matt had previously agreed to go to the nearby Tesco superstore with us to get a few items. I can't remember the last time that he ... came to a supermarket with us and taking us to the market was so out of character that I was convinced that he knew I was keeping this log on that day!

Jim [her son] and Matt spent the rest of the afternoon logging wood. I emptied my collection of kitchen waste on to the compost heap – this is one of the daily tasks of the household. Washed up lunch dishes. Hung some washing on the line, and took in some now dry and ready for sorting. Got in coal. Washed and dried Rebecca's hair. Did as much ironing as I could bear. Drew all the curtains. Prepared dinner. Washed up late in the evening made some coffee and ham sandwiches for supper.

(2)

The amorphousness and endlessness of housework is evident here, as too is the sense that housework involves not just the maintenance of a physical ecosystem but also the primary emotional maintenance of care and concern of the household.[18]

One of the central themes in the document is the relationship between housework and emotions. Implicit within this account is a sense of the duration of emotion-work. For instance at one point in the account she becomes furious with the curtains:

> I had taken the curtain track off the wall to clean it and it took me an hour to work out how to put the blasted system together again. To cap it all I find that one of the curtains have shrunk. Frustration turns into sheer blind rage.
>
> (7)

Whether this felt like an hour or took an hour is difficult to tell, but the sense that an affective state such as rage extends the experiential time of a chore seems very much in evidence.

In ordinary life we often talk about time dragging (in relation to boredom or anticipation) or its fleeting presence (in the context of elation or fun) but a more thorough understanding of the relationship between time and emotional life would have to move beyond the slowing-down and speeding-up of experiential time. Affective states such as anger, frustration, happiness, resentment, bitterness, laughter and guilt do more than slow down or speed up time. In one sense they could all be seen as intensifying a sense of time because they are primarily sensorial intensities themselves. But these intensities have their peculiar durations. Someone's anger might flare up in a second but then might dissipate over hours, days or minutes. Resentment might prolong the inequity of a task by projecting it both backwards and forwards in time. Guilt can hang around, muddying the flow of time, worming its way into the past and unsettling spent time. Happiness and euphoria can expand time, making us feel that this time, our time, connects to an oceanic sense of time as we marvel at cloud formations and take pleasure in everything under the sun.

One way of viewing the relationship between emotions and experiential time is to see it as often resulting from clashes between everyday-time, life-time and large-scale time. At the level of everyday-time intensities may arise because clock time (for instance) clashes with alimentary time (hunger, primarily) or circadian time (the body's need for sleep, play, rest and so on). But the primary affective intensities that are evident in this account of domestic routines concern clashes between all three 'levels' of time. Resentment, or guilt, for instance are not the result of something immanent to everyday-time, but are generated when everyday-time clashes with life-time and large-scale time. The very fact that you might be able to simultaneously experience two affects that are as seemingly conflicting as resentment and guilt suggest that life-time and large-scale time are themselves complexly connecting and disconnecting.

Our Mass-Observation diarist offers a scene that bristles with complex affective intensities, and suggests some of the ways in which emotions shape time:

> Feelings of guilt because I have to ask Matt to collect Rachel from the birthday party. I was in the middle of preparing dinner so if I had gone he would have had to take over that. I felt guilty because I know he hates chasing about in the car after the kids, but I also felt cross with him because I also hate collecting them but usually end up doing it and I think that's the sort of job we should share when possible. Jim offered to go with him and actually call for her so that Matt can sit in the car and be spared making small talk with the birthday child's Father who has a white collar job with the local Water Authority and who Matt thinks is a right shit.
>
> (14)

In a very practical sense guilt and anger can be seen as emotional work that takes up time. So here, even though the diarist is not doing something (picking up the kids) she is temporally involved in this activity through the feelings of guilt and anger that it produces. It is not hard to locate a range of larger narratives here that orchestrate the specific affective states that are being articulated: narratives of class and masculinity (between Matt and the 'right shit'); narratives of 'dutiful' labour; narratives of fairness and justice and so on. But it is not easy to unpick them. The rightful anger of the diarist is clear: within patriarchal family structures it is commonly assumed (by many men at least) that a man might carry out housework in an effort to 'help out', but that the obligation for it rests (tacitly) on the woman's shoulders. But this anger is also peppered with guilt and the guilt is not easy to explain away. On the one hand it could be seen as an internalisation of a gendered sense of duty (even though it is set against the fact that she is preparing dinner), on the other hand the sense of guilt is related to the fact that for Matt picking up the kids involves him in all sorts of class confrontations. And it is here that we can partly make sense of her emotional frustration with both living the specificity of an everyday life (here and now, with these people and routines) and trying to live 'the feminist life'.

In a recent historical account of the relationship between the 'housewife' and feminism, Lesley Johnson and Justine Lloyd have offered a nuanced account of the emergence of second wave feminism in the 1960s and 1970s. Taking a genealogical approach they have positioned the classic works of Betty Friedan (1965), Germaine Greer (1971), and Ann Oakley (1974a) as conduct books.[19] Conduct books tell you how to live and, importantly, how to perform selfhood. These three books demonised the picture of the housewife as the failure of 'self-actualisation': housework and the selfhood of the housewife (what little there was in the dominant picture painted by second wave feminism) stymied the process of actualising a self because it failed to allow for the narrative possibilities of fashioning autonomous, future-looking, intellectually and creatively ambitious selves:

> The texts of early second wave feminists, as conduct books of a kind, thus provided forms of training through which women could learn to understand themselves as self-choosing and acquire the desire to be self-determining, able to order their lives and the world around themselves by planning and making their own selves. Understood in this way, it becomes clearer why Friedan's book sought to make the issues of feminism psychological and primarily personal.
>
> (Johnson and Lloyd 2004: 14)

As conduct books, these examples of second wave feminism performed a 'technology of the self' that was based on future-orientated narrative of self-formation. As such it often 'requires of women that they pursue a fantasy of the feminist subject as fully unified and coherent, able to define herself and her world un-ambiguously' (Johnson and Lloyd 2004: 17). Johnson and Lloyd offer a large, revisionist history of the housewife across the twentieth century (focusing primarily on Australia) and charting organisations such as the Australian Housewives' Association (formed in 1915) as well as specific media formats dedicated to housewives (magazines, radio programmes and so on). Their argument is that the sort of feminist identities that became possible in the 1970s were dependent on much earlier forms of politicisation around housework and the figure of the housewife which had already situated domestic labour as a public issue and, importantly, as a collective issue.

The diarist's sense of time knotted and pinched with intense feelings of guilt, anger and shame (but also elation and satisfaction) is partly a result of the way that the production of life-time (including various versions of feminist life-time) conflicts with everyday-time and large-scale time. On the one hand the feminist self that is being fashioned and performed is much more divided than the one imagined in second wave feminism (in this sense it is much closer to Johnson and Lloyd's sense of the multiple histories of feminism) and on the other hand this is not the only life-work she is doing: she is also establishing a range of commercial craft-based enterprises with Matt that will allow them to be self-sufficient; she is undertaking a university degree; performing a number of community-based duties; and last but by no means least writing as a Mass-Observation correspondent.[20]

The anonymity of Mass-Observation alongside the confessional aspects of much second wave feminism allows for a narrative peppered with conflicting emotional energies. Explaining how frustrating she finds doing house repairs in a household where her husband is a professional builder, and where she feels she is constantly the recipient of a negative assessment of her work, she writes:

> My standards aren't bad enough to make him want to do the job however, but he always has to make remarks like – 'Couldn't you get that bit of paint off that edge?' He's right of course, it's little things like that that make the difference between just doing a job or doing a job well. So I try and compromise by doing it as best I can a bit at a time and then getting him to 'inspect' it for flaws before the seal goes on, just to make my point and if I'm honest probably trying to glean some sort of appreciation from him, or even praise! How pathetic I am at times.
>
> (4)

But while wanting appreciation is a common concern with invisible labour we shouldn't read the decision to have it 'inspected' by Matt as complete supplication to his standards: the inspection is designed, I would assume, to tease him and his perfectionist standards and to embarrass him in his role of overseer.

The undecided nature of emotional work (the ambivalence of combined guilt and anger, for instance) is reflected in the constant misunderstandings that take place between the Mass-Observation correspondent and her husband Matt. The misunderstandings always seem to involve the misrecognition of where affective energy is aimed (for instance the interpretation of laughter as being 'laughing-at' someone, rather than 'laughing-about' something that has happened). Feminism, as we will see, provides the grounds for correcting the apprehension that Matt is dissatisfied with her contribution to the housework, by supplying the means for bringing invisible emotional labour into the foreground, and we find out that he is directing anger at himself for not completing a household task:

> When he put my back up recently by commenting on the generally dirty veneer on our stairs and the surrounding walls, he wasn't implying that I should have been scrubbing every dirty mark off as they appeared, but in fact feeling angry with himself for not sealing all the wood on them as soon as they had been fitted, so that we could have then painted the walls and even if we couldn't afford the carpet at least the surfaces would have been more resistant to dirt and also easier to clean.
>
> (7)

Emotional time is unevenly spread, but it is also shared by the work of never quite doing enough, of having to eke out a living where coming to a workable compromise and getting something finished properly can often be at odds.

Stopwatch, habit and drift

The crucial break in the document comes after ten pages of detailed narration. A week of logging housework is over. After a period of reflection the author decides to repeat the week of logging again but this time using Jim's stopwatch. Timing housework with a stopwatch invokes the scientific management of the domestic sphere which was a central element of the rationalisation of the home at the very end of the nineteenth century and early twentieth century.[21] From the perspective of second wave feminism the rationalisation of housework looks like a further embedding of women within the home (this time as efficient domestic operatives). And yet the scientific management of the home is also part of the history of feminism (or its prehistory), and the desire to rationalise housework was seen as freeing up the sort of spare time that men enjoyed, so as to provide opportunities for hobbies, leisure and self-improvement.[22] The first week of accounting involves a meandering narrative that extends into the wilder territories of affective life. Each time an affective state is described the time of description seems to expand (or its registration as description expands).[23] A more 'scientific' itemising seems to partially block the affective reflection. Narrative continuity is swapped for something that often approaches the qualities of an accounts ledger, for example: 'Hang out completed load of washing, bring some articles in off line, sort and fold ready for ironing or just airing: 6 mins', or: 'Cleaned out oven which had been sprayed with oven cleaner the night before, "jiffed" sink (for future historians' reference this means I used a cream cleansing liquid called "jif"): 31 mins' (14).

But if itemising work is an effective way of decreasing the 'wild' affective states that might animate a narrative it is impossible for these to be totally kept out of the account:

> Set off to change tractor parts that were purchased yesterday. On the way back drop off a chair at a place that runs a paint stripping service. Call at an Antique Restorer's work shop further down the road and leave a washstand – retrieved from a dark corner of the stable – to have the surrounding upstand which had disappeared over the years replaced. Ashamed of myself when, as I'm gingerly reversing the car out on to a busy junction, I contemplate leaning over and locking the passenger door in case the three punks who are walking on the pavement around the front of the car decide to open the passenger door and swipe my handbag off the seat. Call at little farm shop nearby to buy vegetables. Deliver one of the Cub Scout Agenda's: 1 hr 8 mins.
>
> Light fire, get in coal and wood from outside the back door: 4 mins. Prepare lunch: 12 mins. Further preparations for evening meal: 23 mins. Wash, dry and clear away collected items: 9 mins.
>
> (23)

Affective intensities demand a form of description that can't be contained within an itemised ledger. And if there is a correlation between affective energy and the form of description that it demands, then to establish a practice (one more systematic, more quantifiable, more precise in its measurements) that requires a neutral itemising of tasks might also be to produce a practice that lessens the likelihood of affective experience itself.

Rationalisation becomes an effective way of lessening the amount of work being done (both emotionally and physically), but comes with its own physical price. The daily chore of collecting a barrow of logs for the fire is turned into a weekly task:

> So I got in eight barrow loads of wood which should last us a week it took me 36 mins but I reckon that's about half the time I would normally spend in a week if I was getting wood in every day. I did give myself backache doing it but the pile really looks lovely situated on the wall just inside the back door and what bliss to think that I haven't got to worry about it every day. I might also be able to earn a bit extra pocket money doing this job in the future.
>
> (33)

By conducting the sort of time and motion studies employed by scientific management (albeit in an informal way) the author saves time that can now be spent in other ways (in ways that could be more aimed at self-actualisation, for instance) but at the price of more concentrated exertion which results in physical stress.[24] The author's decision to use a stopwatch as well as her decision to rationalise and delegate chores involves a different 'distribution of the sensible', a different way of parcelling out time and distributing affective life. Stopwatches can only measure the physical time of a task, not the emotional investment of time-spent in preparation or in post hoc affect (resentment around a task, for instance, would include forms of procrastination as well as the storehouse of bitterness that might produce a corrosive temporal tail to the task).

Across this account of domestic routines and housework (emotional and practical) the theme of drifting occurs at two crucial moments. The first is during the diarist's reflection on the narrative of the first week and the second is similarly placed at the conclusion of the second week's more fractured account of housework. Even though the two drifts are significantly different (one is about the drifting within housework, the other is describing the drift back towards familiar habits) they are interrelated. At the end of the first week the correspondent offers a description of her method of housework that reads like a practical demonstration of John Dewey's exemplification of non-aesthetic experience (see Chapter 2):

Well, there is my log, I'm sorry I didn't keep a check on actual time spent on these various jobs. I would have found that very difficult and rather depressing. To begin with I drift through the day intending to start one job and finding that I'm involved in another completely different one. For instance I might put some milk on to make yoghourt, then go to the utility room to collect the broom in order to sweep the kitchen floor and seeing a muddle in there, start cleaning that up or perhaps remembering there's some washing to be hung out on the line or the loo wants cleaning. ... I seem to spend my entire day in this sort of muddle and by the end of the day I don't seem to have made any impression. I am often amazed at just how little I do achieve in a day and yet I am still occupied, but just don't seem to have anything to show for it.

(7)

This sense of a busy work-life accompanied by a feeling of never accomplishing anything substantial is a perennial experience found in studies of housework.[25] But in this account it heralds a critical moment that introduced a new way of practising housework. The drifting movement of time would be replaced by a more precise attention to the tasks at hand, a new distribution of chores, and a strong sense that tasks are discrete with distinct beginnings and endings.

The shift to a more precise performing and accounting for tasks is heralded by a dialogue between the diarist and Matt that is also facilitated by a feminist ethos of discussion, fuelled as well by reading feminist literature about housework:

The children are home from school today on an 'occasional' day. Matt and I were both reading to the early hours of the morning and so we both overslept. He is due to start another job today but as it is not pressing we sat and had a long discussion about the feminist movement and how it affects us as a family unit both directly through my feminist ideals and indirectly as a result of the changes that have taken place in society generally because of the movement. This discussion was sparked off by the book I was reading last night – The Guilt Cage by Suzanne Lowry (a study of Housewives and how a decade of so called liberation has affected them), and the feelings of failure, inadequacy and anger I had been mulling over since completing the previous pages of this directive a week or so ago.

(11)[26]

The decision to use a stopwatch is partly designed to introduce a certain amount of objectivity into the log: 'In order to be more objective I have borrowed Jim's stopwatch. I have also determined to concentrate on one job at a time which I have since discovered takes a lot of self discipline' (11). Alongside the rationalisation of tasks, chores have been delegated to the kids and to Matt and some tasks have simply been dropped. But the active refusal of drifting by a new system of self-imposed monitoring is also designed as part of a recognition that tasks take longer when they are accompanied by an emotional outlay that could be redirected.

It seems clear that the stopwatch week had a number of outcomes which improved the experience of housework (for a week, if nothing else). While some of this is no doubt down to the new time-fashioning that is taking place (the stricter parcelling out and demarcating of time and the effective blocking of emotional labour) it is more readily explainable through the new organisation of the household that an explicit feminist agenda has introduced. The resulting assessment is a complex recognition of the potential to redistribute time and tasks and brings together (not in any easy way) a range of different feminist moments:

> The week that I used a stop watch I enjoyed very much. I learnt a lot about myself and my family that week. I also realized that my days being 'Housewife' and Mother are not unproductive even if they feel like it most of the time. One thing that surprised me was just how little time each job does in fact take and that has helped me approach these routine tasks with a slightly different attitude now. If I want to carry on whining about a housewife's lot then that's up to me, but if I take the attitude that these jobs have to be done and so it's much better to rope in help from the rest of the family when and where possible and I have proved to myself that if I actually get up as soon as possible in the morning, get the necessary tasks finished and then I *can* fit in other jobs that I get more pleasure from.
>
> (40)

The classic second wave feminist diagnosis of housework is now rendered as 'whining' (though it is still an option) while a more practical feminism that is associated with earlier moments of domestic politics is elevated. But this does not involve a rejection of second wave feminism, far from it, it actually allows for the realisation of its goals more effectively. To a degree, then, the diarist is working through a history of feminism and the temporal dimensions it generates.

This account of two weeks of housework comes to an end with something approaching narrative closure. Life-time, large-scale time and everyday-time have been renegotiated in a compromise formation that is at least temporarily satisfying (and for the moment temporally satisfying). The household itself has been reworked and the relationship between Matt and the author has altered. What we are left with though is a dizzying array of tasks that seem to explode the possibility of ordering time in a coherent fashion:

After discussing the directive with Matt I find that I get more support from him now when I ask the children to do something. I have also adopted a method of making a list of jobs that I either need to do or want to do but can't somehow get round to them – for instance, phone signwriter to arrange for new business sign, work out what support system I'm going to use for the new raspberry plantation and order the posts etc. repot house plants, finish accounts ready to go into the Accountants for audit, finish decorating utility room which has at last had the quarry tiles laid on the floor and the skirting and architrave fixed etc. finish university work. I find that by having this list it gives me something to aim for, as I cross each job off it gives me a sense of both achievement and relief, and I am aiming to finish the list completely before I draw up another one of more jobs that I want or need to do.

(40–41)[27]

The ambition and drive of the author is never far from the surface of this account. It is evident in the physical presence of the document as a thick neatly typed piece of writing, lovingly and carefully put together. If one narrative that the account describes is of a woman worker negotiating her lack of time, and her relationship with housework, feminism and family, another narrative describes a writer accomplishing a narrative account of housework that is ebullient and proud while also being lightly self-deprecating. While one initial reading of this diary might suggest a sense of obsessive documenting, it seems clear by the end that it hasn't been obsessive enough. Clearly the amount of time-expenditure on housework has to be accounted for in relation to other kinds of work that the correspondent is also undertaking, and it has to be seen in relation to Matt's work. You could imagine the next level of itemising and accounting which sought to include all forms of labour, alongside housework, in a comparison between Matt and the diarist.

The second 'drift' though is telling. This is the drift of habit pulling at her. In many ways it is the victory of everyday-time over life-time and large-scale time, in other ways it suggests that everyday-time has its own rhythm that is ordered to a different notion of life-time than the self-authoring task of detailing intentions:

I must admit that over the last few weeks I have started to drift back into my old habits, I find I'm getting the wood in each day again, and the house is not so clean as it could be, for instance I know there's a layer of dust *everywhere*. During the week I had the motivation of actually completing the directive to keep me going, but since then, other things have taken priority over the house.

(40)

This is, I want to argue, not simply a failure of self-discipline, nor is it to be explained by the profound pull of the narrative sense of emotional life that the drifting performance of housework allows. In many ways it is a historical critique of various versions of feminism played out across the terrain of the everyday. What we are left with is the self-work of a diary writer fashioning a literary self where drifting is part and parcel of a life-time whose formation is ambitious, intricately entwined with various household projects and intellectual projects, which can't be reconciled into an homogenous subjectivity. The return to drift is both a critique of a more instrumental rationalist feminism and a critique of some of the self-actualising demands of the conduct-book aspect of second wave feminism. But it is also reliant on these formations too. If she can't marshal time into a rationally efficient schema, she can't turn her life into a self-sufficient project either. But in this messy and beautifully rendered account of work-life, we get a glimpse of emotionally bountiful time that is both open and constrained, filled with both possibilities and lost opportunities. It is a complex feminist time lived in all its difficulties, in all its real compromises, accomplishments and material affects.

Click, click, click ... the orchestrations and seductions of routine

I want to leave our Mass-Observer diarist here, returning to the drift of the day-to-day. To end this chapter I want to briefly look at the time routines of typists, but again I want to do this via one specific account. The lure of routine is to surrender to a certain temporal rhythm. To see the pleasure in this is perhaps to see the pleasure in a form of self-nullification that is foreign to most intellectual projects (dedicated as they nearly always are to the sorts of self-actualisation that are often necessary for becoming an intellectual with institutional legitimation). The routine work of being a typist is not, then, the goal of those ambitiously striving for self-authorship in whatever form. But as a way of establishing a basic material form of autonomy it was a very real option for many women. For commentators from both the political right and left a common answer to the alienation of housework and the 'lot' of the housewife has been to get a job. For educated women, primarily for single women in the late nineteenth and early twentieth centuries, and particularly those from the lower middle classes, the solution was to get a 'nice' office job. As an advert for typewriters put it:

> the benevolent can, by the gift of a 'Type-Writer' to a poor, deserving young woman, put her at once in the way of earning a good living as a copyist or corresponding clerk. No invention has opened for women so broad and easy an avenue to profitable and suitable employment as the 'Type-Writer,' and it merits the careful consideration of all

thoughtful and charitable persons interested in the subject of work for woman.

(1875 Remington advert cited in Davies 1982: 54)

The rise of the secretary as an *image* of independent woman has to be reconciled with the actuality that for many the job was accompanied by the sort of low pay that made full independence something that was usually impossible to accomplish (see Keep 1997). And because this image of female labour was rendered as a form of 'incidental' economic supplement (to add to the household whose main earner was a man; or to fill in the time before a woman got married) it was difficult to see it as a career that one day would achieve the sort of financial security that goes with full independence.[28] For others, of course, the secretarial pool was not available because the levels of literacy required to operate within it were not evenly distributed across the classes.

The rise of the typist as a female trade is an interesting story not least because, from one angle, it can be seen as a technical, mechanical role that might relate to the male-dominated printing trade. For Margery W. Davies the typewriter in the 1880s 'was such a new machine that it had not been "sex-typed" as masculine' (1982: 55).[29] It seems clear that in the early years of the typist (the late nineteenth century and into the twentieth) a good deal of gender work was performed so that the role of typist became primarily associated with women. One aspect of this was a conscious mechanical association of the typewriter with the sewing machine rather than the printing press. Another aspect of this gender work was the regendering of the job of private or personal secretary away from its role as apprentice executive towards its association as 'office wife'. An employment guide for educated women who didn't want to enter the teaching profession could claim in 1910 that 'a man chooses his secretary much as he chooses his wife, and for much the same reasons' (cited in Davies 1982: 154).

The account of a typist's routine that I want to look at here is from a book published in 1975 called *All the Livelong Day: The Meaning and Demeaning of Routine Work*. In the early 1970s the book's author, Barbara Garson (a community activist and labour organiser as well as journalist, playwright and single mother), went to a number of factories and work situations to interview workers, especially those in routine, repetitive jobs. Towards the end of the book she tries to find out about routine office workers but finds them even harder to get access to than the factory workers. Her final chapter describes her own experience of taking a job as typist at the Kennel Club in New York where she has to type out information about dog owners and their dogs on data cards. But before we get to this description it is worth setting the scene provided by the other chapters.

For a book so obviously about the hardship of poorly paid work as well as about the strain and stress of unrelenting routines (as well as the dictatorial supervisors that implement them) it is a surprisingly musical (or at least a sonorous) one. The way people describe their work is often in relation to noise (the constant boom of the factory; the loud sudden blast of the buzzer); but perhaps what is more surprising is the sense of musicality that people use to describe their own pleasures and pains of routine work. For instance, in the ping-pong factory mentioned earlier, Garson finds packers who have a fine sense of discernment about different types of box that they have to assemble. What gives pleasure or, to put it in the more nuanced language that a ping-pong factory employer might, the boxes that are least horrible to assemble are the ones that allow a smooth rhythmic musicality:

> The UT-2 was Gregg's favorite box. It was the smoothest to assemble and he could do five hundred in a day. Of course he quickly denied an interest in working fast for Paragon. 'Not that I give a fuck how many I get done. But some of the boxes just don't fold right and then you have to fix them. The UT-2 you just flip. Flip, flip, flip ... feels good'.
>
> (Garson 1975: 13)

'Feeling good', in this situation, is about a connected orchestration and ease of rhythm. Rather than feeling happy about work it is directed at the material actuality of work (the boxes feel good).

Repetitive rhythms can lull us into calmness or drag us into machinic compliance against which our creaturely bodies rebel. To guard against the acquiescence with rhythmic monotony another musical figure intervenes. The arrhythmic or syncopated sound interferes with the perpetual monotony of the assembly line's beat to animate the deadening routines:

> Well for one thing lots of people have a special noise they make. Like one guy who welds the screws onto the bracket – every so many pieces he lets out a tremendous yell. Another guy keeps saying 'Sarge,' or something like that, I can't quite make it out. My noise is 'ey-yoo.' I yell it whenever I feel like it.
>
> (Garson 1975: 11)

The sudden shout over the perpetual racket of machinery is enunciated 'whenever I feel like it' and is a bodily reply to the dull orchestration of the factory's soundscape. If it is an exuberant sound it is not one that the machinic world recognises but it is one that the body seems to require in such circumstances.

Barbara Garson's book is an animated and impassioned account of human belittlement by the organisation of labour. It is filled with little pleasures, sonic outbursts or the smooth acoustics of a particular box, set against an environment of structural exploitation. In the final section of the book she turns her attention to the world of office work. To start with Garson interviews women working in insurance companies and banks whose tasks are to input data on special cards that can be read by computers. These are the early years of computerisation and techniques of key-punching make holes in pieces of card that signify numerical information about wages and claims. Like many routine jobs the major complaint is isolation: you may be in a room with dozens of others but essentially you are tied to a single machine, separated from the other workers both by noise and by the concentration necessary to punch accurately. While interviewing various keypunchers Garson finds a common practice of 'racing'. This is Irene describing her races with Aida:

> One thing Aida and I used to do is have races. On the older machines you had to hit harder and they made a louder noise. So we could hear each other and when we were doing the same job we could race. Sometimes we'd synchronise – adjust so that you'd move into the next field exactly together. But you're always pressured to go the fastest with the least errors. So we'd synchronize for a while but it always turned into races. We didn't plan the races but we found ourselves listening to how fast the other person was going and doing it a little faster. At first we didn't know that the other one was racing. We were both doing it but we didn't know.
>
> (Garson 1975: 154–55)

Here a phatic form of communication emerges between two keypunchers: there is no information being communicated, only the basic connection that is being made through the rhythms of keypunching.

One of the more extraordinary accounts of sonic communication involves a keypuncher who is neither a synchroniser nor a racer, but as Garson has it is 'a complex syncopater':

> 'This'll sound crazy,' she said, 'but I like to keep a certain rhythm ... sound going. I mean I'd move forward when the woman next to me was halfway through another field and then she'd move in when I was halfway through the next. So you'd get a constant – like, bum, bum, zing; bum, bum, bum, ba-bum, zing. You could only do that with certain jobs.
>
> ' ... no, no, she didn't know what I was doing. If she slowed down I'd sort of slow down, but if she made a mistake or stopped I'd just have to go on.
>
> 'Sometimes I had it going with three people, so we'd all be doing it exactly together. I don't think the others noticed it. It's like sometimes you notice that three friends will be walking in the street and their footsteps are all the same. It'll last for a while and then it'll get broken

up with nobody noticing. We never planned it. I never mentioned it to the other girls. I don't think they noticed it. Everybody just does their work. I never knew anyone else was listening to my sounds.'

(Garson 1975: 155–56)

The pleasure here is not in communicating to others (the point seems to be that it goes unnoticed) but that the sonic field it produces is some sort of musical commentary on the disordered cacophony in the office.

In a final bid to find out more about office work Barbara Garson takes a job at the American Kennel Club. What she discovers is not the barbarity of routine office work but its mesmeric effects:

After a week I began to feel how relaxing a routine can be. By the second week my thoughts, my conversation, my life after work had modulated to the rhythm and tone of my office. For two years I have been trying to understand how workers adjust. In all that time perhaps the most docile and adjustable worker I have encountered was myself. I still don't understand the process, but at least I can describe it from the inside.

(Garson 1975: 178)

At this point the book changes from a journalistic investigation of work-life to a more descriptive first-person account of her life. The chapter detailing Kennel Club life and the routine tasks of typing data entries is also by far the most humorous in the book as it offers surrealistic juxtapositions between the often flamboyant names of dogs and their owners and the mundane details of getting through the work day.

Garson has to juggle a full-time job as a typist with the care of her daughter, with the needy demands of her lover and with various social commitments to her food co-op, parents meetings, an awareness class about the ecological effects of DDT and so on. The office work is dull and soporific. At times time seems to slide by relatively easily; at other points the afternoon seems locked into a 'go slow'. After work in the evening she is too tired to go to the meetings she had hoped to attend and organising school pick-ups proves to be much more time-consuming than she imagined. Her boyfriend, Lenny, is in publishing and has a penchant for various 'new age' remedies. His main interest is in 'primal scream therapy' which attempts to take you back to your birth and to unblock any childhood traumas along the way. Rather than talking your way out of trauma, primal scream therapy was addressed to the central nervous system with the idea that you could scream your way through trauma. At the moment, though, Lenny is stuck at the birth of his younger sister and can't get past this event.

Life at the Kennel Club is challenging in various ways. Her typing is not as good as she wanted it to be so she ends up making more mistakes than the others. She finds it hard to deal with the boredom, but starts talking with other typists who seem to be very friendly and surprisingly conscientious (which turns out to be the result of a bonus scheme). Most crucially though she starts to feel what she had previously only had second-hand knowledge of:

> I continued painful minute after minute. And then something happened. I looked at the clock at 2:54 and when I looked back again it was 3:20.
>   Oh blessèd unconsciousness.
>   I finally understood the keypunchers who hated to change programs. 'If you can get into the rhythm the time passes. If you have to think about it, it's a drag.'
>   My afternoon passed in alternations. Sometimes I fell into rhythm. Then ten or fifteen or even seventeen minutes would pass without my noticing. But sometimes something would jar me out of suspension. Then the thoughts and daydreams and half fantasies would interrupt. It was terrible. You couldn't really think and you couldn't really type. I was exhausted when I got home.
>
> (Garson 1975: 206)

Exhaustion is a constant presence as the weeks pass. But so too is a sort of lethargic contentment.

As the weeks go by she begins to empty out her life of extraneous and awkward obligations: DDT classes are the first to go and then next is the parents' meeting. The food co-op becomes more haphazard. Lenny is dumped when he backs out of a planned dinner because he is going to try and primal his way past his sister's birth back to his primal impetigo. Life becomes less cluttered and instead centres on home, her daughter, a few friends and work. There is comfort in this simplicity and life at the Kennel Club becomes more enjoyable. Here habit and connecting to a workable rhythm appears as a seductive vacuum beckoning the author towards its comforting but asocial embrace.

Garson's book ends abruptly: she is sacked for incompetent typing and has to return to her more adventurous life. Of course in this context her more 'adventurous' life could be seen as her more established habitual realm. The charms, possibilities and problems of habit are at the heart of ordinary life's complex orchestration. It is the accommodation of the human sensorium to the rhythms of external life. It is also their internalisation. Habit and rhythm release us from the metronome of clock time but connect us as willing (or reluctant) supplicants to the time of labour.

Time is the essential ingredient of everyday life. Its rhythms and markings are what makes time ordinary and extraordinary. Yet ordinary time is not the regular beat of the hum-drum, but the complex weave of time thickened by emotion, by affect. The stretching and truncating of time when it is animated by propulsions of joy or fear need to take their place in an ecology of everyday time. But so too do the looping rhythms of time as it is pulled into new shapes by resentment and guilt or debilitating forms of boredom. This is ordinary life, not set to a metronome, but to the common comings and goings of passion. It is time as social life, lived as intimately as can be.

Notes

1 Of course from the perspective of real material misery, middle-class alienation might seem like a luxury to aspire to. But what Henri Lefebvre referred to as 'the bureaucratic society of controlled consumption' (1984 [1968]: 68–109) implicates everyone in its cycles of alienation, even if it does so unequally and unevenly (which is crucial to its functioning). The popular 1970s TV sitcom *The Fall and Rise of Reginald Perrin* charts a middle manager's mounting despair at the absurdity of such a society, and at the routine exasperations of work-life.

2 For other accounts of assembly line work see Benyon 1973 and Hamper 1992. Berger and Mohr 1982 offer a haunting account of the double alienation of the migrant worker involved in assembly line (and other) work in Germany.

3 The classic work on emotional labour is by Arlie Russell Hochschild; see 2003 [1983] and 2003. Hochschild's primary subjects came from the airline industry and her research was focused on the emotional labour of flight attendants, as well as the emotional management they undertake during training session.

4 The literature on boredom as a modern condition includes Anderson 2004; Goodstein 2005; Petro 1993; and Spacks 1995.

5 The theme of time and the differences between experiential, bodily time and forms of scientific, rational and official time are a constant preoccupation with thinkers particularly from the end of the nineteenth century onwards. For an overview see Adam 2004 and Kern 1983. Classic texts include Bergson 1991 (1908), Heidegger 2008 (1927), Mead 2002 (1932), and Schutz 1972 (1932). The ever-inspiring William James coined the term 'stream of consciousness' (1950 [1890] vol.1: 239) to describe the incessant flow of perception and sensation-response.

6 For a history of the mechanisation of the home see Cowan 1989 and Hardyment 1988.

7 Histories of office work that are directly related to the conditions and fate of female secretaries can be found in: Davies 1982; Gardey 2001; Keep 1997; Strom 1992; and Wershler-Henry 2005. Davies writes that 'the male private secretary might some day sit in an executive's chair; the female was, as a rule, an office wife or servant whose chances of moving up in the corporate world were virtually nil' (Davies 1982: 168).

8 The psychoanalyst and literary theorist Julia Kristeva has influentially argued for an understanding of 'woman's time' as a socio-biological condition: see Kristeva 1981.

9 One of the best demonstrations of this argument can be found in the first chapter of de Lauretis 1987.

10 The denigration of female labour is part and parcel of a patriarchal society and is articulated across social institutions, not least of course by the institution of the family. As Engels pointed out, inside the home the man is the bourgeois and the woman the proletariat (1986 [1884]).

11 The early history of Mass-Observation is discussed in my *Everyday Life and Cultural Theory* (2002: 75–112). For an account of Mass-Observation that is particularly attentive to the period after 1981 see Sheridan, Street and Bloome 2000. During the post-1981 period the number of correspondents has varied from five hundred to a thousand, not all of whom are active at any one time. While these diarists come from a wide range of backgrounds they are never designated as a representative sample of a population. Crucially (and necessarily) they were and are self-selecting investigators of their own social and cultural lives.

12 In the UK the 'Wages for Housework' campaign was launched in 1972 by Selma James (based on a conference address that was later published as a pamphlet, James 1976; see the interview with James in Lowry 1980: 65–78. 'Wages for Housework' echoes a number of earlier campaigns to politicise housework and women's domestic work. For longer histories of housework and feminism see Hayden 1982; Johnson and Lloyd 2004; and Oakley 1974a.

13 This is the tag-line for its website, see www.massobs.org.uk.

14 While this orientation to posterity was an aspect of Mass-Observation in the early years it coexisted with a sense of providing a mass-voice as a form of alternative media for contemporary times. In post-1981 Mass-Observation it is the posterity orientation that takes centre stage.

15 The works of Laura Marcus (1994), Liz Stanley (1992), and Carolyn Steedman (1988) are centrally concerned with the shaping work that narrative, genre, gender and living the 'autobiographical life' can do.

16 The document is the response of correspondent R340 to Autumn Directive, September 1983. It is part of the Mass-Observation Archive which is held in the University of Sussex. Throughout this section I will refer to this document by page number only. I am using extensive quotations from this document, partly because I think it is important to give you, the reader, a strong sense of her written voice, and partly because it is a complex and rich account. Thanks are due to the wonderful archivists at the Library Special Collections Department, University of Sussex and especially to Dorothy Sheridan.

17 I've altered his name to preserve the anonymity of the correspondent. The Mass-Observation project operates on the understanding that correspondents remain anonymous in any published writing.

18 The task of washing children, for instance, is part of an ecology of emotional energy. As Selma James put it, 'we defined housework as the reproduction of *people* rather than the reproduction of *things*. We defined it in the emotional sphere, letting someone cry on your shoulder, kissing the child who had hurt his knee and so on' (James interviewed in Lowry 1980: 72). Later in the Mass-Observation document the correspondent is preparing food: 'Ben, Jim's friend, comes in with a cut leg that needs attention, ask him to hang on while I finish doing Rachel's bunches. Dress his leg and curse Rachel for using up all the Elastoplast etc on her dolls. Fix dressing with sellotape' (11).

19 Describing this work as a genealogical approach is a way for the authors to signal their indebtedness to the work of Michel Foucault, as well as their affiliation to the Foucaultian work of Donzelot 1997 (1977) and Minson 1985.

20 There is a strong sense that post-1981 Mass-Observation allowed correspondents a sense of themselves as anonymous and collective authors, and that the literariness of the project was a crucial aspect for them. As one correspondent put it: 'I wouldn't be so comfortable writing, and I probably wouldn't write so frankly, if I knew that people would be able to identify me, at any time, even in the future, even after I was dead' (correspondent cited in Sheridan, Street and

Bloome 2000: 177). For some anonymous writing was an end in itself; for others it was a dry-run to becoming an author.

21 The pioneers in domestic scientific management were the Americans Charlotte Beecher and Christine Frederick: see Freeman 2004: 25–54.

22 The argument that labour saving never amounted to a general diminishment of labour time is persuasively put forward in Cowan 1989.

23 There is of course no direct correlation between the quantity of words used to describe a phenomenon and the temporal intensity of it. Yet in the example that she is about to give the affective registers of shame and fear seem to summon up words that have a strong temporal tone, in this case the adjective 'gingerly'.

24 For one of the best accounts of time and motion studies and the rationalisation of scientific management see Doray 1988.

25 For first-hand accounts of this feeling see Hobson 1978 and Oakley 1974a and 1974b. For historical work that looks at a range of representations of feelings of non-achievement in housework see Johnson and Lloyd 2004.

26 As well as reading *The Guilt Cage* (Lowry 1980), which contains the interview with Selma James about wages for housework mentioned above, and which may explain the reference to pocket money in relation to stacking wood, the correspondent also buys a copy of Maud Pember Reeves' *Round about a Pound a Week* (1979 [1913]), which is a social exploration of the domestic life of working-class Londoners in the early twentieth century (1909–13).

27 For the gendering of working to a list see Shaw 1998. This essay also uses Mass-Observation as its archival source.

28 Many historians of office workers note that the average wage for typists in the early years of the twentieth century meant that they would have had to share a room with a work colleague, or else live in dormitory-type conditions (see for instance Wershler-Henry 2005, chapter 11).

29 For a technical, commercial and cultural history of the typewriter see Beeching 1974.

Chapter 5

Absentminded media

Scene one

Location: someone's front room. X is lying on a sofa trying to watch TV but her head is too full of worries about tomorrow's interview. X wants the TV show to blot out the voices in her head that fill her with doubt and anxiety, but the show is just not distracting enough. Y is playing a computer game, oblivious to everything around her, drawn into a virtual world where an endless supply of zombies has to be dispatched with hi-impact weapons. Z is buying some train tickets online. She has been following the TV show competently enough and thinks she knows who the murderer is.

Scene two

Location: someone's bedroom. P is trying to get to sleep but the radio seems to be slightly louder than usual. The radio programme appears to be a comedy, or at least there is an audience laughing. P thinks about his day. The programme changes. The radio begins to lull him to sleep:

> ... Biscay Fitzroy Sole Lundy Fastnet: Westerly or southwesterly six to gale eight, occasionally severe gale nine at first, backing southerly five to seven, but cyclonic later in south Fitzroy. High occasionally very high at first, becoming very rough in Lundy and Fastnet. Rain or squally showers. Moderate occasionally poor. Irish Sea: West six to gale eight, backing southwest five or six. Rough or very rough, occasionally moderate later. Squally showers. Good ... [1]

Scene three

Location: someone's train journey. Q is taking her weekly train journey from the South West of England down to the south coast. She is listening to music on her MP3 player. For a while she just couldn't settle on playing anything in particular – a song from here, half a song from there – but has now found something she is comfortable with. Q is also reading a novel. After some time has elapsed she realises that the MP3 player has turned itself off. She can't remember when this occurred, or what music she had been playing.

The question that 'the ordinary' poses for media is not a question of representation but of attention. Or rather: the question that I want to pose for media in everyday life is the question of attention. The little micro-sketches above take for granted the presence of media within everyday life, but they also take for granted that our attention towards media is far from homogenous, and far from straightforward. But if our attentiveness to media is heterogeneous and complex it is also the product of historical interactions between everyday life and technologically driven communication practices. A historical ecology of media could do worse than to plot a movement from scarcity to saturation, from lack to ubiquity. A hundred or so years ago it would not have been too hard to find books to read, music to listen to and photographs to look at. The industry of technological communication and entertainment was already in full swing: if you lived in a metropolitan centre some of this would have been unavoidable (for instance advertising and newspaper headlines). Outside the large cities many of the products of the culture industry would, with a little effort and money, have been readily available. Two hundred years before that though, much more effort and money would have been required to seek out pictures and words to entertain and inform.[2] Today it requires a substantial amount of effort to *avoid* the products of the culture industry.[3] The ubiquity and pervasiveness of forms of media are such that it is not enough to live outside the city to be relatively media-free; we have to have been 'living on another planet' to know nothing of this month's reality TV debacle or not to have caught a glimpse of the most recent advertising campaign for this must-have mobile phone.

If it is a commonplace of academic media studies to claim that we are 'saturated by media' (media-culture, media-texts, media-messages, media-spectacle), then it is still a commonplace worthy of consideration, and of fundamental interest for the study of everyday life. Indeed 'saturation' could be seen as a cognate term for the everyday: when something reaches saturation point it has bled into the everyday, set up home there, colonised the domestic realm. I like to think of 'saturation' literally: I'm walking about shopping malls soaked to the skin in muzak and free newspapers; drenched in the advertising I barely noticed but which flitted by on the edge of my peripheral vision; sopping wet from last night's TV binge of the 'top one hundred most enigmatic moments in US cop dramas'. If we are saturated by media, and if it takes more effort to avoid than it does to succumb to it, then what does this mean for our perceptual attitude towards it? Should we expect indifference and blasé attitudes, new forms of information and entertainment fatigue,[4] alterations in where authoritative communication takes place, blurrings between media formats and between media and non-media actuality? In this chapter I want to concentrate (if this doesn't seem too much of a contradiction) on distraction.

In the 1920s and 1930s German critics Walter Benjamin and Siegfried Kracauer claimed that modern forms of culture (radio, cinema, advertising) solicited a particular form of attention that they called distraction (*Zerstreuung*). Their contemporary 'new media' – cinemas, commercial exhibitions, advertising and so on – were distractions (attractions and entertainments) as well as establishing distraction as the most appropriate mode of perceiving them.[5] Benjamin and Kracauer use the term distraction to mark what they see as a historical shift in attention towards cultural objects and to diagnose the condition of reception of the culture industry within monopoly capitalism.[6] But, in their different ways, they also want to grasp the potential of distraction as a new collective and emancipatory form of perception that could offer a (potentially) critical purchase on the culture industry and on modern life.

Today the term 'distraction' has become a way of signalling a mode of reception that is characteristic of a culture where media saturate the everyday and where a range of media forms constantly and simultaneously demand our attention. A study of radio listening in Mexico City, for instance, associates distraction with both the background presence of media and its ubiquity within domestic space: 'The *distracted* way of relating to the radio, manifested in the attitude of "listening without listening" or keeping the radio on as "background music," constitutes a cyclic mechanism of withdrawal-connection that characterizes communication practices in the domestic sphere' (Winocur 2005: 323). Distraction here is associated with a perception that comes and goes, that is attentive one moment but is inattentive and unfocused another. Such use of the term often assumes that media forms are ongoing (whether you are attending to them or not broadcasting continues); that media are embedded in a network of other activities (chatting, reading, eating and so on); and that media are manifold and ordinary (distraction is often seen as the everyday 'hopping about' of attention as it navigates across a plethora of media formats and possibilities).[7] The over-abundance of media possibilities is evident in the names we have for forms of indecisive media attention: zapping, grazing, surfing, trawling and so on.

As the range and insistence of media communication increases there is a possibility that the idea of distraction will simply become shorthand for the difficulty of concentrating on any one channel, on any one platform, and, as a result, there is a danger of losing the sort of dialectical nuance that Kracauer and Benjamin sought to give to the term.[8] Like most dialectical puzzles, treating distraction as both 'poison and cure' is not always an easy trick to pull off. How do we hold on to the critical possibilities of distraction when it seems so well suited for a cultural industry intent on selling us more and more media formats? What phenomenal qualities can distraction offer that could rescue it from being just a symptom of a hurried culture where sustained attention is a luxury that seemingly few can afford? In a series of notes titled 'Theory of Distraction', Walter Benjamin demands that 'the relation of distraction to absorption must be examined' (1936b: 141). These were notes that were probably written in preparation for the second version of his most famous essay 'The Work of Art in the Age of its Technological Reproducibility' (1936a) (or the 'Work of Art' essay, to give it a shorter title). But in reading this essay, and its later version, it seems clear that the relationship between absorption and distraction, and between concentration and distraction, needs further examination and clarification.

In some regards the very term 'distraction' contains within it a range of contradictions that stop it settling into any fixed condition, even a dialectical one. In everyday usage you can mobilise the term 'distraction' to mean quite different and incommensurable phenomena. For instance you could use it to point to the assumed *misdirection* of attention. This would be the point of claiming that pupils were being distracted or diverted from doing their homework by the sound of the radio, or that the British working class were distracted from overthrowing the bourgeois state by football.[9] There is a moral and political force to this use of the term (the implicit assumption being that homework and insurrection are morally or politically superior to radio and football), one that associates the distracting phenomena with the frivolous and worthless. But it should also be clear that such distractions must also be *attractions* or they would not be able to function as something that could divert and redirect attention. So if distraction is often seen as the inverse of concentration, here it is clearly being used in a way that is much closer to concentration itself (even if it is concentrating on the 'wrong' thing): the worry is precisely that the students are concentrating too much on the radio or the working class are far too absorbed by football.

A similar sense of distraction as a form of concentration is evidenced in another common use of the term. When a police officer, for instance, claims that a defendant 'seemed distracted' she might be suggesting a degree of suspicion in his behaviour, but also pointing to his inability to con-centrate on a set of questions being addressed to him.[10] Yet here we often use the term distraction to signal not a total lack of concentration, but of a concentration already engaged. The distracted person is preoccupied; they are already occupied with concentrating on whatever it is that preoccupies them. To be distracted, in this sense, is to be so taken up with your own concerns that you are unable to focus on the general hubbub around you. In this sense a distracted person appears to be 'somewhere else', or 'worlds away'. But the difference between this use of the term and the first is that here attention can't be shifted whereas in the first case it was the movement of attention from one thing to another that was characteristic.

The third use of the term distraction might best be thought of as another name for a form of absentminded or vacant consciousness. In William James' *The Principles of Psychology* (written before the media phenomena that Kracauer and Benjamin were trying to describe had become an everyday reality) distraction is starkly opposed to forms of attention. For James: 'Focalization, concentration, of consciousness are of its [attention's] essence. ... which has a real opposite in the confused, dazed, scatter-brained state which in French is called *distraction*, and *Zerstreutheit* in German' (James 1950 [1890] vol. 1: 404). Distraction, as a dazed state, is for James a very ordinary daily experience:

> We all know this latter state, even in its extreme degree. Most people probably fall several times a day into a fit of something like this: The eyes are fixed on vacancy, the sounds of the world melt into confused unity, the attention is dispersed so that the whole body is felt, as it were, at once, and the foreground of consciousness is filled, if by anything, by a sort of solemn sense of surrender to the empty time passing.
> (James 1950 [1890] vol. 1: 404)[11]

While James sets 'distraction' in opposition to attention when he claims it as a form of vacancy, distraction is not opposed to attention if we follow the previous examples I have mentioned. Indeed for James the essence of attention is precisely the moving from one thing to another that is seen as crucial to distraction in the first example. For James, attention 'implies withdrawal from some things in order to deal effectively with others' (James 1950 [1890] vol. 1: 404): so if attention is a turning-towards it is simultaneously a turning-away. Distraction as a form of being attracted by something else is precisely the movement that defines attention.

For now it is enough to recognise the variety of states that distraction covers (vacancy, preoccupation, as well as attention itself) and suggest that distraction might most usefully be thought of within an economy of movement and location. The sort of wild distraction that newspaper columnists conjure up to scare us about the dwindling attention span of young people could also describe the speed by which attention can move and the number of places it can move to. To say you are vacant might be another way of saying that the location of attention is elsewhere (that you are not at home to attention). So rather than thinking of distraction in terms of objects (in this case media forms that are supposed to be doing the distracting) I want to suggest that it is more productive to think of distraction as the mobility of attention as it turns-away-from while turning-towards its objects; or the tenacity of attention as it is compelled by its object (perhaps against the odds); or the attention-in-waiting of forms of boredom, vacancy and absentmindedness. These are contradictory formations, yet it is precisely this quality of unresolved contradiction that allows distraction to be a productive description of reception in a culture where surprising and progressive experience can be fleetingly found in a sea of media production that is governed by but not reducible to an ethos of conformity and profit. To claim reception as simultaneously agile and tenacious, vacant and absorbed is to point to the contradictory state of modern media perception in everyday life without condemning it or condoning it. Distraction is the complex, and occasionally exhilarating, condition of ordinary media attention.

In what follows I want to pursue the idea that distraction is often a form of vacillation of attention and sometimes fascination and that it can be a productive state for encountering the new in everyday life. To this end I also want to return to Kracauer and Benjamin and rehearse how they were thinking of distraction. Benjamin's notion that distracted forms of perception (including distracting forms of production) facilitate a new apperception of modernity will be particularly important. Apperception is what allows perception not to have to continually start from first principles. So instead of seeing a new chair and saying 'what is this strange thing?', we can say 'what kind of chair-like thing is this?'. Yet as will become clearer apperception is a habit of mind that only really wants to allow the already known into consciousness. There is, then, something contradictory in expecting distraction to facilitate apperception of the modern and new. Rather than intending to contribute to the vast forests of Benjamin commentary I want to consider the linking of distraction and apperception in order to think about extraordinary moments in everyday life where something new has pushed through the world of apperception and called someone to attention. In many ways this is to link distraction to the moment of aesthetic 'breach' in the distribution of the sensible that Jacques Rancière claims is the task of the aesthetic regime of art to produce. My job here is to show how ordinary such moments are and how they happen at moments of absentmindedness in everyday life.

Towards a theory of distraction

As we have already seen the term distraction covers contradictory meanings while always foregrounding the movement and location (as well as dislocation) of attention.[12] In the English language versions of Siegfried Kracauer and Walter Benjamin's work 'distraction' is the usual translation of the word *Zerstreuung*. The German term, though, is more evidently ambiguous and covers a wider range of meanings than the English 'distraction'. The German term also seems much more insistent on the centrifugal movement of attention: 'the German *Zerstreuung* might mean, at one and the same time, distraction, diversion, amusement, diffusion, preoccupation, absentmindedness, scattering, dispersion, and so on' (Vidler 2000: 82–83).[13] Distraction as a scattering-outward of attention is not opposed to concentration as a mental ability or as a quantity of attention; it is opposed to concentration as a spatially bounded description of attention. If concentration describes a tightly demarcated location for attention, then distraction describes a space that is at once larger, less bounded and requires more nimble forms of attention.

Walter Benjamin takes the term distraction primarily from his friend Siegfried Kracauer and in one of Kracauer's most programmatic descriptions of distraction the term is used not simply to describe a medium (in his case film) but to describe its staging and housing (cinema). Writing about the large picture houses in Berlin, Kracauer describes them as 'palaces of distraction' and understands them as a continuation of Wagner's attempt to produce a 'total artwork' (Gesamtkunstwerk).[14] In fact when Kracauer is describing the multiplicity of means that the picture palace uses to solicit attention, the phenomenon of film seems surprisingly muted:

> This total artwork of effects assaults all the senses using every possible means. Spotlights shower their beams into the auditorium, sprinkling across festive drapes or rippling through colourful, organic-looking glass fixtures. The orchestra asserts itself as an independent power, its acoustic production buttressed by the responsory of the lighting. Every emotion is accorded its own acoustic expression and its color value in the spectrum – a visual and acoustic kaleidoscope that provides the setting for the physical activity on stage: pantomime and ballet. Until finally the white surface descends and the events of the three-dimensional stage blend imperfectly into two-dimensional illusions.
>
> (Kracauer 1926: 324)

There are several interrelating points worth mentioning here that are relevant to any discussion of distraction: first, that the range of material relates to different senses (not just visual but auditory and tactile too); next, the sorts of attention that are being solicited vary significantly (a light flickering on a thick curtain is sensually perceived but doesn't require the sort of sustained cognitive attention that a narrative film requires, for instance); and last, that while some of these phenomena are sequential (the film follows pantomime and ballet) a number of them are simultaneous (the lights and music).

The picture palaces that Kracauer refers to were vast sites of entertainment. By the 1920s movie audiences in big cities were offered cinemas that could seat two thousand spectators or more.[15] The variety format (a night's programme might feature dancing, comedy sketches and film, for instance) was most often employed in these 'palaces of distraction', combining traditions of musical hall, popular theatre and opera with film presentations. Alongside this was the spectacle of the movie theatre itself. Often employing baroque extravagance, cinema theatres mobilised all sorts of sensual effects to attract customers. Loew's Paradise Theatre in New York, for instance, opened in

1929. This 4000-seat theatre employed 'atmospherics' to create the illusion of being in an open-air amphitheatre in Italy: fake gardens and Italianate facades made up the walls of the interior and an illusionistic sky provided a canopy over the auditorium (Bruno 2002: 48–50).

In the context of such spectacles it would be hard to know what to concentrate on: the luxurious carpet under your feet might be your first taste of such opulence, while the light show could be the most spectacular thing you have seen. And of course there are the films themselves. For Kracauer these movie theatres and their programmes of entertainment evidenced an ambivalent politics: reactionary elements mixed with progressive potential.[16] Palaces of distraction offer a new form of attention that might easily be described as a negative form: they encourage a more 'superficial' engagement with phenomena. In a context where so much sensorial material is clamouring for attention the result is that spectators distance themselves from being caught up in a single element. Bombarded from all sides, the audience (bankers and labourers momentarily unified by being positioned as a mass audience) adopt new forms of attention that don't offer the opportunity for reflection, but acquire a new habit of mobile attention while not being subsumed by the artwork:

> The interior design of movie theatres serves one sole purpose: to rivet the viewer's attention to the peripheral, so that they will not sink into the abyss. The stimulations of the senses succeed one another with such rapidity that there is no room left between them for even the slightest contemplation. Like *life buoys*, the refractions of the spotlights and the musical accompaniment keep the spectator above water. The penchant for distraction demands and finds an answer in the display of pure externality.
>
> (Kracauer 1926: 325–26)

'Pure externality' is also Kracauer's description of cinema, and by this he means that films, most of the time (either by design or default) refuse the pseudo-internality of much art that tries to carry the viewer away on a wave of emotional sympathy. By producing emotionally thinner stories, cinema usefully inoculates itself against the false conception of a unified image. But, as the above quotation suggests, what blocks the audience from being carried away isn't just the result of the media of film: distraction is the form of reception that is demanded by the glut of effects, all pressing forward to be noticed, that is cinema in its entirety.[17]

Ten years later, Walter Benjamin takes up and develops some of these themes in his 'Work of Art' essay (1936a and 1939). By this time Benjamin was also heavily involved in the theatrical aesthetics of another friend, Bertolt Brecht, who similarly proposed a theatrical form that refused to let the audience get carried away by an illusion of emotional depth. The theatre of Brecht favoured distraction in as much as it promoted a spectatorship analogous to the sort of enthusiastic amateur critic that Brecht found in sporting arenas where involvement in the action was accompanied by informal commentary, cigar smoking and a lack of illusionism.[18]

As we have seen 'illusionism' wasn't something that was lacking in Loew's Paradise Theatre (nor would it have been lacking in many of the films shown there), yet by combining incompatible forms of illusion and by offering a startling array of sensation the audience are drawn towards a condition of comparison rather than singularly directed empathy. Benjamin links distraction to the birth of a mass audience that has become a body of social critics and this leads him to one of his most famous formulations: 'the audience is an examiner, but a distracted one' (Benjamin 1939: 269). For Benjamin the age of technological entertainments has brought about a sea-change in perception: in a previous age, cultish and auratic art demanded concentrated and sacral attention; in the modern age a much more agile and less reverential reception is appropriate.

The difference pivots on the direction and locus of absorption:

> Distraction and concentration form an antithesis, which may be formulated as follows. A person who concentrates before a work of art is absorbed by it ... . By contrast, the distracted masses absorb the work of art into themselves. Their waves lap around it; they encompass it with their tide.
>
> (Benjamin 1936a: 119–20)

If the traditional artwork demanded absorption by the onlooker (being 'carried away' by its 'majesty', for instance), then the objects in a culture of distraction are, more usually, absorbed into the concerns of the mass audience. You can see this today in the plethora of online platforms for consumer and fan reviews: from online bookshops and music stores (for instance Amazon online stores and Apple's iTunes) to film reviews on the internet movie database. Ordinary reviewers aren't cowed by an established hierarchy of taste but evaluate culture according to their own concerns, needs and tastes.

But Benjamin's bigger hope was that distraction would transform the reception of culture and would establish an audience more critically active. While evaluation is very much part of a culture of distraction there is no reason to assume that evaluation is expanded towards social criticism. Today our reception of culture is probably more 'distracted' than it was in Benjamin's day (adverts interrupt film, publicity banners flutter across the top of web pages and pop up during the viewing of video feeds) yet the assumption that this enhances social critique seems to be unjustified. Does an active evaluative attitude (that we can associate with a culture of distraction) lead to a consideration of the relationship between the latest

Hollywood blockbuster and the position of the USA in the global military-industrial-complex, for instance? Indeed there may be good reason for assuming the opposite: evaluation might be expected to reinstate the sorts of response that curtail such criticism. In a world suffused with cultural products and orchestrated by much more complex forms of misery, distraction might provide succour as much as criticism. For an exhausted and confused mass audience evaluation might have its own agenda: this film gets five stars because it is the perfect relief for tired nerves; this TV series is loved because of its ameliorative affects in the face of so much gloom; this computer game offers the heightened sensations that are missing in my ordinary world.[19]

Benjamin's essay was programmatic; it was designed to encourage the production of culture that didn't 'carry away' its audience and instead allowed for critical dialogue. This would, of course, necessarily entail the production of critical content as well as new forms of reception.[20] In 1936 Benjamin sent his essay to Adorno, whose response was scathing; he accused Benjamin's essay of pedalling an 'anarchistic romanticism which places blind trust in the spontaneous powers of the proletariat within the historical process – a proletariat which is itself a product of bourgeois society' (Adorno to Benjamin, March 1936, in Lonitz 1999: 130). For Adorno the 'Work of Art' essay is far too Brechtian, and not nearly dialectical enough:

> I am very doubtful of the expertise of the newspaper boy in discussing sport, and in spite of its startling seductiveness, I cannot find your theory of 'distraction' at all convincing – if only for the simple reason that in a communist society, work would be organized in such a way that human beings would no longer be so exhausted or so stupefied as to require such distraction.
>
> (Adorno to Benjamin, March 1936, in Lonitz 1999: 130)

In a world where the highest viewing figures are for reality TV series and the neo-liberalism that they seem to deliver, and where 'mass distraction' is part of the spectacle of a culture that endlessly marches to the beat of the commodity, it is hard not to side with Adorno in all this.

Yet there was another aspect to Benjamin's appraisal of distraction that focused on habit and was much more dialectical: it was also an aspect of distraction that was much harder to harness for a progressive cultural politics. In the end it is this aspect of distraction that has the most to offer to an account of media in everyday life. For Benjamin the example of 'reception in distraction' that emphasises habit rather than evaluation is architecture: 'Architecture has always offered the prototype of an artwork that is received in a state of distraction and through the collective' (Benjamin 1936a: 119–20). The reasons why Benjamin chooses architecture are two-fold: on the one hand he recognises that when a building becomes part of our habitual realm we no longer have to be attentive to it; and on the other (and this is a related point) when we are habituated to it we 'know' the building tactilely as much as optically. A much-used building is 'known' by its users through their feet and hands as much as it is through their eyes: we 'know' which floorboards creak, which door handles are stiff: our body seems to 'know' the whereabouts of the light switch without us having to look for it.[21] Habit calls on the entire human sensorium to perform tasks, freeing up cognitive capabilities for dealing with new phenomena, and it is this that Benjamin sees as the promise (and the problem) of distraction:

> For the tasks which face the human apparatus of perception at historical turning points cannot be performed solely by optical means – that is, by way of contemplation. They are mastered gradually – taking their cue from tactile reception – through habit.
>
> (Benjamin 1936a: 120)

This understanding of habit is reflected in our everyday speech where we call on the sense of tactility and haptic perception to describe the process whereby something becomes habitual: we talk of 'getting to *grips* with something' or 'getting a *feel* for it'.

Habit, it may seem obvious to say, is the essential ingredient of ordinary life: without it there would be no room for day-dreaming, no space for the new. For William James, '*habit diminishes the conscious attention with which our acts are performed*' (1950 [1890] vol. 1: 114 italics in the original); for Benjamin 'the ability to master certain tasks in a state of distraction proves that their performance has become habitual' (1939: 268).[22] Distraction is the test of habit's accomplishments, and successful habituation marks out a space for distraction. But the conundrum that faced Benjamin, and faces us, is that habit both allows for the new while preparing us for the old. Habit delegates perception and cognition to motor reflexes, muscle groups and automatic sensorial responses and by doing so enables us to attend to a more and more complex environment: at the same time habit trains the body and trains our perceptive faculties to look for the old in the new, to automate our tastes and responses, to take the well-worn path. And it is this that makes distraction both poison and cure: distraction conspires with habit in the realm of perception simultaneously making space for new experiences while constantly privileging the already-known. Philosophers and psychologists called the mind's storehouse of established perceptions 'apperception' and it was a term that Benjamin subtly relied on in his 'Work of Art' essay.

Bad-scissors: apperception, habit and mass culture

For Benjamin, distracted reception performs in the field of apperception. The task of 'reception in distraction' was the preparation of an accommodating subject for a dislocated world (a world that was more fragmented, more unsettled, more chaotic) and this task had to be accomplished by apperception. Apperception was an idea that had been central to the work of Kant and had been a mainstay in the fields of psychology and philosophy that had informed the work of Kracauer and Benjamin. If we perceive the world through our senses, we don't do so as empty vessels. We are prepared receivers, so to speak, and this preparation is designated as the field of apperception. William James, though he is sceptical of the value of the term apperception (he prefers the words assimilation and association), offers a particularly vivid example of apperception that also gets to the heart of why it was such an urgent problematic for Benjamin:[23]

> My child of two played for a week with the first orange that was given him, calling it a 'ball.' He called the first whole eggs he saw 'potatoes,' having been accustomed to see his 'eggs' broken into a glass, and his potatoes without the skin. A folding pocket-corkscrew he unhesitatingly called 'bad-scissors.' ... Most of us grow more and more enslaved to the stock conceptions with which we have once become familiar, and less and less capable of assimilating impressions in any but the old ways. Old-fogyism, in short, is the inevitable terminus to which life sweeps us on.
>
> (James 1950 [1890] vol. 2: 110)

James' son perceives the world through the stock of already-perceived understandings. For James an original moment of sensation is quickly followed by a sketchy and provisional ordering of perception (through the way one sensation can evoke another) which takes place in the first weeks of life; the hardening of the apperception field occurs at about the age of twenty-five according to James (1962 [1899]: 79).

Habit, for James, is a phenomenon that demonstrates human abilities to adapt to the new and the complex, while also being evidence of an insistent old-fogyism. Take, for example, James' understanding of the development of human cognition. In James' account 'pure sensation' is only possible in the 'earliest days of life' (1950 [1890] vol. 2: 7). The baby's 'next impression' produces a reaction 'in which the awakened vestige of the last impression plays its part'. This is 'another sort of feeling and a higher grade of cognition ... and the complication goes on increasing till the end of life' (1950 [1890] vol. 2: 8). James offers an image of the human subject collecting more and more impressions, developing capacities for greater and greater complexity. This has to be juxtaposed with the previous claim that we grow 'more and more enslaved to stock conceptions' and 'less and less capable of assimilating impressions' in new ways.

Habits of the body and habits of the mind are the way that we 'get to grips' with the complexity of life: but in getting to grips with it we carry with us the imprint of that 'grip'. And the way we do this is via repetition:

> Our dressing and undressing, our eating and drinking, our greetings and partings, our hat-raisings and giving way for ladies to precede, nay, even most of the forms of our common speech, are things of a type so fixed by repetition as almost to be classed as reflex actions. To each sort of impression we have an automatic, ready-made response.
>
> (James 1962 [1899]: 33–34)

Habit shows how capable we are of getting a feel for new and complex practices (including the practice of comprehending new genres of media communication), but in the process it indelibly shapes us and our futures: 'All our life, so far as it has definite form, is but a mass of habits, – practical, emotional, and intellectual, – systematically organized for our weal or woe, and bearing us irresistibly toward our destiny, whatever the latter may be' (James 1962 [1899]: 33). Habit is essential and useful, but can make us ossified. The process of making something habitual needs to be distinguished from the trace that it makes across our sensorium. And this is why James ends up recommending that we develop habits of regularly doing things that we find hard because they are new:

> be systematically heroic in little unnecessary points, do every day or two something for no other reason than its difficulty, so that, when the hour of dire need draws nigh, it may find you not unnerved and untrained to stand the test.
>
> (1962 [1899]: 38)

The conflict between perceptual and bodily ossification through repetitious routines and the flexibility to accommodate the new is made explicit in James' understanding of the plasticity of the human sensorium:

> I believe that we are subject to the law of habit in consequence of the fact that we have bodies. The plasticity of the living matter of our nervous system, in short, is the reason why we do a thing with difficulty the first time, but soon do it more and more easily, and finally, with sufficient practice, do it semi-mechanically, or with hardly any consciousness at all. Our nervous systems have ... *grown* to the way in which they have been exercised, just as a sheet of paper or a coat, once creased or folded, tends to fall forever afterwards into the same identical folds.
>
> (James 1962 [1899]: 33)

We gain new habits (which can be habits of vice or virtue) and we can lose habits. Our plasticity allows what was once complex and difficult to become a reflex, to become second nature, but that plasticity bears the crease of our repetitions, the stamp of our behaviour.

For Benjamin 'the hour of dire need' was now. His wager was that there was something in the culture of distraction that prepared us for this more productively than the cult value of traditional art. We could write Benjamin's task or problem (the task that he requires apperception and distraction to address) in a number of ways. The central theme of it concerns modernity and the constant transformation of the experiential world. One version of it would be to say that the sorts of traditional cultural resources that could give some shape to modern experience and allow for some reflection on it are no longer fit for purpose.[24] Storytelling, for instance, inadequately attends to the sensual delirium of the modern city or the chilling scale of industrial warfare. Put another way, we could say that our field of apperceptions (our habits of mind, our social conceptions of the world) prevent us from registering the new dynamics and instabilities of modern life. The difficulty here, and one that Benjamin recognised, was that merely replacing the content of apperception would no longer do: to swap one set of conceptions for another was to inevitably miss the essential ingredient of the modern world: its erratic and often violent alterations of experience. If a more productive field of apperception was required its shape would have to be more amorphous and shifting, it would need to include a proclivity for improvisation, and to be 'systematically heroic in little unnecessary points'. In other words a modern apperception would have to alter the form of apperception as much as its content.

Distraction is the name for the alteration of the form of apperception in Benjamin's 'Work of Art' essay, and its most significant means is film: *'Reception in distraction – the sort of reception which is increasingly noticeable in all areas of art and is a symptom of profound changes in apperception – finds in film its true training ground'* (1939: 268–69 italics in the original).[25] Film, with its constant alterations of scale (from long-shot to close-up in the blink of an eye), its jump-cuts (from Moscow to Paris in a snap of the fingers), and its complex soundscapes (orchestral music and the sounds of industrial culture welded together), is a training ground in a new form of apperception. And what is so startling is that the 'shocks' that film delivers twenty-four times a second become ordinary, become part of the habitual realm of our daily perceptions. It's as if film (and distraction culture more generally) had taken up the advice that James gave by being 'systematically heroic in little unnecessary points', so that we don't flinch at loud bangs, or bat an eye when presented with startling juxtapositions, and so that we can cross busy roads with nonchalance and indifference.[26] Such new forms of apperception allow us to experience our bewilderingly complex and violently sensationalist world in a state of absentmindedness. And of course it also allows us to attend to our complex media environment as absentminded perceivers.

Being called to attention

Habit and apperception (and apperception is sensorial and cognitive habit) are radically ambivalent. On the one hand they are deeply conservative; on the other they are an accomplishment that frees-up the sensorium, giving it space for new sensations (even if they are likely to be met by old conceptions). Distraction, at its most progressive, is the training ground for more mobile forms of habit and apperception, more flexible, fluid and improvised forms of perception. At its best it allows for a taste for the new and the unexpected; at its worst it promulgates a taste for the already known, the readily digestible. A cultural politics that is based on distraction has to recognise this ambivalence. In the face of the sheer volume and complexity of today's media and information platforms the very fact that we can perceive this in a state of distraction (as absentminded spectators) should be seen as a human accomplishment. To bemoan this fact or celebrate it might be beside the point: it might be better to start by recognising it and investigating its problems and potential.

An absentminded disposition towards complex media environments means that our senses have adjusted to intricate and heterogeneous genres, platforms and formats of media. As Benjamin suggested, distracted perception is partly the proof of habit. Habit, as we have seen, is a form of delegation: habit frees up consciousness by delegating 'knowledge' to the hands, the feet, the nervous system and to the field of apperception. And habit allows for absentmindedness, for semi-automatic reflexes, for taking things 'in our stride' and 'with a pinch of salt'. Absentmindedness delegates the work of culture to our sensorium, to our already-known stock of experience. A culture that wants to profit out of this might want to address us as already habit-formed, or in our capacities to attend to the new. I think it does both and that it does so in ambivalent ways. In ordinary life a complacent conciliatory world of culture rubs shoulders with the odd and the innovative. We can sit, dreamily, in front of multilayered TV series taking it all in without having to concentrate. We know the format; we know the moral ambiguities of the police detective, the torn sympathies we have for vics and perps (victims and perpetrators), the departmental politics, the montage sequences of jagged camerawork and rock soundtrack. We know this culture and this culture know us and it happily peddles us more of the same.

Distracted culture produces culture that knows us in advance: it has got the hang of us; it has got to grips with our apperceptions which it produced in the first place. Writing about the new class of petite bourgeois employees that emerged across industrial nations in the beginnings of the twentieth century Kracauer finds a degraded culture of ameliorative fixes for impoverished, harried and distracted workers. His ethnography of Berlin's 'salaried masses' (secretaries, clerks, department store employees and so on) describes a culture of aspiration and limited resources, of people wanting to 'live the promised life' but without the money or the energy to fulfil the promise. For these Berliners saccharine songs of love and heartbreak pepper their ordinary lives:

> I recall a girl whom her friends nickname 'Cricket'. Cricket is a prole-tarian child who lives not far from Gesundbrunnen and works in the filing room of a factory. The magic of bourgeois life reaches her only in the meanest form, and she accepts unthinkingly all the blessings that trickle down from above. It is typical of her that, in a dancehall or suburban café, she cannot hear a piece of music without at once chir-ruping the appropriate hit. But it is not she who knows every hit, rather the hits know her, steal up behind her and gently lay her low.
>
> (Kracauer 1998 [1930]: 70)

Kracauer, as usual, casts his analysis as a gendered attack on culture: his constant targets are 'little shop girls'.[27] Nevertheless we can also recognise a form of truth here: a feeling of déjà vu and déjà entendu pervades modern culture. We can hum along to the radio without knowing the song; we can often predict endings to movies or guess the next line on a TV show. And we can do so with little or no concentration (indeed concentrating on this sort of activity is often counter-productive). Yet it can also be this absent-minded attention to culture that allows us to perceive the new and the challenging.

As we saw in chapter two, for enlightenment thinkers the best way to have an unfettered commerce with sensual life is when we are least 'inter-ested' in it. As Archibald Alison suggested in 1790: 'the emotions of taste' require a state of mind 'in which the attention is so little occupied by any private or particular object of thought, as to leave us open to all the impressions ... . It is upon the vacant and unemployed, accordingly, that the objects of taste make the strongest impression' (Alison 1815 [1790]: 10–11). Distraction can often be this state of mind, though it can also be, as I have suggested, 'preoccupied' with apperceptions and thoughts that are hard to shrug off. For Immanuel Kant disinterest on the part of a perceiver allows for the sensual material to produce its own interest: 'a judgement upon an object of our delight may be wholly *disinterested* but withal very *interesting*, i.e. it relies on no interest, but it produces one' (Kant 1988 [1790]: 43–44). While these claims may be open to dispute it is not hard to find some very ordinary evidence that point to their (partial) validity: how often have you been disappointed by a film or a song that you took an interest in precisely because it had been hyped or recommended to you? And conversely, how often has the most precious music come to you by way of a chance encounter and without any prior preparation that would shape a particular disposition towards it? Enlightenment aestheticians argued that aesthetic taste could be taught: a theory of distraction might argue that the pedagogy of taste requires being 'systematically heroic in little unnecessary points' as a way of unlearning apperceptions, of remaining open to the new. If 'chance favours the prepared mind' it can also be said that preparation can take various forms and that the preparation that distraction can sometimes achieve is a preparation of absentminded openness for the unprepared encounter.

A number of autobiographical accounts of distracted listening offer what, I think, is a familiar tale. The stories relate to music and are told not just by musicians and those who have made a career in music but also by those for whom music has been an important ingredient in a life that has never been defined by it. The stories differ in their content but the form is similar: one day when nothing special is happening something special this way comes. These are stories that are not daily occurrences, but are ordinary aspects of life for all that. The stories often involve TV or radio. The writer is not really listening to the radio, or is just routinely watching a TV show, when a song comes on that hadn't been anticipated.[28] It was the first time they heard Elvis Presley, or saw Little Richard perform, or saw Prince.[29] The form is often couched in terms of a languid vacancy or an aimless preoccupation of some sort that is suddenly broken: something out there calls them to attention.

Regular listeners to the late night John Peel BBC Radio One show in the 1970s and 1980s were treated to a distracted education: you never knew what was going to be played next. A dub reggae song was followed by a punk record from Switzerland, an old blues song and an up-tempo number from Swaziland. John Peel had devoted followers who wanted to listen to every song, but even for the most vociferous fan of the DJ the chances are that they spent a good deal of time 'tuned out', not really listening to what was played. To listen to Peel was to try and be 'systematically heroic in little unnecessary points': it was hard to like even half of it, but that didn't matter because there would always be something that you loved, and listening to it among such an impossibly eclectic selection added to the joy. In his autobiography, half-written before he died unexpectedly and completed by Sheila Ravenscroft his partner, he offers an example of the power of the chanced-upon song:

> I had been driving for some time and it must have been two or three a.m. as I started through the richly forested area of East Texas known as the Piney Woods. There was little traffic on the roads and, as the road rose and fell through the trees and past tiny towns that were often barely more than a handful of bedraggled shacks, the moon, which shone brilliantly directly in front of me, turned the concrete to silver. I was listening, I imagine, to Wolfman Jack from XERB, over the border in Mexico, and as I came over the top of a hill to see another tiny town below me, he played Elmore James' 'Stranger Blues', 'I'm a

stranger here, just drove in your town,' Elmore sang, and I knew that I would never forget the perfect conjunctions of place, mood and music. Nor have I.

(Peel and Ravenscroft 2005: 192)

The drive from New Orleans to Dallas was a lonely and dispiriting one, transformed by hearing one song. Here the distracted reception recognises the way a constellation of elements line up to produce a glorious event: driving very late at night, tired and preoccupied, enchanted by a country and a culture that was still unfamiliar enough to produce moments of exhilaration, being in the process of discovering African-American blues and so on.[30] In some ways Peel was 'primed' to hear this song coming over the airwaves as something special, but he was also distractedly primed for the beauty of the unexpectedness of this chance collision of music and place.

Powerful moments of listening and seeing can crop up precisely when the interested expectations that you had brought to something are refused, leaving you 'vacant' and receptive. Lavinia Greenlaw, growing up in rural Essex in the 1970s, remembers watching the Marc Bolan show (*Marc*) on TV in 1977:

A man who sported ringlets and a leopardskin catsuit talking in a floppy voice about three boys who buttoned down their collars and measured the turn-ups on their trousers. While Bolan lounged on a fluffy pink throne, The Jam posed rigidly – black suits, white shirts, black ties, black-and-white shoes – in front of a plain black backdrop. Clean-shaven, short-haired and with emphatic estuary accents, The Jam played 'All Around the World' and here was a speeded-up, pared-down sound that I knew could take me further and faster than any boy in his car. Bolan cooed and drawled but The Jam shouted: 'All around the world I've been looking for new … ' I was looking for 'new' and it lay in such collisions and detonations and two-minute songs, and in a new kind of colour.

(Greenlaw 2007: 121)

In the context of what had become a lethargic pop legacy, a 'glam' and hippy mix, the Jam cleaves a path of working-class vowels and frenetic musical urgency. Of course you could imagine the same narrative taking place half a dozen years earlier with Marc Bolan's T-Rex as electric warriors opening up a path of fresh, camp vitality in the arid landscape of pre-packaged heteronormative, asinine pop.[31] In one sense it doesn't matter much where the breach occurs and in what directions the sensorial world is opened up; in another sense, though, nothing matters quite as much.[32] In this example the tightly held exuberance of punk alters the 'distribution of the sensible': 'Punk didn't just change what I listened to and how I dressed. It altered my aesthetic sense completely. This is what music could do: change the shape of the world and my shape within it, how I saw, what I liked and what I wanted to look like' (Greenlaw 2007: 123).

Jacques Rancière's aesthetic thought is useful here. For Rancière the aesthetic regime continually replays a moment of rupture, a breach. It is a moment that is similar to the opening up of equality that is performed by the political: what had previously been excluded becomes included, what had previously been deemed noise becomes sound, what had previously been a form of identification becomes rearranged in a moment of disidentification that allows for a new subjectification. To listen to the stories of distracted encounters with significant musical moments is often to get a sense that the liberation that is performed is pure potentiality. These are not moments that confirm, reassert or cement, but breaches that undo, redirect and occasionally derange. Sexuality, class and sound coalesce, but not as a 'new paradigm' or a 'new identity' (or at least not at first) but as a break with the old. It is not recognition that triggers the encounter but a sense of the new.

For pop-loving kids growing up in Britain in the 1970s the weekly dose of *Top of the Pops* was the one time you got to see the musicians in the flesh, so to speak. David Bowie performing his song 'Starman' in July 1972 was a significant moment in the history of that show, not least for the sexual uncertainty of Bowie's stage performance, particularly when he puts his arm around guitarist Mick Ronson. It is hardly surprising that this musical moment features in some of the biographies of gay musicians and non-musicians who were boys at the time.[33] But these stories are rarely about a straightforward identification: usually they are couched in relation to an attraction that undoes the fixed regime of sexuality and music that were in place at the time. The song 'Starman' was other-worldly, as were the clothes and the look of David Bowie and his group. As a moment of musical and sexual disidentification it would be a significant moment for someone as insistently heterosexual as the radio DJ Mark Radcliffe:

> I first saw David Bowie on *Top of the Pops* doing 'Starman' in his tinsel and tat with his arm around the shoulder of the equally otherworldly, though less convincingly androgynous, guitar 'hero' Mick Ronson. To the adolescent Boltonian grammar school boy in 1972 they appeared to have arrived from another planet where men flirted with each other, made exhilarating music and wore Lurex knee socks. I had no idea where this planet was, and wasn't sure I wanted to flirt with men, but it certainly seemed like a world that was worth visiting.
>
> (Radcliffe 2009: 58)

This sense of 'another planet' echoes across the stories people tell of their encounter with new music, and with the forms of attraction and distraction (rather than identification) they solicit.

Broadcast media (television and radio, in particular) are collective phenomena, even if that collectivity is often virtual. Viewers of Bowie's performance of 'Starman' might well feel that they were watching him alone or together: there would be time to tell the following day in the play-grounds and canteens ('did you watch *Top of the Pops* last night?').[34] One of the best descriptions of distracted listening places the collectivity of broadcast media at its core. Greil Marcus' *Like a Rolling Stone: Bob Dylan at the Crossroads* focuses on, you won't be surprised to hear, Dylan's 1965 song 'Like a Rolling Stone'. Marcus describes a moment of languid boredom and distracted attention, in a holiday resort in Maui in 1981, that is broken when the Dylan song comes on the radio:

> People were talking quietly; even small children were lolling in the heat. Everything seemed to move very slowly. There was a radio playing tunes from a local FM station, but it was almost impossible to focus on what they were. Then 'Like a Rolling Stone' came on, and once again, as in the summer of 1965, sixteen years gone, with 'Like a Rolling Stone' supposedly safely filed away in everyone's memory, the song interrupted what was going on: in this case nothing. As if a note were being passed from one table to another, people raised their heads from their pine-apple and Bloody Mary breakfasts; conversation fell away. People were moving their feet, and looking toward the radio as if it might get up and walk. It was a stunning moment: proof that 'Like a Rolling Stone' cannot be used as Muzak. When the song was over, it was like the air had gone out of the room.
>
> (Marcus 2006: 98–99)

For Marcus this wasn't a scene of nostalgia, of people remembering the song, but of listening to the song as if for the first time. Marcus' account of 'Like a Rolling Stone' recognises it as something that causes a breach in time and music. It can't be filed away as completed and known. To hear it again is to hear its ambition, its refusal of history. More crucially, though, rather than seeing the collectivising energy as simply being 'in' the song, Marcus' account persuades us that it is the song (and not just any song, of course) encountered under conditions of distracted listening that allowed 'Like a Rolling Stone' to produce this breach in the languid vacancy of the scene. To sit down and listen to the song with 'an agenda' might well result in the feeling that the song had indeed been 'filed away'.

'Like a Rolling Stone' might not do it for you. My guess is that there are songs out there that have done it for you. In Rancière's writing you get a sense that the aesthetic regime opens up a caesura for the possibility of equality. A novel, for instance, might write of a group of people never previously given subjectivity, having had to make do with the walk-on parts of history; a painting might heroicise the condition of peasants; a song might be animated by the voice of the people. You also get an implicit sense of how quickly this gap might be closed, as identification is restored, and how a new item might now be added to the list of aesthetic subject matter. In other words apperception quickly adjusts to the potentiality of the aesthetic breach, making it a completed addition to the world rather than a portal through which a revolution might pass. Yet it is too easy to historicise such breaches and too neat to assume an ecological process that sees revolutionary art quickly reabsorbed into conservative and commercial culture. For Marcus to listen to Dylan's song again is to hear that breach again, not the memory of it. And this is perhaps the possibility that a distracted culture can most forcefully offer: the best of it is forever new, partly because its promises for equality were always rescinded. To hear it again is to encounter equality as a possibility.

Ordinary distractions

The micro-sketches of ordinary media reception that I began this chapter with, point to a diversity of forms of attention that are circulating today. But what is perhaps so striking about our media reception is not that it encourages inattention but that 'reception in distraction' is so successfully and commonly achieved. I can perform fairly complex operations on a computer while also successfully following a TV show that has a number of intertwined narrative threads. Media reception in a world saturated with diverse formats doesn't encourage a lack of concentration; rather it makes available a scattering of attention and a mobile and absentminded concentration. It might be better, then, to see distraction as a form of promiscuous absorption, of attention flitting from one thing to another, and multiplying its objects. The ability for sustained concentration has not been lessened by the new technologies and cultures of media: anyone who has been absorbed by a computer game, or watched as the hours whizz by while someone else navigates the dungeons and palaces of a virtual world will know that absorption is very much part of the distractions of new media.

The same culture that has turned music consumption into a form of shopping also provides the conditions under which an excoriating screech of guitar feedback can reach out across the airwaves and alter your sensorial world. A musical form that perhaps should seem ugly and abrasive (choppy chords, fragmented melody, distortion and reverb, harsh, aggressive rhythms, off-key jangles and barely on-key singing) can reach us as the most interesting and wonderful sound. Partly this is because our collective field of apperception includes so much and, potentially, excludes so little. Such a culture favours the ability to find beauty in unlikely places. But this same culture also prioritises the unsustainable rhythms of commerce, whereby the new becomes outmoded before it has even settled into custom, and where we are encouraged to constantly upgrade everything under the sun (computers, kitchens, clothes). The recently new is often disposed of while still being in a state of 'nearly new'. And yet a Dylan track from 1965 still has the power to present itself as a breach in time, creating a gap we can fall through to rediscover a thickly resonant soundscape full of disillusionment, promise and relentless cascades and clatter.

Notes

1 This is an example of the shipping forecast broadcast on BBC Radio Four (UK). The forecast is issued by the Met Office on behalf of the Maritime and Coast-guard Agency (which is part of the Ministry of Defence). Radio Four has an obligation to issue the shipping forecast (which is intended to be of service to sailors and ships' pilots) as part of the BBC's Royal Charter. Due to the seemingly poetic content of the forecast and the abstract quality it has for those unfamiliar with the conventions of the bulletin (e.g. which qualities refer to wind or visibility) it has been used in a range of pop cultural forms (songs, plays, comedy sketches, etc.).
2 For a useful social history of the media see Briggs and Burke 2002.
3 One of my students tried to do a media 'detox' for a week, swearing-off all forms of modern media communication. He ended up going early to bed, not through boredom, but through the additional energy it required.
4 I have in mind a slighter, less obviously violent, version of David Bowie's alien in *The Man Who Fell to Earth* (Nicholas Roeg, 1976), watching a bank of TVs at the same time, in the hope of receiving a message from 'his' planet, and despairing at the effects of so much media.
5 This is Walter Benjamin writing about international exhibitions: 'World exhibitions glorify the exchange value of the commodity. They create a framework in which its use value recedes into the background. They open a phantasmagoria which a person enters in order to be distracted' (1999: 7).
6 *Mass Art under Monopoly Capitalism* was the name that Theodor Adorno gave to a planned collection of essays that would have included writing by Adorno, Benjamin and Kracauer. Other contributors would have included Ernst Bloch, Siegfried Giedion and Max Horkheimer (see Lonitz 1999: 195–203).
7 There is a massive literature on media and everyday life. For some examples of work that has looked at the experiential aspects of media in relation to their capacities for altering perception, attention and the material environment see Bull 2000 and 2007; Fornäs et al. 2007; Galloway 2004; Goggin 2006; McCarthy 2001a and 2001b; Moores 2000; Scannell 1996; Silverstone 1994; and Wise 2004.
8 For commentary that is specifically attentive to the dialectics of distraction (and attuned to the work of critical theory) see Abbas 1996; Aitken 1998; Eiland 2003; Hake 1987; Hansen 1987; Latham 1999; McLaughlin 2005; Morse 1998; Petro 1989 and 2002; Rutsky 2002; Schwartz 2005; Vidler 2000; and Waters 2003.
9 This would be Trotsky's belief in the 1920s, for instance: see Trotsky 1975.
10 The notion of hysteria and neurosis is often seen as a form of chronic pre-occupation (by unruly reminiscences) that results in debilitating distraction.
11 For James it is clear that such 'vacancy' is associated with 'lower' forms of consciousness and has little value: 'It is difficult not to suppose something like this

scattered condition of mind to be the usual state of brutes when not actively engaged in some pursuit' (James 1950 [1890] vol. 1: 404).

12 Distraction as a form of dislocated attention is pursued in Abbas 1996.

13 *Zerstreuung* is sometimes translated as entertainment or amusement when the context suggests it. 'Diversion' is Sabine Hake's preferred translation because, for her, it is better at maintaining the ambivalence that Kracauer and Benjamin sought to invest in the term. I have stuck with 'distraction' mainly because this has become the most common translation and because it has become a dominant term used by conservative critics for describing a presumed lack of attention (particularly among young people). Because of this it seems important to try and restore the sense of ambivalence to 'distraction'. See Hake 1987: 147, footnote 3.

14 At the time when Kracauer was writing (the mid-1920s) Berlin witnessed a spectacular growth in large-scale picture houses. For the German context of Kracauer's work in relation to Berlin cinema see particularly Ward 2001. Other relevant accounts of Kracauer in relation to distraction can be found in Gilloch 2007 and Hansen 1991a and 1995.

15 The largest theatres held over five thousand. For more discussion of early cinema and other forms of popular amusement see Gunning 1986; Hansen 1991a; McKernan 2007; McNamara 1974; Nasaw 1999; and Rabinovitz 1998; as well as the collections edited by Charney and Schwartz 1996 and by Hark 2002.

16 Patrice Petro glosses Kracauer's account of distraction in the following way:

> On the one hand, Kracauer argues that cinematic distraction has potentially progressive effects, since it translates modes of industrial labor into a sensory, perceptual discourse which allows spectators to recognise the need for collective action under changed conditions of modern social reality ... . On the other hand, Kracauer insists that cinematic distraction contains reactionary tendencies, since it rationalizes perception to such an extent that spectators fail to recognize forms of exploitation and therefore lose the ability to act.
>
> (Petro 1989: 64–65)

17 Kracauer's insistently dialectical approach can't leave the cinema in such a purely positive light: just as distraction is effected through the combination of these elements, each one in turn tries to restore the semblance of wholeness: the interior design through the use of sacral elements; the films by aspiring to the image of universal wholeness.

18 Bertolt Brecht in a notebook entry from 1922: 'I've avoided one common artistic bloomer, that of trying to carry people away' (1964: 9).

19 This is also part of Benjamin's understanding of distracted culture and comes to the fore much more successfully when he is writing about world exhibitions and trade fares. But perhaps the most successful account of how a distracted and spectacular culture is both a poison and a cure is offered by Georg Simmel's account of the Berlin Trade Exhibition. Spectacular distractions are part of the cause of sensorial fatigue as well as being the only thing that can address sensorial fatigue:

> Every fine and sensitive feeling, however, is violated and seems deranged by the mass effect of the merchandise offered, while on the other hand it cannot be denied that the richness and variety of fleeting impressions is well suited to the need for excitement for overstimulated and tired nerves.
>
> (Simmel 1991 [1896]: 120)

20 The example of Brecht is useful again: if Brecht's only interest had been in establishing non-illusionistic popular culture he could have just become a boxing promoter. For Brecht's theatre non-illusionistic forms had to present antagonistic representations of the social world that required social evaluation.

21 People who touch-type (and the phrase connects directly to Benjamin's privileging of the tactile) often can't remember the position of the keys on the keyboard and have to ask 'their fingers' where they are (by virtually rehearsing hand movements). Our daily sense of 'knowing' is often biased towards forms of consciousness (especially related to hearing and seeing) oftentimes ignoring other ways of knowing the world and re-establishing splits between mind and body. We might talk about the 'mind's eye', but never of the 'mind's hand'.

22 As Graeme Gilloch glosses it: 'complete mastery of a practical activity is indicated precisely when one can perform tasks competently without thinking about them – that is, while distracted. Habit is not forgetfulness as such, but rather a form of accomplishment amidst amnesia' (2002: 191).

23 In bringing the work of William James to bear on Benjamin and Kracauer's theory of distraction I am not claiming that the two Germans were informed by this American psychologist. I am claiming (after the work of Jonathan Crary) that James, Benjamin and a host of others belong to the same longer history of the problem of modern attention: see Crary 1999, particularly chapter one, 'Modernity and the Problem of Attention'.

24 Benjamin's account is partly directed at our ability to tell productive stories about modern life:

> With the [First] World War a process began to become apparent which has not halted since then. Was it not noticeable at the end of the war that men returned from the battlefield grown silent – not richer, but poorer in communicable experience? ... A generation that has gone to school on a horse-drawn streetcar now stood under the open sky in a countryside in which nothing remained unchanged but the clouds, and beneath these clouds, in a field of force of destructive torrents and explosions, was the tiny, fragile human body.
>
> (Benjamin 1982: 83–84)

25 In the earlier version of the 'Work of Art' essay Benjamin wrote: '*The function of film is to train human beings in the apperceptions and reactions needed to deal with a vast apparatus whose role in their lives is expanding almost daily*' (1936a: 108) emphasis in the original.

26 This training can be compared to Simmel's understanding of a blasé attitude permeating modern industrial and metropolitan culture (Simmel 1903).

27 The best critique of Kracauer's gendered reading of cultural practices is Sabine Hake's (1987).

28 Distraction might be defined in this context as often taking the form of hearing without listening.

29 For a great account of distraction and watching and listening to Elvis on the *Steve Allen Show* on 1 July 1956 see Waters 2003.

30 Car journeys and music were a central theme in the reinvigorated genre of road movies in the 1970s, in particular in the early films of Wim Wenders. I remember first hearing David Bowie's *Low* while travelling through the night from outer London to North Wales. Squeezed into the back of an over-stuffed car, the second side of the album seemed to perfectly echo the lunar landscape of an end-of-the-world Anglesey.

31 To listen again to (and to watch) the early songs of T-Rex ('Jeepster', 'Get it On', 'Hot Love', 'Children of the Revolution' and so on) is to hear and see an electric polymorphous sexuality sweeping aside all in its path. Punk would pay its homage to Bolan and T-Rex: Siouxsie and the Banshees, for instance, would cover '20th Century Boy'.

32 It wouldn't be hard, for instance, to insert the names of other artists such as Dick Gaughan, Gill Scott-Heron, the Last Poets, Jimmy Hendrix, Kate Bush, Mike Ladd, Stephen Malkmus, Howlin' Wolf, Ali Farka Touré, Nina Simone, Nirvana and a seemingly unlimited supply of other musicians, into these tales of musical moments. My knowledge of music is limited, no doubt provincial and regionally specific. I perhaps should admit to having a deep sentimental and aesthetic attachment to the music of the Raincoats and the Slits, for instance, which no doubt primes me in quite specific ways.

33 See for instance accounts by Pete Shelley of the Buzzcocks and the writer Jake Arnott.

34 With the exponential rise of channels such collective discussion is much rarer, though not infrequent. When Bowie sang 'Starman' on British TV there were three channels that you could watch.

Chapter 6

Senses of the ordinary

It starts by spreading a mask of steam over your features. Long before your tongue touches the spoon, your eyes have started to water and your nose is dripping with borscht. Long before your insides have gone on the alert and your blood has become a single wave that courses through your body with the foaming aroma, your eyes have drunk in the red abundance in your bowl. They are now blind to everything that is not borscht, or its reflection in the eyes of your table companion. It's sour cream, you think, that gives this soup its rich texture. Perhaps. But I have eaten it in the Moscow winter, and I know one thing: it contains snow, molten red flakes, food from the clouds that is akin to the manna that also fell from the sky one day.

(Benjamin, 1930: 361)

In this, the last substantive chapter, I want to bring together some of the major themes of this book around the varied meanings and associations of 'sense': the senses (touch, taste and so on), sensuality, sensibility, sense (good sense, common sense, etc.) and sensitivity. I want to use this orientation to continue to explore ordinary aesthetics and its relation to the habitual and the becoming-habitual. As many of those who write on the senses quickly point out, the categories we have for distinguishing the 'five senses' quickly break down when we start to think about specific phenomena. Or rather: we begin to see how imbricated the various senses are when we apprehend something as ordinary as eating. Clearly, if we are in possession of all our senses (or they are in possession of us), there is a good deal of sensual overlap occurring when we eat. The visual aspect of food adds or takes away from its allure (we 'eat with our eyes' as the saying goes); the sound of crunch adds to our sense of the freshness of a vegetable or a crisp; the textures of food are part of what we enjoy or detest. Do we taste or smell herbs? I remember school biology lessons where we were taught the flavour-map of the tongue: this bit of the tongue tasted salt, this area was good for sourness, go here for sweetness. We dropped saline solution and lemon juice on our tongues to show this happening. Although it turns out that this tongue-mapping was a myth, it was always the case that eating could never be reduced to such flavour maps. Food, common sense might tell us, is about smell and taste, yet whatever else we do when we eat we always touch food with our mouth and particularly our tongue, and the softness or abrasiveness of food is part of its pleasure (indeed for spicy food the abrasiveness of the chilli is part of what produces the experience of 'hotness').

But the imbrications of sense are not limited to the overlapping of the five senses. The intermingling of emotions and sensual experience, for instance, is evident in the blurring of meanings associated with words such as bitter, sweet, sour, bile, acrid, acid, rough and so on. It wouldn't be hard to see this as simply a metaphorical use of a world of sensations: clearly the taste of bitterness is different from the emotional feeling of bitterness.[1] Yet we live our metaphorical worlds in intimate and material ways to the point where metaphorical meanings flavour material experience (a sour taste, endlessly pleasurable, will never have the comforting ease of sweetness for a society that equates sweetness with kindness and gentleness). We live a synaesthesia that hitches the metaphorical to the material (and vice versa) and makes it impossible to purify our experience into scientifically exact biological activity or, alternatively, into pure discursiveness.

Emotions and memories, sense and sensitivity, energy and affect, congregate and congeal in complexly singular ways. A tired parent washes a small baby. The baby is teething: his red face is crunched up in displeasure. The parent struggles with the sympathy he knows he should be feeling, but sympathy is too mixed-in with last night's broken sleep and the vague animosity that he knows he shouldn't be feeling. Yet somehow the mixture of cutaneous contact, mediated by water and soap, and the baby's buoyancy, which requires the merest touch of support, allows animosity to dissipate, allows a bond to be remade. A teenager returns home after the long walk from school. Fractious and cold, and mulling over the various exchanges that have knitted and unknitted the day, she takes a shower. The full-blast of almost scorching hot water drills into the shoulders and neck, marshalling the muscles and nerves, galvanising the body for the tasks ahead. The masochism of the drilling heat, prickling shoulders and back, assembles the muscles and nerves against the emotional toxins of the day. Tired limbs relax. Can we simply see these complexes of sensual and emotional relations as an intermingling of metaphor and materiality? Are adverts for bath salts that will 'wash away anxiety' simply analogies? Or are there partial truths in those soapy solutions?

Recent cultural inquiry has witnessed a marked increase in studies that focus on what might loosely be called immaterial material: affect, emotion and the senses.[2] Such an orientation might seem unsurprising given cultural studies' privileging of experience as a central locus for inquiry.[3] This orientation has often resulted in a partial abandonment of the stalwarts of critical inquiry so central to cultural studies (ideology critique and discourse analysis, predominantly), as investigation moves towards arenas less obviously ripe for critical purchase: the body, everyday life and the sensorial. This arena (mundane, bodily and sensorial life) seems less amenable to critical assessment because inquiry often starts out by querying the very object of study. Sensual, bodily, mundane life throws standard epistemologies into disarray, revealing the mentalist foundations of dominant forms of attention in the human sciences: forms of attention, then, that would remainder a world characterised by its non-ideational aspects. What often characterises the best recent work in this area is the way that inquiry favours description over prescription, exploration rather than assessment. Alongside this what should also be noted is the way that such an orientation towards 'immaterial' objects has often been undertaken in the name of a renewed materialism; a materialism that seeks to recognise the phenomenal materiality and collectivity of those aspects of culture that have been seen as ineffable, or irredeemably subjective.

This chapter began life many years ago when I first tasted fresh coriander (the herb) in cooking. To begin with I found it to have a soapy taste that I couldn't stand. Now I can't get enough of coriander. What happened? Obviously I got the hang of it, learnt to love it, just as children learn to love (or at least not detest) the taste of bitter things as they get older. But if I had managed to reorientate myself toward coriander, to move from loathing to loving, then what had achieved this pedagogic function; what had made the reorientation possible? I forget the circumstances of how I was introduced to coriander and I'm sure that there wasn't a 'eureka' moment when it went from being something I didn't like, to being something that I did. It crept up on me. As far as I can see the coriander itself was an agent in all this, a pedagogic guide that trained my taste buds, reorchestrated my sensorium to a new taste and aroma. But it did so not as a solitary and timeless material ingredient; it did it as part of a much larger cultural and sensual shift that could be called (somewhat blithely, I have to admit) multiculturalism.

Indian food in Britain has become part of the ordinary landscape of everyday food. The history of Indian cooking in Britain goes back at least to the end of the eighteenth century and while it has had a large presence throughout the twentieth century it was in the 1970s and 1980s that it really took off in the British high street.[4] An aesthetic approach sensitive to the migrations and diasporic communities that produce the multicultural foodscape of somewhere like Britain, would want in the end to look at a whole range of culinary negotiations: the changing landscape of restaurants; the domestic food culture of diasporic communities; the food practices of British 'natives' and so on. There isn't the space to do all this here so I want to concentrate on a very specific, but also culturally dominant, example of ordinary Indian-food eating in Britain. In a recent essay on Indian food in Britain, Elizabeth Buettner relays one of many accounts:

I started to go out for curries. It was a bit of fun in that you'd try the hottest curry, even if it was so fiery it blew the roof of your mouth off … You'd always try to have the hottest curry, you'd have a Madras, or a vindaloo or a tindaloo. … Going for an Indian was very much a boy's thing, a boy's night out.

(Jim Taylor in Buettner 2008: 878)

It is events like this that I'm interested in here.

For intercultural studies of ordinary eating an orientation towards mundane bodily and sensorial life is destined to be extremely productive. After all, differences between national cultures (or local cultures) are often registered at precisely this level: the advertising hoardings and the TV programmes of another country *look* different; talk, music and noise *sound* unfamiliar; climates and cooking provide a *tactile* and *olfactory* environment peculiar to this place and not another. And of course the very first element that any holiday maker, any refugee, any migrant has to overcome is the urgency of food, of sustenance. The sensorial is the accompaniment of what is initially deemed 'foreign': phenomena are foreign precisely because they offer a different orchestration of sight, sound, smell, touch and taste.

Where there is difference, there is unevenness: seemingly inevitably there is inequality, and that acute mixture of fear and fascination that marks so many encounters with the new and the 'foreign'. Taste and smell play an inexorable role in everyday forms of racism.[5] They are also central components for convivial and cosmopolitan intercultural, interethnic exchange. Such radical ambivalence might suggest that smell and taste are incidental ingredients in a series of cultural scenes that need to be explained by recourse to the 'harder stuff' of political and sociological discourse. But what playground racism – 'you smell', 'urgh, what are you eating?' for instance – shares with convivial cosmopolitanism is a non-ideational resonance that exists alongside (sometimes in support of, sometimes in opposition to) competing forms of ideology. Whether that ideology promotes neo-liberal integrationist policies, forms of xenophobic isolationism, libertarian 'open borders' policies or racist responses to migration, sensual and sensorial intercultural exchange is not simply governed by ideological persuasion. Argument won't persuade the taste buds to enjoy or dislike unfamiliar foods: taste or distaste is not simply a matter of cultural capital, but of the body's orientation and disposition towards specific sensorial orchestrations.

In *de facto* multicultural society eating a range of diasporic and 'native' cuisines is an ordinary activity of embodied sensual life. For marginalised ethnicities, as well as those ethnicities more powerfully placed, cross-cultural food consumption can be both pleasurable and problematic. Food spaces (shops, restaurants and so on) can be seen, for some social agents, as a potential space where new worlds are encountered. How these potential spaces are negotiated – the various affective registers of experience (joy, aggression, fear) – reflect the multicultural shapes of a culture (its racism, its openness, its willingness to embrace difference). These negotiations offer a barometer of lived everyday multiculturalism but they are also themselves transformative negotiations (they are *potential* spaces) that will in turn shape the multicultural pattern of a culture, a society. In all this the material agency of the food itself will play its part – the taste of fresh coriander can train an unfamiliar palate to like it (it can take possession of the new taster).

The spice of life

It is becoming something of a generic characteristic for authors who write about the cultural success of Indian food in Britain to mention the fact that England's unofficial football anthem is called 'Vindaloo' and that Britain's favourite meal is said to be chicken tikka masala (Basu 1999 and Monroe 2005). In these accounts it is enough to mention these facts as a sign of the general cultural currency of the 'curry' in Britain.[6] Some commentators go further to mention that a liking for curry and a disliking for people considered to be foreign is not mutually exclusive:

> Although the British eat vast amounts of curry, they are not always welcoming towards the Asians who make it for them. The lager-loutish tradition of rolling, uproariously drunk, into an Indian restaurant and proving one's machismo by ordering the hottest vindaloo or phal, is one of the disturbing sides of the British relationship with Indian food. The consumption of large quantities of curry has not necessarily made the British any less racist.
>
> (Collingham 2005: 236)

What is left underexplored, though, is the way that eating curry (in a specific register) might constitute a xenophobic practice (of sorts), or the way that the contradictions between liking curry and being unwelcoming to Asians might get played out at these moments of consumption. More significant to my mind is the way that eating curry might include within it a processual and pedagogic function that could (potentially at least) alter the aggressive and xenophobic contact with both a food culture and a social culture. Let me start by putting more detail on this moment of aggressive food consumption: first the football anthem.

In 1998 the comedian and actor Keith Allen, the artist Damien Hirst and Alex James, the bassist from the pop group Blur, collaborated to produce an 'England' football anthem (for that year's FIFA world cup). The song was released as 'Vindaloo', and the threesome called themselves 'Fat Les'. It has gone on to be the unofficial anthem for the England football team and its supporters, and is sung in football terraces wherever England is playing. The song is assertively masculine and working class as well as mockingly ironic and absurd. The song (with the help of a promotional video) conjured up a world of grotesques chanting the chorus of 'Vindaloo' and shouting 'we're going to score one more than you'. The song wore its nationalism on its sleeve at the same time as it parodied it, stereotyping 'Englishness' yet keeping strict control of what would count as English (tea drinking, knitting, cheese and vindaloo): 'Where on earth are you from? We're from England. Where do you come from? Do you put the kettle on?'

The central chorus, which is the simple refrain 'vindaloo, vindaloo, and we all like vindaloo', is first introduced after some semi-spoken doggerel: 'Me and me Mum and me Dad and me Gran, we're off to Waterloo. Me and me Mum and me Dad and me Gran, and a bucket of vindaloo.' These lines perform a sense of nationality based on the actuality of the present and on real and imagined past 'victories' (Waterloo is both the name of a symbolic national victory and the train station that, when the song was written, took you into mainland Europe). Does the derogatory figuring of 'vindaloo' in a bucket also point to an imagined victory and a prosaic actuality – an overcoming of South Asian subcontinental culture in Britain (by working-class whites), while also acknowledging the real and undisputed presence of Asian Britain? Connecting Waterloo and vindaloo is a nation-alism that can only be fashioned in relation to other nations, and only by means of conquest and denigration (a bucket of food). But crucially, here, it is as a marker of working-class machismo (parodied or celebrated) that an England supporter would regularly eat the hottest curries supplied by the high street Indian restaurant. The song 'Vindaloo' is a sign of the popularity of Indian high street food in Britain to the point where it is an ironic marker of English ethnicity. But it is also a sign of the aggression that sur-rounds this food culture: to see a crowd of English football supporters, waving the St George flag and chanting 'Vindaloo' would not, I assume, summon up feelings of inclusion among British-Asians.

But this scene of exuberantly aggressive food consumption is not just, of course, a feature of the imaginative culture of songs and sitcoms: it is there in the British high street too. One of the first Bangladeshi restaurateurs in Bristol, for instance, remembers the nightly fights in his restaurant in the 1960s and 1970s: 'There was a fight every night. We used to make curry and rice for 3/6d [about 17 pence] – they used to eat and then they'd run! We used to catch them! At that time we were young, 18–25 year olds. They used to throw rice and curry at each other' (Ahmed 1998: 104). The long quotation that follows is taken from Ahmad Jamal's ethnographic study of food con-sumption in Bradford (UK) undertaken in the mid-1990s with informants from British-Pakistani and Anglo-Celtic communities. This is Javed, who is remembering a time (unspecified) when he owned a restaurant in Bradford:

> Once another *angraiz* [an English person] came into my restaurant. He was accompanied by a group of friends. He asked [the] waiter for a

vindalu dish. I was listening to him. I went to my chef and asked him to make a special *vindalu* dish for him. You know a *vindalu* dish is made by pouring lemon juice over lots of green chillies so that the dish becomes strong and bitter. So we gave him the dish. But he complained and told that the dish was not hot enough. I was astonished. I asked my waiter to bring back the dish. Then I poured a big tablespoon full of chillies. My chef and other persons started to say, 'Oh uncle! Are you mad! Do you want to kill him!' And I said, 'Oh no he is not going to die'. I swear I put so much red chillies and then green chillies as well. I added lemon juice and some garlic as well because garlic is also hot. So when he was eating that dish, his friends were laughing at him. After finishing his meal he came towards the counter. He was completely wet with his sweat. He asked who had cooked that dish. I pushed my chef backwards because I thought he might fight. You know it was one o'clock in the morning. I told him that I had cooked that dish and I asked him whether he had any complaints. He moved forward, shook hands with me and told me that he had never eaten such a strong dish in his entire life. He told me that he had really enjoyed eating that dish. And finally he thanked me very much. I told him that it was alright. But in my heart I said, 'Son you go to you home tonight and then you will come to know' [laugh].

(Jamal 1996: 23)

Javed recounts that the man returned a couple of weeks later and said 'For God's sake, don't give me that poison again' (Jamal 1996: 23).

This is a dense passage of memory, and there is much to note. It is also humorous, and the overlying threat of physical violence, from the white customer towards the restaurant staff, is consistently deflected towards the consumption (and excretion) of chillies. The time is one o'clock in the morning and we can assume (or at least speculate) that the customer is here partly to eat and partly to carry on drinking (Indian restaurants have been a customary haunt for late-night drinkers, especially during a period when UK licensing laws meant that bars and pubs closed at 10.30 p.m. on week nights or 11 p.m. at weekends). We should note that everyone mentioned (and we don't know the genders of the group of friends) is male. When an image of the customer springs to mind you would be forgiven if you imagined him unsteady on his feet, erratic and unreadable in behaviour, in a word, drunk.

The eater chooses the hottest dish on the menu (a vindalu/vindaloo) and complains when it arrives that it is not hot enough.[7] The restaurateur remakes the dish, making it catastrophically hot. The eater eats this dish (that will become poison for him), congratulates the restaurateur and shakes his hand. The restaurateur is accommodating and paternal ('son'), but is also (not necessarily happily) conducting a lesson of 'moral' and gustatory instruction. The subtext suggests that the eater is aggressive, but what is relayed is not an aggression against other people – he shakes hands, is effusive in his thanks (though we don't know the 'full story' of this scene) – but against the cuisine and against himself. In this the main agent of the story is the chilli itself: without the chillies there would be no sweat, no pain and no pedagogy, no corporeal lesson.

To recount this scene from the perspective of the chillies it could be argued that the eater (intoxicated, full of vim and machismo) enters the restaurant and picks a fight with chilli. Here the chilli is both a (strong) foodstuff and a synecdoche for South Asian culture. He orders the 'strongest' dish (and it hardly matters if this term is the one that the eater uses, as opposed to 'hottest', or if it is the restaurateur's term). When it arrives he feels that this dish is no match for him (it is a weakling) and returns it. When a new opponent arrives (the vindalu with copious chillies) the match is on. The chillies make him sweat (they drench him in his own sweat) and no doubt they inflict pain on his tongue and mouth. At last the eater has finished: he has literally overcome the strongest chilli dish possible – it has been ingested, contained, incorporated. The chilli, though, hasn't finished with him; it is still continuing its alimentary journey. The next morning (we presume) it is ready to inflict its anal pain. The eater's victory is pyrrhic and two weeks later he admits defeat.

Such a scene of bravado, inebriation, trepidation, ignorance and hunger are given a brilliant reverse image in the British-Asian television comedy show *Goodness Gracious Me*. In its pilot episode the comedy team turned the white enthusiastic aggression towards South Asian food on its head. With a prelude that mimicks 1970s cinema advertising, the sketch starts with an invitation to eat at the Mountbatten restaurant in Bombay for 'the authentic taste of England right here in India'. Once inside the restaurant a raucous group of Indians are getting ready to order. Asking themselves why the come here every Friday one of them replies, 'You go out, get tanked up on lassis and go out for an English. It wouldn't be Friday night without going for an English.' Clearly drunk and patronising towards the waiter (who is called James, but who the customers call Jáhmés) the two conscious men (one man is slumped face down on the table) ask what the 'blandest thing on the menu' is, the waiter replies that 'the scampi is particularly bland'. One of the men goes so far as to order scampi with a prawn cocktail on the side, much to the consternation of some of his friends. The women want to order a 'chicken curry' but are cajoled into ordering something English, with the compromise being that they can order something that isn't 'completely bland'.

But the actual scene in Javed's restaurant goes further than staging a one-off encounter between an eater and cook that is articulated across cultural inequalities. In the restaurant scene, the eater returns, changed and seemingly contrite (perhaps). Whether or not his body has learnt something is, of course, impossible to know. Has the chilli taught him a material respect for the food culture? Does he ask the restaurateur what he would eat in his Bradford home? Or what he had eaten as a younger man? Does he continue his food aggression? Has the chilli reconfigured the man's sensual orchestration, opening him up to the pleasures and pain of chilli, to the culinary density and opacity of the spice, to the way it might mesh and counterpoint with coriander, or garlic, or vinegar? Aside from these speculative questions, what for me is crucial here is that this 'discussion', this event, that takes place between the eater, the restaurateur and (I insist) the chilli, is not taking place on the level of discourse, or ideational material. If persuasion happens, it is material in the most prosaic use of that term. The multicultural scene that is being conducted is not simply of hearts and minds, but of guts too. And it is here that thinking about ordinary food consumption in relation to the psycho-social material subject can play a significant role.

The world in small doses

Bodily enthusiasm towards various cuisines may seem at first to be a turning outward of the sensate self to the outside (and multicultural) world. Some kinds of gustatory relish take this form, where savouring new orchestrations of taste and smell are characteristic of an eater giving themselves over to a savoury experience and a sensual culture. If disgust works to protect and reaffirm the boundaries of the cultural self, then sensual relish could be seen as an opening out of these boundaries to extend the cultural self. Yet it might make sense to be wary here; after all the British colonial administration in India were often enthusiastic about the local cuisine, preferring it to the blander, less savoury traditional English cuisine (Procida 2003). Lisa Heldke, for instance, a self-confessed 'food adventurer', argues that her enthusiasm for 'exotic' cuisines (cuisines originating predominantly from the southern hemisphere) is intricately entwined with colonialism:

> Eventually, I put a name to my activity, to my penchant for cooking and eating ethnic foods – most frequently and most notably the foods of economically dominated 'third world' cultures. The name I chose was 'cultural food colonialism' because, as I had come to see, my adventure eating was (and continues to be) strongly motivated by an attitude with deep connections to Western colonialism.
>
> (Heldke 2003: xv)

Heldke's analysis is a useful corrective to those accounts which might naively associate (Western-directed) cosmopolitan food consumption with a progressive attitude towards multiculturalism, but it leaves unaddressed the material contact with food, and its possible agency in reorientating sensual perception. It would, of course, be a fantasy to assume that intercultural food exchange could possibly be even and equal given the social structures in place that work to privilege Eurocentric culture. As Keya Ganguly notes: 'Even today, when multicultural tastes are asserted with great élan, haute cuisine may call up French food; Italian food; perhaps even variants of *nouvelle* cooking with mild combinations of Thai, Chinese, or Indian spices; but hardly ever subcontinental offerings alone' (Ganguly 2001: 127).

While the general contact with various food cultures might inevitably be conducted under the awning of neo-colonial formations, this does not mean that they are reducible to this. Nor does this awning explain or describe what takes place between the specific agencies involved, agencies which might include the eater, the cook and (crucially) the cooked. As a counter-argument to Heldke, but one that is similarly sensitive to the neo-colonial structures that frame intercultural food consumption, it is worth mentioning Uma Narayan's less mentalist account of the possibilities of gustatory relish:

> Where prejudiced attitudes, as well as large social structures such as *de facto* occupational and residential segregation, still conspire to restrict the contacts many of us have with members of other ethnic groups, as friends, as neighbours, as fellow students and workers, as fellow citizens, the recognition that these separations diminish the collective possibilities of all our lives is imperative. In such situations, gustatory relish for the food of 'Others' may help contribute to an appreciation of their presence in the national community, despite ignorance about the cultural contexts of their foods – these pleasures of the palate providing more powerful bonds than knowledge. We risk privileging the mind too much if we ignore the ways in which a more carnal relish may sometimes make for stronger appreciation than intellectual 'understanding'.
>
> (Narayan 1997: 184)

For Narayan 'carnal relish' allows for a sensual immersion (even if contained within a limited duration and carried out under specific circumstances) that allows a non-ideational form of contact with another culture. For Narayan this is fundamental, both in countering the physical alienation between ethnic communities and in fostering what might be called 'thick' multiculturalism.

What I want to argue for here is a social aesthetic approach to intercultural food exchange that would include psychoanalysis as an element within its forms of attention. While I don't for a moment think that this is the only approach that could or should be taken (and in many ways there are a number of more urgent approaches that are presently being developed [for an indicative collection see Watson and Caldwell, eds 2005]) I would argue that it is particularly well suited to the experiential density of ordinary lived multiculturalism.[8] This would be an approach alert and sensitive to aspects of perception, to the orchestration of the sensual, and to the living experience of subjects. This would be an approach that combines sociological elements with new and established approaches to the senses, emotion and affect, and with socially orientated psychoanalytic work.

Clearly, from a social aesthetic point of view, changes in the smells, tastes and flavours of a social environment would be of crucial import. But perhaps more important still would be the routines and habits that would accompany them: the habit of savouring or turning your nose up, the practices of eating and cooking, the routines of what is eaten and what is not eaten. It was Walter Benjamin who recognised most profoundly that you cannot separate habit from the sort of exotic, playful intensity with which new substances and practices are introduced:

> For play and nothing else is the mother of every habit. Eating, sleeping, getting dressed, washing have to be installed into the struggling little brat in a playful way, following the rhythm of nursery rhymes. Habit enters life as a game, and in habit, even in its most sclerotic forms, an element of play survives to the end. Habits are the forms of our first happiness and our first horror that have congealed and become deformed to the point of being unrecognizable.
>
> (Benjamin 1928: 120)

Food arriving on spoons pretending to be aeroplanes and trains is designed to delight babies to the point where they can accept this strange substance that is clearly from an alien world.

Psychoanalytic accounts of eating, and the role of food, provide, I think, a viscerally rich opportunity for a more outward-directed psychoanalysis, one not just capable of registering personal histories or social history, but profoundly desirous of contact with the concrete sensual realm of socio-cultural experience. The work of Donald Winnicott (as I hope I began to show in chapter three) is, I think, particularly useful here. But first it is worth following, very briefly, Jean Laplanche in his book *Life and Death in Psychoanalysis* for a reading of Freud that repositions food at the centre of psychical material life. Crucially in his reading of Freud he reasserts the primacy of the drives (the instinctual and material drives) whose animating energy provides the supportive intensity for subsequent desires (primarily sexual, but more generally the subject's orientation to others). Thus for Laplanche (and, as he would argue, for Freud): 'it is precisely hunger, the feeding pattern, which the "popular conception" assumes to be the *model of every instinct*' (1985 [1970]: 17). For Laplanche the original drive is the hunger instinct, and it is driven towards an object: not the mother, nor the breast, but sustenance, milk:

> We thus have an 'impetus', an accumulation of tensions [hunger]; a 'source' as well, the digestive system, with − to localize and restrict

things further – those points in which appetite is most specifically felt. A specific 'object' is similarly introduced into the discussion. Shall we identify it as the breast? Well, no, since it is not the breast which procures satisfaction but the nourishment: milk.

(1985 [1970]: 17).

Thus, in Laplanche, 'it should be understood that the real object, milk, was the object of the function, which is virtually preordained to the world of satisfaction' (1985 [1970]: 17).

The positioning of food (milk) does much to move psychoanalysis away from an abstract understanding of desire. It also suggests pathways for understanding why food consumption can be so pleasurable and problematic, so intense and so visceral. But in the end Laplanche returns us to the dynamics of sexuality and the family. The earlier and less textual work of Winnicott (which shares some similarities with Laplanche), while continuing the focus on sexuality and the family, crucially suggests a way that the privileging of food can take us out into the bigger, social and multicultural world. Winnicott's work follows on from a tradition in psychoanalysis pioneered by Melanie Klein that is concerned with the way babies become mature subjects. Central to this tradition is a concern with the world and the bodies within it (including the child's) as a series of connected and disconnected objects. One of the major contributions that Winnicott was to make was to look at the way that subjects, infant babies through to adults, negotiate their affective environment and extend themselves from a world of control, outwards towards a larger sense of the environment.

The most famous example of this is the soft toy, or piece of blanket, that babies often use to comfort themselves. For Winnicott these transitional objects are the baby's 'first "not-me" possessions' (1974: 1). In Winnicott's world babies gradually experience 'the world in small doses' (1964: 69), but this movement away from a maternal imbrication to the greater world-at-large is anxious, filled with loss, as the baby becomes a social being. While toys and blankets are the first 'not-me' *possessions*, they are not the first 'not-me' objects. As babies are weaned, start to eat solid foods, the really central 'not-me' object is food – and importantly these are 'not-me' objects that can't be possessed (or can't be possessed for long). The first intense moments of discovering the world beyond the baby are through small doses of food. And this is a process that continues from the food given to a child in its home environment, to the food it might encounter at friends' homes, to the food it might come across at school and so on.

Winnicott has a real sense of the agency of food and hunger. This is him describing a baby's feeling of hunger: 'When babies begin to feel hungry something is beginning to come alive in them which is ready to take possession of them' (Winnicott 1964: 35). And when food enters into the alimentary tract, that sense of being possessed (rather than possessing) continues. Feeding, weaning, starting to eat solids, experimenting with new foods, are profoundly social and cultural acts that are accompanied by feelings of anxiety and anger – weaning is after all a refusal to allow the baby satisfaction. In an essay titled 'The Location of Cultural Experience', Winnicott suggests that the most intense experiences are had in 'potential space':

> From the beginning the baby has maximally intense experiences *in the potential space between the subjective object and the object objectively perceived*, between me-extensions and the not-me. This potential space is at the interplay between there being nothing but me and there being objects and phenomena outside omnipotent control.
>
> (Winnicott 1974: 118, emphasis in original)

The intensity is there, in other words, in the contact with the unfamiliar, the new, the 'foreign'. The world that a subject controls (the world of 'me-extensions') meets a new order outside omnipotence.

In Winnicott's account of the child gradually opening up to the world ('in small doses') the intricate relationship between what is self and what is world is rendered as a complex entanglement: the extending of the self outwards is coterminous with incorporating the world into the self. In this Winnicott's theories inherit something of the social psychology of William James, and something of the humanist philosophy of David Hume. For James habit has to be understood as the most intimate accommodation of the social world into the nervous system and the field of apperception. For Hume our most characterising ingredients of selfhood are nothing more and nothing less than the shape of our social entanglements. The self stretches out into the world so as to become a self. The emphasis on food for a writer such as Winnicott is an emphasis on process: the child gradually steps into the social world by taking small bites of culture, by rejecting and then accepting solid foods, and gradually gaining confidence in its physical commerce with the world. For Winnicott the eater is not a fully constituted subject, but a subject constantly becoming constituted through their orientations towards things like food. Food, then, always has the potential to join in the act of reconstituting the subject.

Authenticity, habit and diasporic popular culture

Habit (eating habits, cooking habits, washing habits and so on) are simultaneously world-embracing activities and world-containing ones. In the realm of multicultural food this particular dialectic is never simply given as a neutral negotiation. The dialectic is played out across a historical field that is made up of passionate intensities. We can name them as forms of aggression and forms of carnal relish (as well as forms of indifference), and recognise that they are dynamic features where one can slip into the other. But we can also see another side of this which is the policing activity of such negotiations that go by the name of authenticity. The discourse of authenticity has to be contrasted with the complex actuality of historical processes.

Food, as might be expected, is an important marker in migrant and diasporic culture, primarily because it is a portable practice that can materially (and sensually) remake a 'home' culture that has been left behind. For the generations of diasporic peoples for whom 'home' is a multicultural existence where they are figured as a 'minority', food culture is the complex site of negotiations, of continuities and discontinuities, between a cultural present and cultural heritage. It is hardly surprising, then, that food should play such an important role in recent diasporic novels such as Nadeem Aslam's *Maps for Lost Lovers* (2004), Monica Ali's *Brick Lane* (2003) or Zahid Hussain's *The Curry Mile* (2006). Nor given the sensual propensities of food and its relationship to memory is it surprising to see the emergence of diasporic autobiography centred around food memories (for instance Rohan Candappa's *Picklehead* [2007]), offering an alternative to the Raj-orientated food memories found in memoirs like Jennifer Brennan's *Curries and Bugles* (1990).

The dissemination of 'Indian' food, as both idea and actuality, occurs across a range of registers. If the physical restaurant exists at one end of this range (presenting a material food culture and a setting), and at the other end, concerned with the symbolic and affective meaning of diasporic food, exist novels and films, then between them lies a 'literature' that is both representational and practical. Recipe books, television cooking programmes, restaurant journalism and food guides constitute material which is clearly intended for use; to instruct the reader (or viewer) in how to enact and consume a food culture (by visiting certain restaurants, or by performing certain cooking practices). This material is particularly important for thinking about South Asian food in Britain as a form of diasporic popular culture because it is so often centred on the notion of authenticity – a value closely associated (though contentiously) with both popular culture and diasporic culture. Diasporic popular culture is often contradictorily based on what might be called artificial or improvised authenticity: a cultural form that out of necessity has had to adapt a diasporic food culture to a specific non-diasporic audience and context. In the literature of recipe books and food guides this diasporic working-class adaptability has usually been scorned as a form of inauthentic and impoverished cuisine.

The ubiquitous curry of the high street Indian restaurant was almost structurally incapable of being seen as achieving gastronomic standards equivalent to European-influenced cooking. In the London listings of the 1982 *Good Food Guide*, for instance, only five 'Indo-Pakistani' restaurants are listed, in relation to forty-two restaurants serving versions of French cuisine (Driver 1983: 90). More crucially the Asian restaurants that are noted are never simply 'Indian' restaurants (in the tradition of the dominant high street curry house): the *Good Food Guide* lists them as Gujerati (Gujarati), Tamil and Bengali. To be 'Indian', in the way that was first constituted by imperialism, was to already admit to inauthenticity.

While the predominant food culture of the high street restaurant was Bengali (Bangladeshi), regional specificity was never a characteristic of the restaurant's promotion or self identity. The standard menu of the Indian restaurant was and still is regionally, historically and socially promiscuous; incorporating Punjabi, Mughlai and Goan cuisines, for instance, with dishes designed for (white) Anglo-Indians during the Raj (for instance, the madras) and inventions peculiar to the UK high street itself (chicken tikka masala and the balti) (see Achaya 1998 and Collingham 2005). Ideas of gastronomic excellence combine contradictory prescriptions for authenticity and invention: the standardised variety and anglicised food culture of the high street Indian restaurant would fail on both counts, even though the history of its emergence as standardised cuisine was nothing if not inventive.

Recipe books (which are rarely if ever directed to poor and working-class audiences) similarly establish the coordinates of authenticity (and hence of gastronomic value) precisely by stressing regional variety and denigrating the transformation of cuisines as they migrate across national borders. While the very first mention of curry in British cookbooks in 1747 (see Monroe 2005: 63) offered a cuisine filtered through colonial experience, this continues alongside an insistence that the recipes have been taken from authentic 'natives' from the subcontinent. For the British middle and upper classes curry was a standard component of most domestic cuisines (and of the cookbooks that they relied on) from the mid-nineteenth century (Humble 2005: 24 and Basu 1999: xxiv). While cookbooks offering instruction in how to cook Indian food often declared the authenticity of their recipes, it was in the 1970s where the question of authenticity became decisive. Madhur Jaffrey, in England in the 1960s to promote her film *Shakespeare Wallah*, sampled the food of Indian restaurants and started to learn to cook via letters from her mother (Hardyment 1995: 142–44). Jaffrey's upbringing was highly privileged and far removed from the working-class culture of the pioneering Indian restaurateurs during the twentieth century, and her critique of the high street Indian restaurant is inflected with class connotations:

> On a recent visit to London, I was astounded to see Indian restaurants flourishing in practically every neighbourhood. Mistakenly, I took this efflorescence to signify an increased supply of good quality, authentic, regional Indian foods. ... Upon visiting the restaurants, I found most of them to be second-class establishments that had managed to underplay their own regional uniqueness as well as to underestimate the curiosity and palate of contemporary Britons.
>
> (Jaffrey 1973: 519)

While Jaffrey is well aware that 'the cooks in these proliferating Indian, Pakistani, and Bangalee restaurants are often former seamen or untrained villagers who have come to England in the hopes of making a living, somehow or other, in alien surroundings', she is simultaneously amazed that she 'saw no roe fritters, or fish smothered with crushed mustard seeds and cooked gently in mustard oil or *bhapa doi*, that creamy, steamed yogurt' – the regional foods of Sylhet (Jaffrey 1973: 519–20).

This critique of the standardised (and anglicised) cuisine of the high street Indian restaurant, in the name of authenticity, is now a classic strategy in recipe books promoting South Asian cuisine. In one sense it is presumably a justified reaction to the imperialist and capitalist inflection that has been central to the emergence of this food culture in Britain, yet at the same time it fails to recognise that *all* South Asian cooking has been affected by colonialism (the chilli only came to the subcontinent through Spanish and Portuguese colonialism), and fails to recognise the extraordinary success and specificity of the high street restaurant. In a recent and highly successful recipe book, *Cooking Like Mummyji: Real British Asian Cooking*, Vicky Bhogal echoes the words of Jaffrey, from the perspective of a British-Asian:

> I grew up really confused about Indian restaurants in this country. When I was young I could not understand why the food served up in such establishments was labelled as Indian – it bore no resemblance to anything I ate at home. ... I have spoken to many Indian restaurant chefs around the country about why the food is so different from the food we cook at home. They were completely honest and explained that, back when the first Indian restaurants in England appeared, there were no rules. There were no real Indian grocers and so they used little in the way of fresh ingredients. Powders were cheap and long lasting and chefs used powdered garlic, ginger, coriander, onion and chilli. A lot of Indian restaurants still do. They make a base of tomato and oil which forms the basic sauce for every dish and they add a little more chilli or maybe some cream depending on what the dish requires. After all, the more sauces you make, the more skilled manpower you require, all of whom need a wage.
>
> (Bhogal 2003: 124)

While Bhogal recognises the pragmatics involved in Indian restaurant culture, the critique of inauthenticity is still the main priority. Perhaps, though, what is most ironic is that Bhogal sold her brand (Cooking Like Mummyji) to the international conglomerate Tesco, thereby ensuring that her recipes would become industrialised, batch-produced products.

In recipes and writings sympathetic to and excited by the possibilities of cultural transformation offered by intercultural exchange, hybridity is often championed against claimed authenticity. Thus Sophia Ahmed can introduce her recipe for the 'invented', hybrid dish that is chicken tikka masala by suggesting that it represents a 'third space':

> Chicken tikka masala, which existed neither in South Asia nor in Britain, occupies a distinct 'third space' between the purities of South Asian and British cuisine. It exists only because of the fusion of these cultural experiences and as a consequence is now eaten both in Britain and throughout South Asia.
>
> (Ahmed 2006: 62)

Yet this celebration of hybridity and bricolage is itself premised on a false notion of the authenticity that it departs from (the assumed and fantasised purities of South Asian and British cuisine). An understanding of the Indian restaurant as popular culture is only obscured if it is greeted either by mourning the loss of authenticity or praising the new hybrid cuisines of a postcolonial 'multiculture'. Rather it is only through the mapping of force-fields, by tracing the material and historical circumstances within which processes of adaptation and 'making-do' take place that it can be understood. For the high street Indian restaurant in Britain, this force-field is the conjunction of the social and historical actuality of Indian restaurants.

History, class and the Indian restaurant

As something of a corrective to the tales of authenticity and inauthenticity routinely paraded in cookbooks, it is worth historicising the emergence and consolidation of the high street Indian restaurant. The commercial history of South Asian cuisine in Britain follows two distinct but overlapping strands. For instance, the earliest record of 'curry' being commercially sold is usually cited as the Norris Street Coffee-House in Haymarket, London, which had curry on its menu from 1773 (Monroe 2005: 61). This was a coffee-house run by entrepreneurs eager to capitalise on the burgeoning trade of coffee-houses in London, and catering to a clientele of prosperous and aristocratic Londoners and visitors to the capital. This was not, however, the first 'Indian' restaurant, if by that it is meant a restaurant owned or organised by migrants from South Asia. The first commercial outlet for South Asian food, run by an Indian restaurateur, was Dean Mahomed's 'Hindostanee Coffee-House'. Thus right away it is possible to get a sense that 'curry' comes to Britain via an appropriation by a 'host' culture (Britain), at the same time as it is promoted as a diasporic cuisine (by migrating South Asians). Yet while this might suggest a necessary distinction, the overarching culture of colonialism mobilised a common imperial style that was utilised across this divide.

The Hindostanee Coffee-House was Dean Mahomed's business from 1810 to 1812, and while he was declared bankrupt in 1812, the business carried on for many years after (his Anglo-Celtic backers were not cited in the bankruptcy). In 1811 he took out an advertisement in *The Times* which gives some indication of the atmosphere of the coffee-house:

> Hindostanee coffee-house, No. 34 George-street, Portman square – Mahomed, East-Indian, informs the Nobility and Gentry, he has fitted up the above house, neatly and elegantly, for the entertainment of Indian gentlemen, where they may enjoy the Hoakha, with real Chilm tobacco, and Indian dishes, in the highest perfection, and allowed by the greatest epicures to be unequalled to any curries ever made in England.
>
> (*The Times* 27 April 1811, cited in Fisher 1996: 258)

We should note here that Dean Mahomed's address to 'Indian gentlemen' was not an invitation to fellow migrants but to white Anglo-Indians living in London. This address is to an imagined audience who might want to experience the imperial pleasures of a fantasised image of India as either nostalgia or as adventurism.

What can be seen in the Hindostanee Coffee-House is a repertoire of effects that brings together subcontinental, colonial and orientalist simulations addressed to British imperial culture. It was usual for the coffee-houses of London (and elsewhere in Britain) to trade on the orientalist associations of coffee (for instance the coffee-house that was in direct competition with the Hindostanee was called the Jerusalem [see Ellis 2005]), it was also quite common for coffee-houses to trade in anything except coffee (the drink favoured in the Hindostanee was wine). What is so specific about the Hindostanee was its detailed construction of 'India' under commercial and imperial rule. The food and the interior were caught in an 'imperial imaginary' that would constitute central motifs for the later emergence of the high street Indian restaurant:

> Dean Mahomed prepared a range of meat and vegetable dishes with Indian spices served with seasoned rice. He constructed bamboo-cane sofas and chairs on which the patrons would recline or sit. He adorned the walls with a range of paintings including Indian landscapes, Indians engaged in various social activities, and sporting scenes set in India.
>
> (Fisher 1996: 257)

This is an imperial *mise-en-scène*, where the experience of a food culture is heavily associated with a range of other sensual experiences. What makes the Hindostanee paradigmatic of later restaurants is the way that taste and smell (the cuisine) connects to the visual realm (the décor of the restaurant) as well as to sound and touch (the creaking bamboo furniture, for instance, the bubbling sound of the hookah, etc. – later replaced by music). The material presentation of Indian-ness is conducted across all the senses.

But while these two examples from the late eighteenth and early nineteenth centuries (the Norris street café and the Hindostanee Coffee-House) provide fascinating material, showing the longevity of subcontinental cuisine in Britain, the history of the high street Indian restaurant as popular culture in Britain properly belongs to the twentieth century. The first crucial wave of developments occurs in the 1920s and 30s. While the Hindostanee Coffee-House offered a fantasised image of India, a more grassroots food culture emerged as a response to increased migration from the subcontinent. From the time the East India Company was given a royal charter (in 1600) to monopolise British commercial exploitation of 'India', British shipping took on Indian seaman ('lascars' in the vernacular). Sylhet, a district in Bengal (in the part of Bengal that would become Bangladesh in 1971), would supply British shipping with ranks of deck-hands, galley workers and later, when steamships were dominant, with engine-hands and fireman. Life as a lascar was unpredictable and hazardous, and with the advent of industrial shipping, famously noisy and dangerous (with boilers regularly blowing up, workers dying of heat stroke and so on). From the start it was assiduously under-rewarded (lascars earned about one-fifth of the wages of their white counterparts [Collingham 2005: 217]), with large time-lags between voyages. Many understandably jumped ship or found that there was no return voyage, and communities of lascars (many of whom were Sylhetti) emerged and continued to grow, particularly in areas close to the docks of East London, Cardiff, Liverpool and Glasgow (see Visram 2002: 14–33, 54–69).

During the eighteenth and nineteenth centuries thousands of lascars found themselves in Britain (for instance between 1803 and 1813 10,050 lascars arrived in Britain, with Indian seamen constituting roughly twenty per cent of the British maritime workforce by 1919 [Fisher, Lahiri and Thandi 2007: 65 and Visram 2002: 225]). Many became destitute, while others undertook menial work of various kinds. Initially these men were, officially, the financial responsibility of the East India Company, which would pay for their shelter and (eventually) their return passage to India (often as working crew). For instance in 1804 the Company gave Abraham Gole the contract of sheltering and feeding destitute lascars, for which he constructed a purpose-built barrack-style depot (Fisher, Lahiri and Thandi 2007: 66). In 1834 the Company's charter was rescinded, thus ending its financial responsibility to care for its former 'employees' (although many argued for the continued moral responsibility of the Company). The loosening up of trade restrictions, of course, did nothing to better the material life of Indian seamen; it did, however, increase the numbers involved in maritime trade. In 1857 a missionary organisation set up The Strangers' Home for Asiatics in London, with the express purpose of repatriation and for the recruiting of crews (the cost of lodging would have been beyond the means of a lascar wage).

But it was the lodging houses established by former lascars and other migrants that were central to the welfare of South Asians in Britain, and fundamental to the emergence of the Indian restaurant. Unlike the official lodging houses, the more informal housing, very often established by Sylhetti men, was community based and combined cheap, sometimes free, accommodation with cafés serving South Asian food (Choudhury 1993: 49). The boarding houses were often large and the cafés not only served necessary sustenance, they were also social meeting places: as one Sylhetti boarder remembered, the cafés were like 'a Community centre for the Syhletis' (Collingham 2005: 218). The lodging-houses and associated cafés represent diasporic enclaves of mutual assistance in the context of deplorable circumstances. As well as shelter and sustenance, informal networks emerged informing new arrivals of possible jobs. To take just one example, Ayub Ali's lodging-house was intricately connected to his café:

> For many a Sylhetti sailor, the house of Ayub Ali, in Sandy Row, east London, known simply as 'Number Thirteen', was a place of refuge and help, as well as a lodging-house. Born in Sylhet in 1880, and an ex-sailor himself, Ali, who had jumped ship in the USA in 1919, came to London in 1920, and set up a café (Shah Jolal Restaurant) at 76 Commercial Street, east London. Generous and helpful, he provided shelter and food without charge, 'for as long as was necessary'.
>
> (Visram 2002: 257)

This sense of the café as public sphere for a diasporic community was a fundamental aspect of its nineteenth- and early twentieth-century incarnations.

This more 'organic' food culture (so to speak) continues alongside the consolidation of the imperial image of Indian food culture. Nowhere was this imperial imaginary more successfully achieved than in Veeraswamy's. In 1927 Edward Palmer (a British citizen with Anglo-Indian heritage) opened what would soon become the most famous Indian restaurant in Britain, Veeraswamy's – or as it was also known to intimates, simply 'the Indian Restaurant' (Monroe 2005: 83). Palmer had made a name for himself during the British Empire Exhibition in 1924 where he had run the Mughal Palace restaurant. Veeraswamy's in Regent Street (London) conjured up a fantasmatic vision of imperial opulence, where there were tiger skins on the wall, where punkah wallahs worked the fans and where Indian doormen held umbrellas as customers returned to the rain-soaked streets of London (see Monroe 2005: 82–87 and 104–6). Veeraswamy's addressed itself unapologetically to a nostalgic imperial past; or as Yousuf Choudhury (historian of Bangladeshi migration to Britain) succinctly and caustically put it: 'The kitchen and other staff were brought direct from India. They were dressed in traditional clothes, worn with imperial flare, just right to receive and satisfy their old masters' (Choudhury 1993: 65).

Both Veeraswamy's and the boarding-house cafés employed subcontinental cooks, many of whom came from Sylhet. Many of the Sylhettis had learnt to cook on board ship or learnt on the job. The difference between Veeraswamy's and the cafés was that Veeraswamy's was designed for fine dining while the cafés were concerned with cheap meals, that heeded the more pragmatic needs of what, with limited means, it was possible to cook. Two important Indian restaurants (with subcontinental proprietors), that bridge the chasm between Veeraswamy's and the lodging-house cafés, opened in the interwar period: the Shafi in 1920 and the Kohinoor in the late 1920s or early 1930s (the exact date is unknown). The Shafi continued the tradition of an Indian restaurant catering to a migrant population: but this time instead of catering for the working-class Sylhetti boarders the Shafi catered for middle-class Indian students studying at the universities of London. And it was through the more mixed student populations that Indian restaurants first developed a clientele that crossed over into white populations with little experience of the British Raj. For instance the anthropologist Jack Goody remembers studying at Cambridge in the 1930s:

> When I first went to Cambridge University in the year before the out-break of war [1938] there were already a number of Indian restaurants in the town, and one Chinese-American establishment. The Indian restaurants were generally run by Bengalis and served a standard menu of curries and pilaus of the kind that had been directed to British servicemen abroad.
>
> (Goody 1998: 161)

As Nicola Humble claims, the exponential rise of the high street Indian restaurant in the decades after the Second World War was facilitated, in part, by a population of students and young single people:

> The success of Indian restaurants in the 1960s and 1970s was very largely the result of their appeal to a generation of young people living away from home for the first time: students benefiting from the massive expansion of the universities in the late 1960s, and the bedsit dwellers in the big cities. Prices were cheap, the food was excitingly exotic (but cunningly adapted to British palates), and perhaps most crucially, the restaurants were open long after other establishments had shut their doors.
>
> (Humble 2005: 189)

Importantly the Shafi continued the sense of the restaurant as community centre that had been established in the boarding-house cafés.

In the period after the Second World War the figures for Indian restaurant growth are phenomenal and mark a significant change in the shape of restaurant food in Britain:

> By 1946 there were 20 restaurants in London and they began to spread all over the country until in 1960 there were 300 Indian restaurants in Britain and in 1980 over 3,000, of which the vast majority are owned by families from Sylhet. The names of many of the restaurants are tried and tested names of the early successes, *Anglo-Asia*, *Koh-i-Noor*, *Taj Mahal* and their distinctive red flock wallpaper style is a survival of their luxurious air in postwar austerity.
>
> (Adams, ed. 1987: 52)

Caroline Adams, in the above quotation, is referring to the growth in high street Indian restaurants. It is worth remembering that the less conspicuous (as far as restaurant listings are concerned) subcontinental cafés are still very much in evidence during this period in the poorer areas of port cities, so much so that in 1944 in the area of Stepney (a small and poor district in the London borough of Tower Hamlets) there were thirty-two cafés run by 'coloured' men (Visram 2002: 256).

While the growth of high street restaurants was geographically uneven across Britain, there are a number of characteristics that represent a family resemblance for the Indian restaurant in the second half of the twentieth century and into the present. These characteristics point to the way that Indian restaurants are not merely determined by patterns of neo-colonial sociality, but also, and crucially, intervene in this sociality. The first central component of the high street Indian restaurant is that it establishes itself in sites that had previously provided fairly cheap food (former working-class cafés, Chinese restaurants, fish and chip shops and so on). Thus the first restaurants usually took over food establishments where the clientele would expect inexpensive food. Immediately then there is a class association with the Indian restaurant that needs to be seen alongside the obvious ethnic character. Second, this restaurant culture was nearly exclusively male in ownership and in day-to-day running. While this was partly due to religious and cultural prohibitions on women's activities, it was more materially connected to the patterns of migration and the impediments to working-class family migration. Third, the restaurants were often rented and changed hands fairly frequently. Often changes in restaurateurs would be within a network of family, friends and associates. This was not a result of business failure, but because, for many, the restaurant business was not a career but a means to an end (which might include returning to Bangladesh, providing the funds to start other businesses, paying for higher education and so on). Thus while many Indian restaurants were out to provide high quality food, gastronomic excellence was neither an aim nor a realistic possibility.

Fourth, like many other forms of diasporic commerce, it was driven by what has been called a form of self-exploitation. To achieve autonomy, by remaining profitable within a market that demands low cost restaurants and takeaways, waiters, cooks and cleaners have had to work extraordinarily long hours and pay themselves (or get paid) very small amounts. This self-exploitation is continuous throughout the twentieth century and into the present. Thus one chef in an Indian takeaway in the midlands in 2003 would 'at the end of every gruelling 55-hour week' take 'home the reward of £150, working out at rather less than £3 per hour' (roughly £2 per hour under the national minimum wage) (Jones et al. 2006: 362). While this might seem like exploitation by the employer, the proprietor of the takeaway only earned £180. 'South Asian restaurants are now increasingly confronted by fast-food outlets, pubs and chain restaurants ... . Drastic price-cutting is often the only perceived means of survival, a measure inevitably aggravating the problem of low pay and poor working conditions' (Jones et al. 2006: 360).

Fifth, as the Indian restaurant came to be an established part of the urban and the suburban (and also rural) landscape the menu became standardised to the point where the customer would expect all menus to include the same range of dishes (biryani, madras, korma and more recently, balti and so on). This menu is partly based on the food established by a restaurant such as Veeraswamy's but will also contain dishes that emerged in Britain as the Indian restaurant became a significant part of British food culture. Sixth, though the restaurants continue to be largely aimed at an Anglo-Celtic culture, the restaurants themselves have also continued to serve a role as social-community centres.

Coda

This is, no doubt, a schematic history of British Asian curries, but I hope it qualifies and reframes something of the debates about authenticity. It hardly explains, though, the phenomenon of Anglo-Celtic Britons demanding and consuming the fieriest food available. It should however add context to the telling of this story, placing it within a much longer history of Indian and British connections. More crucially, though, it can alter the perspective for viewing aggressive eating. From Winnicott's perspective expanding the world through such mundane acts as eating is not an end in itself, it is processual, gradually expanding the world of the not-me as it is incorporated into the self. Disdain, disgust, aggression and desire are not fixed passionate attitudes, but are mutable orientations to the outside world. Aggression *can* turn into something else. What seems clear is that the aggressive involvement with Indian cuisine belongs to a passionate economy that is a world away from the liberalism of 'tolerance'. Tolerance speaks of a failure to connect to the other, to keep others at arm's length. And this is why the phenomenon of 'going for an Indian' seems a world away from what

Heldke described as 'food adventuring' (see Heldke 2003) and what others have described as 'boutique multiculturalism' (see Fish 1997).[9] Such description could be accused of viewing all intercultural food exchange as inevitably and irrevocably structured in advance by imperialism. I want to follow Fish's insistence that we start from the position of seeing 'multiculturalism as a demographic fact' (rather than as a philosophical problem) (Fish 1997: 385), and that we should follow Uma Narayan's lead in tracing both the problems *and* opportunities that intercultural food exchange allows (Narayan 1995). In this regard the mundane and ordinary facts of multiculturalism, which redistribute the sensory in very real ways, can be found partly in such everyday materials as clothing and food. These are objects of conflict, but also of consolidation and adaptation. In one way multiculturalism (that complexity of diasporic culture, migration and national identities) becomes a fact in the alimentary practices of a population, in the supermarkets and shopping baskets of Asians and non-Asians conducting their ordinary lives.[10]

A historical account attentive to the various roots and routes of South Asian cuisine as it has percolated across and within British culture should thicken the account of the enthusiastically aggressive curry eater mentioned above. So too should the various forms of popular cultural representation (from cookbooks to comedy sketches). It is hard to know if such routine displays of alimentary machismo are now a thing of the past. What is clearer is that the gastronomic landscape of the high street has changed considerably. Pubs throughout the UK, for instance, now host curry nights; whereas the high street Indian restaurant rarely decks itself out in the Raj-style décor so familiar in the 1970s and 1980s. Similarly, regional specificity has become a regular feature of a much more varied set of restaurants.

But what of the foolhardy customer who bathed in the sweat of a seemingly lethal dose of chillies? Would he have moved house because he disliked the smell of curry? Has he developed a connoisseurial and informed appreciation of the subtle flavours and regional varieties of Bangladeshi, North Indian and Southern Indian cuisines? Is he searching out vindaloos that are closer to that hybrid mix of Portuguese and Goan flavours? Is he an enthusiast for all things Indian, a generous spirit welcoming to all sorts of diasporic culture? Who knows? The density of the initial incident, fuelled no doubt by alcohol, might be seen through an optic that refracts class as much as ethnicity in what were often suppliers of cheap food for working-class and student customers. There is a cultural density to the ordinary occasions of 'going for an Indian' that mixes xenophobia and openness. In the sensorial scene of excessive chilli eating the cultural work was performed across bodies (the customer, the restaurateur, the chef) and it was performed in the exchange of flavours and intensities. The sweat from the chillies and the 'carnal relish' of the eater show signs of trepidation and bravado, of xenophobia and misplaced enthusiasm; they also show signs of an alimentary journey that was, perhaps, just beginning.

Such signs are not the sort that can support a cultural politics of multiculturalism, but without such non-ideational signs, multiculturalism is merely virtual, framed in the aspic of 'tolerance'.

Notes

1 And you could quite easily imagine a culture where the taste of sourness was associated with a more uplifting emotion than the one that circulates alongside it in the English-speaking world.
2 For an indicative sample see: Ahmed 2004 and 2006; Howes ed. 2005; Korsmeyer ed. 2005; Probyn 2005; and Wise and Chapman 2005.
3 For historical and thematic overviews of experience as a category of inquiry, see Ireland 2004 and Jay 2005.
4 For historical work on Indian (and Pakistani and Bangladeshi) food see: Buettner 2008; Collingham 2005; Monroe 2005; Panayi 2002 and 2008; and Sen 2009. While the majority of 'Indian' restaurants in Britain have been run by Bangladeshi British restaurateurs I have stuck with the term 'Indian' to describe them. This is because 'Indian' is the term that the restaurateurs themselves use and the food that they provide is not a reflection of any particular region but is a diasporic food relating to migration from the whole of the South Asian subcontinent and to the colonial histories that pertain to it. I will give a more sustained account of this history later in the chapter.
5 For instance, Elizabeth Buettner cites the following quotation from the *Birmingham Evening Mail* in 1976:

> I want to get away from the Asians ... It's not the colour I'm against far from it. I have an Asian couple living next door to me and they are the loveliest people you could meet ... [But] all the houses reek of cooking curry.
>
> (2008: 876)

6 The idea that chicken tikka masala is Britain's favourite dish is often repeated by politicians and the press (as well as in everyday speech). According to Monroe this is simply a myth. The fact that it is a myth, of course, doesn't make it any less pertinent. The fact that the dish is also of mythic and of British-Asian origin only adds to its cultural density. See Monroe 2005.
7 Because South Asian words in English are transliterations, spelling of dishes and places is sometimes inconsistent; I have attempted to stay true to the context rather than systematically adopt the latest transliterations.
8 Of course this is to pursue multiculturalism in only one direction. The other direction would be to look at the pleasures and problems of generations of British Asians eating across cultures.
9 Stanley Fish describes 'boutique multiculturalism' as 'the multiculturalism of ethnic restaurants, weekend festivals, and high profile flirtations with the other ... Boutique multiculturalism is characterized by its superficial or cosmetic relationship to the objects of its affections' (Fish 1997: 378).
10 And of course such multiculturalism is desperately uneven. For instance, Somali migration has not had the same impact on food culture in Britain as Polish migration. A comparative study of food and multiculturalism would be particularly informative about the unequal shape of multiculturalism in Britain or anywhere else, and would have to offer a nuanced account of the interrelationships between economic and cultural factors.

Chapter 7

Conclusion

Towards a political aesthetics of everyday life

This book has been an attempt to put into practice 'a science of singularity'.[1] Throughout I've tried to stay as close as possible to the specificity of examples and these examples have often been microscopic in scale and may seem irreducibly particular in detail. The Habitat chair; the 'housewife' timing the chores she performs; the teenager being enamoured by the music of the Jam; the drunk white guy demanding the hottest curry in the restaurant: these items are not standing here as flag bearers, representing a world of chair sitters, music listeners, female and feminist domesticity, and neo-colonial eating. They are all they can be: instances of ordinary life intricately entangled with more ordinary life and with forces that we only see when they shape our practices and our passions.[2] But looking back, now, at the substance of this book I realise that there is a greater degree of commonality across these specific examples than I had been aware of while I was writing: all these instances of ordinary life (which seem to me to be extraordinary when you get up close to them) congregate around the 1970s and 1980s, and nearly all take place in England. The time and place is not incidental (though I must admit that the temporal synchronicity felt accidental): I was a teenager in the 1970s and became an adult in the 1980s. These were formative times for me that have left their creases and traces in the finite plasticity of my apperceptions and sensorial dispositions.

But if the 1970s and 1980s were formative years for me, they were also formative for the neoliberalism that Britain, under the leadership of Margaret Thatcher, was busily fashioning at the time. In 1979 Thatcher became Prime Minister of that conflictive amalgam of countries and provinces called The United Kingdom of Great Britain and Northern Ireland, and set about implementing policies that violently undid the infrastructure of state social care, while providing the conditions for forms of entrepreneurial individualism that are still shaping global finances (and global culture) even in the wake of economic collapse. 'There is no such thing as society' was one of Thatcher's most chilling statements and when she made it in 1987 she'd already had eight years to help bring this condition about. Characteristically the violence of social and cultural dismantling is framed in a language of aesthetics and putative care:

> There is no such thing as society. There is [a] living tapestry of men and women and people, and the beauty of that tapestry and the quality of our lives will depend upon how much each of us is prepared to take responsibility for ourselves and each of us prepared to turn round and help by our own efforts those who are unfortunate.
>
> (Thatcher in Keay 1987: 8–9)

Translated into a social sentiment this meant that now you only had yourself to blame for failure and could take all the credit for your (financial) success. The idea of care was returned to 'cap-in-hand' charities and Anglican ideas of doing good, while the notions of structural support and a more equal redistribution of resources were effectively demonised.

In David Harvey's *A Brief History of Neoliberalism* the years 1978–80 are seen as the crucial ones. The four protagonists in Harvey's history are Deng Xiaoping, Paul Volcker, Margaret Thatcher and Ronald Reagan (Harvey 2005) and Harvey argues that while neoliberalism might have taken different forms in specific regions it needs to be thought of as a global (and global-ising) phenomenon. Neoliberalism isn't simply the name we give to specific governments (named as the government of the Conservative Party or the Republicans, or a new form of Communism, for instance) but is a political form that stretches across state, commerce and culture. Michel Foucault named the scattered and heterogeneous (yet still cohesive) distribution of cultural and social management 'governmentality' (and for this the clear similarities between a Labour Party and a Conservative Party or Republican and Democrat would be more significant than their differences). As Anna McCarthy suggests:

> governmentality is a concept that provides a powerful model for understanding the cultural and political manifestations of neoliberalism, in which state policies synchronize with cultural practices to apply market-based individualism as a governmental rationale across the institutions and practices of everyday life.
>
> (McCarthy 2007: 21)

Neoliberalism is the name for a collective fashioning of the self, which is experienced as anything but collective (its processes involve constant separating and specialising in the name of competitive individualism).

Such social self-fashioning works on an aesthetic register, shaping emotional and sensorial experience. Writing about the larger history of the modern as the prevalence of stories of disenchantment Jane Bennett writes that: 'The story of disenchantment represents and sustains a specific range of aesthetic sensibilities; it enters into the moods, temperaments, habits, perceptual comportments, and somatic predispositions that find expression or resistance in political choices, alliances, and policies' (Bennett 2001: 16). This work of sensorial orchestration (a distribution of the sensible) is of course political and it is of course ordinary. But this is not to say that it exhausts the ordinary: it has its effects on the ordinary but it also marginalises what might be a much larger and more diverse set of feelings. This is Bennett's point too as she sets about recovering stories of enchantment as an alternative account of the modern world that would allow for the recognition of those (extra)ordinary aspects of life that disenchantment narratives have remaindered. In a recent book the historian Barbara Taylor and the psychoanalyst Adam Phillips follow the plight of kindness. Kindness, like enchantment, has had to face a concerted effort aimed to disabuse us of its ordinariness. Ordinary acts of generosity and care face a world where selfishness is taken as the norm and kindness is seen as extraordinary. Since at least Hobbes' *Leviathan* (1651) the idea that human nature is self-centred has been taken as common sense.[3] It would be a mistake, though, to see this as a self-fulfilling prophecy and we should always be wary of mistaking overarching explanations of social life for adequate accounts of actuality. For Phillips and Taylor the result of ubiquitous accounts of selfishness is not the eradication of kindness, but its submergence: 'people are leading secretly kind lives all the time, but without a language in which to express this, or cultural support for it' (2009: 2).

This book (the one you are reading now) joins a number of others in calling attention to the affective life of people, and it joins others in wanting to provide more sensual and phenomenological descriptions of social and cultural life. But it also wants to connect the turn towards affect and emotion with an interest in the senses and with the experience of such seemingly nebulous phenomena as time and memory in the name of a more general social aesthetics. Here (at the end) I want to pose a final question: does such an orientation occlude politics? More emphatically I could ask whether 'a science of singularity' is actually symptomatic of neoliberal culture itself. After all, the stress on the singular person and occasion, an emphasis on sensual experience (rather than social structures, for instance) and emotions (rather than political economy, for instance) might not, in the end, be incompatible with the individualising tendencies of neoliberalism. This is, I think, a pertinent point and something worth confronting. Personally I think that the concerns of what might be thought of as a 'new materialism' in cultural theory (a materialist turn towards the immaterial, towards affect, towards thinglyness, the senses and so on) are necessarily determined by the social world that produced them. It would be very odd if that wasn't the case. Determinism, though, is not a straightforward causal movement that has predictable outcomes, and intellectual debates are dialogically (rather than causally) related to the world that they try and apprehend and comprehend. The concerns of those who pursue a form of social aesthetics often explicitly recognise the extent to which neoliberalism has shaped a social self that is deeply entangled in the affective realm of neoliberal values and moods, where arguments about the systematic increase in the gap between rich and poor seem to be treated as a natural fact. But this is a tale that needs a fuller telling and one that will have to wait for another day.[4]

My concern in these last few pages is to ask: what sort of a politics could 'a science of singularity' carry on its necessarily narrow shoulders? The answer is short, modest (I hope) and experimental and involves, as should be fairly clear by now, a sense of how an aesthetics of ordinary life could be invoked for a world that seems simultaneously fragile, capricious and conformist. A science of singularity also provides a critical attitude towards social and cultural theories that have established paradigms of interpretation in advance of the encounter that we might have with the world. One of the benefits of a science of singularity is that it doesn't have to go in search of material that would be usable for an interpretative framework already established. A science of singularity would hitch its cart to the refashioning of the distribution of the sensible because it would have a commitment to the empirical and wouldn't have already answered the question 'what is the difference that makes a difference?'.

Ordinary habits: keep calm and carry on

Ideas about the ordinary, about habit and about everyday life are often mobilised in the name of governmentality. Keeping up habits, altering habits and establishing new habits, is the work of cultural politics in its most ordinary form. For instance, in 2004, in the wake of the 9/11 attacks in New York and Washington, the British government sent out a booklet to every household in the UK alerting them to the procedures that were in place should a catastrophic event occur (either by design or as a natural disaster). The television advertising campaign that promoted the booklet addressed itself to an audience governed as much by habit as by the anxieties that were circulating at the time:

> We're surrounded by things that are there just in case – they don't worry us, but we know that if we ever needed them they'd help us and keep us safe. Like the *Preparing for Emergencies* booklet that you'll be receiving in the next few weeks. It will give you common sense advice on what to do in an emergency, like a major accident or an act of terrorism, as well as telling you what's being done by the government to protect the country as a whole. So look out for the booklet, read it and keep it somewhere safe – and then get on with your everyday life.
> (British government television advertisement, July 2004)[5]

If the threat of disaster produced fear, then (given the right measures) such fear could be absorbed into a habit of simply getting on with the business of everyday life. Habit, that centrally ambivalent characteristic of the everyday, could delegate anxiety to a kitchen draw or could closet it away in the recesses of the mind so that it doesn't clutter up the day-to-day job of 'getting on with things'. As I am writing this (and the news broadcasts remind me daily of an international inability to tackle climate change, as well as insistently telling me the extent of the global financial crisis) one of the latest bits of fashion is a piece of retro graphics from the Second World War simply saying 'keep calm and carry on'. It seems to be everywhere: on t-shirts, mugs and posters. At once nostalgic, ironic and literal, its message seems to be redundant: calm or not what can we do but 'carry on'?

The ability to 'keep calm and carry on' is both an accomplishment and a worrying ability to absorb the latest injustice or iniquitous set of circumstances into the realm of the ordinary. It speaks of a stunning ability to quietly adjust to new situations while evidencing a tenacious refusal to let the new alter the fabric of the ordinary. Towards the end of the same war that produced this seemingly odd piece of advice George Orwell bemoaned the political apathy it seemed to articulate. In a letter to *Partisan Review* he wrote about how consistently people seem to live their everyday lives under conditions of catastrophe:

> In the face of terrifying dangers and golden political opportunities, people just keep on keeping on, in a sort of twilight sleep in which they are conscious of nothing except the daily round of work, family life, darts at the pub, exercising the dog, mowing the lawn, bringing home the supper beer, etc. etc.
>
> (Orwell 1945: 435)

You can hear the political frustration in Orwell's prose; but isn't there also a sense of him recognising a powerful ability not to let the extraordinary overcome the world of the ordinary? Habit (taking the dog for a walk, going to work each day) is figured as a resource of hope at the same time as it's criticised for its inability to grasp opportunities for more radical and progressive change ('don't rock the boat', 'don't upset the apple cart').[6]

For William James the social and political conservatism of habit was its most socially relevant feature:

> Habit is thus the enormous fly-wheel of society, its most precious conservative agent. It alone is what keeps us all within the bounds of ordinance, and saves the children of fortune from the envious uprisings of the poor. It alone prevents the hardest and most repulsive walks of life from being deserted by those brought up to tread therein. It keeps the fisherman and the deck-hand at sea through the winter; it holds the

miner in his darkness, and nails the countryman to his log-cabin and his lonely farm through all the months of snow; it protects us from invasion by the natives of the desert and the frozen zone. It dooms us all to fight out the battle of life upon the lines of our nurture or our early choice, and to make the best of a pursuit that disagrees, because there is no other for which we are fitted, and it is too late to begin again. It keeps different social strata from mixing.

(James 1950 [1890] vol.1: 121)

Without habit, James seems to be saying, fishermen would think twice about going off into dangerous environments, impoverished *favela*-dwellers might refuse to return to their shanties each night and instead rise up and occupy the homes of the well-to-do. It is clear that, for James, habit is what maintains the status quo and the inequalities of its structure and expression.

Yet to simply cast habit in the role of political conservatism misses out on the ambivalence of it that elsewhere James is so attuned to. Habit might be the mechanism that allows for the continuation of 'business as usual', but in other ways it is the name that recognises the phenomenal ability of human life to be transformed. From one perspective the last fifty years has witnessed the growing impossibility for many people to think positively about revolutionary change; the idea of a revolution that would shrug off the yoke of capitalism, for instance, seems to belong to a distant memory of leftist politics.[7] But from another perspective the last fifty years has been nothing but a constant revolutionising of everyday life, forcing through fundamental changes in the life-world. And here habit has been the instrument that has worked in the name of change, not stability. Dramatic changes in day-to-day living can be recognised by looking at the increasing rates by which new technologies and new forms of media are taken up. It was only about fifteen years ago when it seemed other-worldly to see someone in the street appearing to be talking to themselves: today most people don't bat an eyelid as strangers conduct their personal lives on mobile phones in among groups of strangers. When I was growing up no one could have imagined how entire nations (seemingly) have come to feel comfortable interacting with computers and the internet. Who could have imagined that such things would become ordinary?

Habit, as James knew, has had a bad press: we're more likely to associate it with the bad than with the good. When we think of habits, James reminds us, we tend towards thinking about spitting or smoking, rather than politeness or consideration. I guess that it would be hard to imagine that we (humankind in general) haven't been picking up 'bad habits' over the last fifty years or so. Perhaps the world is meaner, and ruder (as Adorno thought), perhaps people have been developing habits of perception that treat the glut of culture as just more disposable commodities, perhaps a habit of profligate consumption is something that has been disseminated far and wide. I guess though it would also be true to say that good habits have also been encouraged if by that we mean healthier habits of eating and exercise, a more ordinary concern with the environment (establishing recycling as part of ordinary routines), for instance. But accounts of society as acquisitive or narcissistic, as politically correct or environmentally conscious might well miss something of the fine grain of the ordinary.

The moral and ethical implications of habit are of course a political matter, but it is worth noting something else about habit: it allows for substantial sensorial change in a way that often fails to be recognised. The process of something becoming habitual is often difficult and viscerally evident (the early days of recycling wasted food in Britain were often accompanied by complaints of physical revulsion), yet once it has become habit it falls away into the peripheries of experience. The transformation of large numbers of people who went from being physically repulsed by putrefying food, to 'not minding' or coping with it is worth considering. On the one hand this might evidence the ability of habit to accommodate the new and turn it into the age-old (recycling food just becomes part of putting out the trash). On the other hand a considerable sensorial trans-formation has taken place, whereby fundamental lines of sensual acceptance (and acceptability) have been withdrawn. In many ways this is the invisible work of the 'distribution of the sensible' as new moods and senses, new feelings and dispositions become absorbed into the ordinary. Not noticing the extent of our transformation is what guarantees the success of this work.

Yet to start to notice sensorial transformation (and to get a taste for it or a habit for it) has far-reaching consequences. This too is part of the ordinary world and the enjoyment that is experienced by people who are regularly experimenting with their lives through the use of new technologies is evidence of this (scattering themselves hither and thither on social networking sites, for instance). There is a materialist actuality to habit that belies the sense of it as merely a tenacious continuity of the age-old: to develop new habits always alters concrete existence and relationships even when it appears to be business as usual. While the last fifty years have witnessed the continuity of gender inequality and renewed instances of 'acceptable sexism' (particularly in the media), alterations to the distribution of the sensible with regard to gender have occurred that most of the time would seem invisible: male parents are more active in bringing up children, girls have aspirations that would have been impossible half a century ago. While the processes of reorchestrating gender were fiercely contested and difficult to achieve (and so obviously incomplete) the materiality of its actuality is, I think, a resource for hope.

In her powerful account of *The Ethics of Waste* Gay Hawkins attempts to shift the ground for thinking about our relationship with rubbish. Rather than alter habits in the name of moral sanction (don't do that it is bad for the planet), Hawkins suggests a potential pleasure that can be found in altering our relationship with the world:

> politics driven by the logics of moral imperatives and guilt can go only so far. A politics of becoming proceeds from those responses to waste that unsettle mastery, those intensities that signal not our difference from waste but our profound implications with it.
>
> (2006: 41)

The sensual and sensorial pleasure in learning a foreign language or a musical instrument is everywhere apparent: getting the hang of trombone, or getting the habit of speaking Spanish, recalibrates us, adds to us, extends us outwards, altering our material capacities and orientations. The same could be true about our relationship with trash. The idea of habit as accommodating the new in the name of the old misses the fundamental transformation of the being that is doing the accommodating. The politics of multiculturalism is often aimed at encouraging an accommodating attitude on behalf of a host nation while assuming the action of transformation (assimilation, for instance) taking place by the 'guests'. Transformations are of course the material consequence of migration and resettlement: the process is painful and pleasurable. But the pleasurable sensorial transformation of a host culture is rarely something that is evident, and rarely something that is embraced and enjoyed as more than the spectacle of 'diversity'.

Habit's potential for change, for adjustment (the 'becoming' of habit), is coupled with its conventionalising and conservative power. This conflict is irreconcilable. To imagine culture is to imagine a culture of habit as a dynamic set of features that includes established habits and the becoming of the habitual. If we live in a time dedicated to the perpetuating of habits of fear (of 'others'), of emotional isolation and habits of self, we also live with many more invisible habits that tell their secret stories. The work of an aesthetic politics of the ordinary may be to produce imaginative acts for thinking the seemingly impossible: a culture that encourages habits of generosity and world-enlarging improvisation and adaptation, while also maintaining habits of comfort and stability.

Notes

1 The phrase 'a science of singularity' is Michel de Certeau's and it is central to my study *Michel de Certeau: Analysing Culture* (Highmore 2006).

2 The issue of the representativeness of cultural material exercises methodological theory in the social sciences. Here the discussion of ordinary aesthetics follows another model that hopefully fetishises neither the abstractions of social theory nor the uniqueness of the detail, but seeks to draw out the cultural grammar of the singular (its sensorial and affective realm) by close reading so as to connect it to the cultural world more generally. Such a grammar wouldn't purport to

establish a set of universal truths; rather it would seek to show connections and orchestrations that will always take local forms.

3 It was David Hume who was most vocal in his rejection of Hobbes' position. In Hume's philosophy there isn't a coherent self that could be self-centred: only acts of sporadic self-alignment. Similarly pride, a seemingly selfish orientation, is, for Hume, outward facing and community minded.

4 The planned sequel to this book is provisionally titled *Cultural Feeling: Mood, Mediation, and Cultural Politics* and will pursue this line of inquiry. This conclusion, then, is not so much a re-emphasis and consolidation of *Ordinary Lives* but a sketch of work still to do.

5 The booklet can be found at www.direct.gov.uk/en/Governmentcitizensand-rights/

6 Orwell overstates his case. It is more likely that those living through catastrophic moments develop a split-focus that couples anxious concern with the 'keep on keeping on' of daily life. Ann Cvetkovich, for instance, describes this split-focus:

> more recently, at another public UT [University of Texas] event, this time to discuss reactions to Hurricane Katrina's devastations, many participants described a sense of divided attention, the movement back and forth between the everyday business of the semester's beginning and the urgency of the disaster.
>
> (Cvetkovich 2007: 460).

7 A discussion of revolutionary transformation (and the transformation of the idea of the revolutionary) is outside the scope of this book. It is worth noting, however, that ideas about the 'end of history' (i.e. ideas that suggest that social upheavals have now settled into a stable and durable form) often occur during periods of intense social upheavals (e.g. the break-up of the Soviet Union and the internecine ethnic conflicts that followed). It is also worth noting that the idea of progressive dramatic change might itself have altered in as much as a conservationist agenda would alter the sense of the forward motion that is associated with it. Walter Benjamin had a sense of this back in 1940: 'Marx says that revolutions are the locomotive of world history. But perhaps it is quite otherwise. Perhaps revolutions are an attempt by the passengers on this train – namely, the human race – to activate the emergency brake' (Benjamin 1940: 402).

Bibliography

Abbas, Ackbar (1996) 'Cultural Studies in a Postculture', in *Disciplinarity and Dissent in Cultural Studies*, edited by Cary Nelson and Dilip Parameshwar Gaonkar, New York: Routledge, pp. 289–312.

Achaya, K. T. (1998) *A Historical Dictionary of Indian Food*, New Delhi: Oxford University Press.

Adam, Barbara (2004) *Time*, Cambridge: Polity.

Adams, Caroline, ed. (1987) *Across Seven Seas and Thirteen Rivers: Life Stories of Pioneer Sylhetti Settlers in Britain*, London: Tower Hamlets Arts Project.

Adburgham, Alison (1975) *Liberty's: A Biography of a Shop*, London: George Allen and Unwin.

Adorno, Theodor (1989 [1951]) *Minima Moralia: Reflections from Damaged Life*, translated by E. F. N. Jephcott, London: Verso.

Ahmed, Feroze (1998) 'Opening Soon', in *Origins: Personal Stories Crossing the Seas to Settle in Britain*, Bristol: Origins, pp. 104–6.

Ahmed, Sara (2004) *The Cultural Politics of Emotion*, Edinburgh: Edinburgh University Press.

——(2006) *Queer Phenomenology: Orientations, Objects, Others*, Durham, NC: Duke University Press.

Ahmed, Sophia (2006) 'Chicken Tikka Masala', in *A Postcolonial People: South Asians in Britain*, edited by N. Ali, V. S. Kalra and S. Sayyid, London: Hurst, pp. 62–63.

Aitken, Ian (1998) 'Distraction and Redemption: Kracauer, surrealism and phenomenology', *Screen* 39, 2, pp. 124–40.

Akrich, Madeleine and Bruno Latour (1992) 'A Summary of a Convenient Vocabulary for the Semiotics of Human and Nonhuman Assemblies', in *Shaping Technology/Building Society: Studies in Sociotechnical Change*, edited by Wiedee E. Bijker and John Law, Cambridge, MA: MIT Press, pp. 259–64.

Alison, Archibald (1815 [1790]) *Essays on the Nature and Principles of Taste, Volume 1* (fourth edition), Edinburgh: Archibald Constable.

Althusser, Louis (1963) 'Marxism and Humanism', in *For Marx*, translated by Ben Brewster, London: Verso, 1982, pp. 219–41.

Anderson, Ben (2004) 'Time-Stilled Spaces-Slowed: How Boredom Matters', *Geoforum* 35, pp. 739–54.

Appadurai, Arjun ed. (1986) *The Social Life of Things: Commodities in Cultural Perspective*, Cambridge: Cambridge University Press.

——(2006) 'The Thing Itself', *Public Culture*, 18, 1, pp. 15–22.

Aslam, Nadeem (2004) *Maps for Lost Lovers*, London: Faber and Faber.

Attfield, Judy (2000) *Wild Things: The Material Culture of Everyday Life*, Oxford: Berg.

Barilli, Renato (1993) *A Course on Aesthetics*, translated by Karen E. Pinkus, Minneapolis: University of Minnesota Press.

Basu, Shrabani (1999) *Curry in the Crown: The Story of Britain's Favourite Dish*, New Delhi: HarperCollins.

Baumgarten, Alexander (1750) 'Prolegomena' [to *Aesthetica*], in *Art in Theory, 1648–1815: An Anthology of Changing Ideas*, edited by Charles Harrison, Paul Wood and Jason Gaiger, Oxford: Blackwell, 1998, pp. 489–91.

Beeching, Wilfred A. (1974) *Century of the Typewriter*, London: Heinemann.

Benjamin, Walter (1928) 'Food Fair: Epilogue to the Berlin Food Exhibition' translated by Rodney Livingstone, in *Selected Writings: Volume 2, 1927–1934*, Cambridge, MA: Harvard University Press, 1999, pp. 135–40.

——(1930) 'Food', translated by Rodney Livingstone, in *Selected Writings: Volume 2, 1927–1934*, Cambridge, MA: Harvard University Press, 1999, pp. 358–64.

——(1936a) 'The Work of Art in the Age of its Technological Reproducibility' [second version], in *Selected Writings: Volume 3, 1935–1938*, Cambridge, MA: Harvard University Press, 2002, pp. 101–33.

——(1936b) 'Theory of Distraction' in *Selected Writings: Volume 3, 1935–1938*, Cambridge, MA: Harvard University Press, 2002, pp. 141–42.

——(1939) 'The Work of Art in the Age of its Reproducibility' [third version], *Selected Writings: Volume 4, 1938–1940*, Cambridge, MA: Harvard University Press, 2003, pp. 251–83.

——(1940) 'Paralipomena to "On the Concept of History"' in *Selected Writings: Volume 4, 1938–1940*, Cambridge, MA: Harvard University Press, 2003, pp. 401–11.

——(1983 [1966]) *Understanding Brecht*, translated by Anna Bostock, London: Verso.

——(1982) *Illuminations*, translated by Harry Zohn, London: Fontana.

——(1999) *The Arcades Project*, translated by Howard Eiland and Kevin McLaughlin, Cambridge, MA: Harvard University Press.

Bennett, Jane (2001) *The Enchantment of Modern Life: Attachments, Crossings, and Ethics*, Princeton, NJ: Princeton University Press.

Benyon, Huw (1973) *Working for Ford*, Harmondsworth: Penguin.

Berger, John (1977) 'Why Look at Animals?', in *About Looking*, New York: Vintage Books, 1991, pp. 3–28.

Berger, John and Jean Mohr (1982) *A Seventh Man: A Book of Images and Words about the Experience of Migrant Workers in Europe*, London: Writers and Readers.

Bergson, Henri (1991 [1908]) *Matter and Memory*, translated by N. M. Paul and W. S. Palmer, New York: Zone Books.

Berlant, Lauren (1997) *The Queen of America goes to Washington City: Essays on Sex and Citizenship*, Durham, NC: Duke University Press.

——(2008) *The Female Complaint: The Unfinished Business of Sentimentality in American Culture*, Durham, NC: Duke University Press.

Berlant, Lauren, ed. (2000) *Intimacy*, Chicago: University of Chicago Press.

Bewes, Timothy (2002) *Reification or The Anxiety of Late Capitalism*, London: Verso.

Bhogal, Vicky (2003) *Cooking Like Mummyji: Real British Asian Cooking*, London: Simon and Schuster.

Brecht, Bertolt (1964) *Brecht on Theatre*, translated by John Willett, London: Methuen.

Briggs, Asa and Peter Burke (2002) *A Social History of the Media: From Gutenberg to the Internet*, Cambridge: Polity.

Brown, Bill (1996) *The Material Unconscious: American Amusement, Stephen Crane, and the Economics of Play*, Cambridge, MA: Harvard University Press.

——(1998) 'How to Do Things with Things (A Toy Story)', *Critical Inquiry* 24, pp. 935–64.

——(2003a) 'The Secret Life of Things: Virginia Woolf and the Matter of Modernism', in *Aesthetic Subjects*, edited by Pamela R. Matthews and David McWhirter, Minneapolis: University of Minnesota Press, pp. 397–430.

——(2003b) *A Sense of Things: The Object Matter of American Literature*, Chicago: University of Chicago Press.

——(2004) 'Thing Theory' in *Things*, edited by Bill Brown, Chicago: University of Chicago Press, pp. 1–22.

——(2006a) 'Reification, Reanimation, and the American Uncanny', *Critical Inquiry*, 32, pp. 175–207.

——(2006b) 'Object Relations in an Expanded Field', *differences* 17, 3, pp. 88–106.

Bruner, Edward M. (1986) 'Experience and Its Expressions' in *The Anthropology of Experience*, edited by Victor Turner and Edward Bruner, Urbana: University of Illinois Press, pp. 3–30.

Bruno, Guiliana (2002) *Atlas of Emotion: Journeys in Art, Architecture, and Film*, New York: Verso.

——(2007) *Public Intimacy: Architecture and the Visual Arts*, Cambridge, MA: MIT Press.

Buettner, Elizabeth (2008) '"Going for an Indian": South Asian Restaurants and the Limits of Multiculturalism in Britain', *Journal of Modern History*, 80, pp. 865–901.

Bull, Michael (2000) *Sounding Out the City: Personal Stereos and the Management of Everyday Life*, Oxford: Berg.

——(2007) *Sound Moves: iPod Culture and Urban Experience*, London: Routledge.

Burke, Edmund (1998 [1759]) *A Philosophical Enquiry into the Origin of our Ideas of the Sublime and Beautiful*, second edition, Oxford: Oxford University Press.

Charney, Leo (1998) *Empty Moments: Cinema, Modernity, and Drift*, Durham, NC: Duke University Press.

Charney, Leo and Vanessa R. Schwartz, eds (1996) *Cinema and the Invention of Modern Life*, Berkeley: University of California Press.

Choudhury, Yousuf (1993) *The Roots and Tales of the Bangladeshi Settlers*, Birmingham: Sylheti Social History Group.

Classen, Constance (1993) *Worlds of Sense: Exploring the Senses in History and Across Cultures*, London: Routledge.

Collingham, Lizzie (2005) *Curry: A Biography*, London: Chatto and Windus.

Conran, Terence (1974) *The House Book*, London: Mitchell Beazley Publishers.

——(2001) *Q & A: A Sort of Autobiography*, London: Harper Collins.

Cowan, Ruth Schwartz (1989) *More Work For Mother: The Ironies of Household Technology from the Open Hearth to the Microwave*, London: Free Association Books.

Crary, Jonathan (1999) *Suspensions of Perception: Attention, Spectacle, and Modern Culture*, Cambridge, MA: MIT Press.

Cvetkovich, Ann (2007) 'Public Feeling', *South Atlantic Quarterly*, 106, 3, pp. 459–68.

Daston, Lorraine and Gregg Mitman, eds (2005) *Thinking with Animals: New Perspectives on Anthropomorphism*, New York: Columbia University Press.

Davies, Margery W. (1982) *Woman's Place is at the Typewriter: Office Work and Office Workers 1870–1930*, Philadelphia, PA: Temple University Press.

de Beauvoir, Simone (1997 [1949]) *The Second Sex*, translated by H. M. Parshley, London: Vintage Books.

de Certeau, Michel (1984) *The Practice of Everyday Life*, translated by Steven Rendall, Berkeley: University of California Press.

de Grazia, Victoria and Ellen Furlough, eds (1996) *The Sex of Things: Gender and Consumption in Historical Perspective*, Berkeley: University of California Press.

de Lauretis, Teresa (1987) *Technologies of Gender: Essays on Theory, Film, and Fiction*, Basingstoke: Macmillan.

Dewey, John (1958 [1929]) *Experience and Nature*, New York: Dover.

——(1980 [1934]) *Art as Experience*, New York: Perigee Books.

Dilthey, Wilhelm (1976) *Selected Writings*, edited and translated by H. P. Rickman, Cambridge: Cambridge University Press.

Dixon, Thomas (2003) *From Passions to Emotions: The Creation of a Secular Psychological Category*, Cambridge: Cambridge University Press.

Donzelot, Jacques (1997 [1977]) *The Policing of Families*, translated by Robert Hurley, Baltimore, MD: Johns Hopkins University Press.

Doray, Bernard (1988) *From Taylorism to Fordism: A Rational Madness*, translated by David Macey, London: Free Association Books.

Driver, Christopher (1983) *The British at Table: 1940–1980*, London: Chatto & Windus.

Duggan, Lisa (2003) *The Twilight of Equality: Neoliberalism, Cultural Politics, and the Attack on Democracy*, Boston, MA: Beacon Press.

Eagleton, Terry (1990) *The Ideology of the Aesthetic*, Oxford: Blackwell.

Eiland, Howard (2003) 'Reception in Distraction', *boundary 2*, 30, 1, pp. 51–66.

Elias, Norbert (1992) *Time: An Essay*, translated by Edmund Jephcott, Oxford: Blackwell.

Ellis, Markman (2005) *The Coffee-House: A Cultural History*, London: Phoenix.

Engels, Frederick (1986 [1884]) *The Origin of the Family, Private Property and the State*, Harmondsworth: Penguin.

Felski, Rita (2000) *Doing Time: Feminist Theory and Postmodern Culture*, New York: New York University Press.

Fish, Stanley (1997) 'Boutique Multiculturalism, or, Why Liberals are Incapable of Thinking about Hate Speech', *Critical Inquiry*, 23, 2, pp. 387–95.

Fisher, H. Michael (1996) *The First Indian Author in English: Dean Mahomed (1759–1851) in India, Ireland, and England*, Delhi: Oxford University Press.

Fisher, H. Michael, Shompa Lahiri and Shinder Thandi (2007) *A South-Asian History of Britain: Four Centuries of Peoples from the Indian Sub-Continent*, Oxford: Greenwood World Publishing.

Fisher, Philip (2002) *The Vehement Passions*, Princeton, NJ: Princeton University Press.

Fornäs, Johan, Karin Becker, Erling Bjurström and Hillevi Ganetz (2007) *Consuming Media: Communication, Shopping and Everyday Life*, Oxford: Berg.

Foucault, Michel (1974 [1966]) *The Order of Things: An Archaeology of the Human Sciences*, London: Tavistock.

——(1982) *Discipline and Punish: The Birth of the Prison*, translated by Alan Sheridan, Harmondsworth: Penguin.

Freeman, June (2004) *The Making of the Modern Kitchen: A Cultural History*, Oxford: Berg.

Freud, Sigmund (1914) 'On Narcissism: An Introduction', in *On Metapsychology: The Theory of Psychoanalysis*, Harmondsworth: Penguin, 1984, pp. 61–97.

——(1920) *Beyond the Pleasure Principle*, in *On Metapsychology: The Theory of Psychoanalysis*, Harmondsworth: Penguin, 1984, pp. 269–338.

——(1927) 'Fetishism', *On Sexuality*, Harmondsworth: Penguin, 1983, pp. 351–57.

Friedan, Betty (1965) *The Feminine Mystique*, Harmondsworth: Penguin.

Fuller, Matthew (2005) *Media Ecologies: Materialist Energies in Art and Technoculture*, Cambridge, MA: MIT Press.

Galloway, Anne (2004) 'Intimations of Everyday Life: Ubiquitous Computing and the City', *Cultural Studies*, 18, 2–3, pp. 384–408.

Gamman, Lorraine and Merja Makinen (1994) *Female Fetishism: A New Look*, London: Lawrence & Wishart.

Ganguly, Keya (2001) *States of Exception: Everyday Life and Postcolonial Identity*, Minneapolis: University of Minnesota Press.

Gardey, Delphine (2001) 'Mechanizing Writing and Photographing the Word: Utopias, Office Work, and Histories of Gender and Technology', *History and Technology*, 17, pp. 319–52.

Garson, Barbara (1975) *All the Livelong Day: The Meaning and Demeaning of Routine Work*, Harmondsworth: Penguin.

Gasparini, Giovanni (1995) 'On Waiting', *Time & Society*, 4, 1, pp. 29–45.

Gilloch, Graeme (2002) *Walter Benjamin: Critical Constellations*, Cambridge: Polity.

——(2007) 'Urban Optics: Film, Phantasmagoria and the City in Benjamin and Kracauer', *new formations*, 61, pp. 115–31.

Gleason, Tracy (2007) 'Murray: The Stuffed Bunny', in *Evocative Objects: Things we think with*, edited by Sherry Turkle, Cambridge, MA: MIT Press, pp. 170–77.

Goggin, Gerard (2006) *Cell Phone Culture: Mobile Technology in Everyday Life*, Abingdon: Routledge.

Gomez, Lavinia (1997) *An Introduction to Object Relations*, London: Free Association Books.

Goodstein, Elizabeth S. (2005) *Boredom and Modernity: Experience without Qualities*, Stanford, CT: Stanford University Press.

Goody, Jack (1998) *Food and Love*, London: Verso.

Greenlaw, Lavina (2007) *The Importance of Music to Girls: A Memoir*, London: Faber.

Greer, Germaine (1971) *The Female Eunuch*, London: Granada.

Gross, Daniel M. (2006) *The Secret History of Emotion: From Aristotle's Rhetoric to Modern Brain Science*, Chicago: University of Chicago Press.

Gross, Steffen W. (2002) 'The Neglected Programme of Aesthetics', *British Journal of Aesthetics*, 42, 4, pp. 403–14.

Gumbrecht, Hans Ulrich (2006) 'Aesthetic Experience in Everyday Worlds: Reclaiming an Unredeemed Utopian Motif', *New Literary History*, 37, pp. 299–318.

Gunning, Tom (1986) 'The Cinema of Attraction: Early Film, Its Spectator, and the Avant-Garde', in *Film and Theory: An Anthology*, edited by Robert Stam and Toby Miller, Oxford: Blackwell, 2000, pp. 229–35.

Hake, Sabine (1987) 'Girls and Crisis – The Other Side of Diversion', *New German Critique*, 40, pp. 147–64.

Hammermeister, Kai (2002) *The German Aesthetic Tradition*, Cambridge: Cambridge University Press.

Hamper, Ben (1992) *Rivethead: Tales from the Assembly Line*, London: Fourth Estate.

Hansen, Miriam (1987) 'Benjamin, Cinema and Experience: "The Blue Flower in the Land of Technology"', *New German Critique*, 40, pp. 179–224.

——(1991a) *Babel and Babylon: Spectatorship in American Silent Film*, Cambridge, MA: Harvard University Press.

——(1991b) 'Decentric Perspectives: Kracauer's Early Writings on Film and Mass Culture', *New German Critique*, 54, pp. 47–76.

——(1995) 'America, Paris, the Alps: Kracauer (and Benjamin) on Cinema and Modernity' in *Cinema and the Invention of Modern Life*, edited by Leo Charney and Vanessa R. Schwartz, Berkeley: University of California Press, pp. 362–402.

Hardyment, Christina (1988) *From Mangle to Microwave: The Mechanization of Household Work*, Cambridge: Polity Press.

——(1995) *Slice of Life: The British Way of Eating Since 1945*, London: BBC Books.

Hark, Ina Rae, ed. (2002) *Exhibition, the Film Reader*, London: Routledge.

Harvey, David (2005) *A Brief History of Neoliberalism*, Oxford: Oxford University Press.

Hawkins, Gay (2006) *The Ethics of Waste: How We Relate to Rubbish*, Sydney: University of New South Wales Press.

Hayden, Dolores (1982) *Grand Domestic Revolution: History of Feminist Designs for American Homes, Neighbourhoods and Cities*, Cambridge, MA: MIT Press.

Heidegger, Martin (2008 [1927]) *Being and Time*, translated by John Macquarrie and Edward Robinson, New York: Harper.

Heldke, Lisa (2003) *Exotic Appetites: Ruminations of a Food Adventurer*, New York: Routledge.

Hemingway, Andrew (1989) 'The "Sociology" of Taste in the Scottish Enlightenment', *Oxford Art Journal*, 12, 2, pp. 3–35.

Highmore, Ben (2002) *Everyday Life and Cultural Theory: An Introduction*, London: Routledge.

——(2006) *Michel de Certeau: Analysing Culture*, London: Continuum.

——(2009) *A Passion for Cultural Studies*, Houndmills: Palgrave.

Hirschman, Albert O. (1997 [1977]) *The Passions and the Interests: Political Arguments for Capitalism before its Triumph*, Princeton, NJ: Princeton University Press.

Hobbes, Thomas (2008 [1651]) *Leviathan*, Oxford: Oxford University Press.

Hobson, Dorothy (1978) 'Housewives: Isolation as Oppression', in *Women Take Issue: Aspects of Women's Subordination*, edited by the Women's Studies Group, Centre for Contemporary Cultural Studies, London: Hutchinson, pp. 79–95.

Hochschild, Arlie Russell (2003 [1983]) *The Managed Heart: Commercialization of Human Feeling*, Berkeley: University of California Press.

——(2003) *The Commercialization of Intimate Life: Notes from Home and Work*, Berkeley: University of California Press.

Howes, David (2004) *Sensual Relations: Engaging the Senses in Cultural and Social Theory*, Ann Arbor: University of Michigan Press.

Howes, David ed. (2005) *Empire of the Senses: The Sensual Culture Reader*, Oxford: Berg.

Humble, Nicola (2005) *Culinary Pleasures: Cookbooks and the Transformation of British Food*, London: Faber.

Hume, David (1985 [1739–40]) *A Treatise of Human Nature*, London: Penguin.

——(1757) 'Of the Standard of Taste', in *Selected Essays*, Oxford: Oxford University Press, 1998, pp. 133–54.

——(1777) 'Of the Delicacy of Taste and Passion', in *Selected Essays*, Oxford: Oxford University Press, 1998, pp. 10–13.

——(2007 [1748]) *An Enquiry Concerning Human Understanding*, Oxford: Oxford University Press.

Hussain, Zahid (2006) *The Curry Mile*, London: Suitcase.

Hutcheson, Francis (2008 [1725]) *An Inquiry into the Original of Our Ideas of Beauty and Virtue*, Indianapolis: Liberty Fund.

Illouz, Eva (2007) *Cold Intimacies: The Making of Emotional Capitalism*, Cambridge: Polity Press.

Ireland, Craig (2004) *The Subaltern Appeal to Experience: Self-Identity, Late Modernity, and the Politics of Immediacy*, Montreal: McGill-Queen's University Press.

Jaffrey, Madhur (1973) 'Introduction' to *An Invitation to Indian Cooking*, in *The Madhur Jaffrey Cookbook*, London: Tiger Books International, 1992, pp. 517–38.

——(2006) *Climbing the Mango Trees: A Memoir of a Childhood in India*, London: Ebury Publishing.

Jamal, Ahmad (1996) 'Acculturation: The Symbolism of Ethnic Eating Among Contemporary British Consumers', *British Food Journal*, 98, 19, pp. 12–26.

——(1998) 'Food Consumption Among Ethnic Minorities: The Case of British-Pakistanis in Bradford, UK', *British Food Journal*, 100, 5, pp. 221–27.

James, Selma (1976) *Women, the Unions and Work: Or What is Not to be Done*, New York: Falling Wall Press.

James, Susan (1997) *Passion and Action: The Emotions in Seventeenth-Century Philosophy*, Oxford: Oxford University Press.

James, William (1884) 'What is an Emotion?' *Mind*, 9, 34, pp. 188–205.

——(1950 [1890]) *The Principles of Psychology*, two volumes, New York: Dover.

——(1962 [1899]) *Talks to Teachers on Psychology and to Students on Some of Life's Ideals*, New York: Dover.

Jay, Martin (2005) *Songs of Experience: Modern American and European Variations on a Universal Theme*, Berkeley: University of California Press.

Jervis, John (1998) *Exploring the Modern: Patterns of Western Culture and Civilization*, Oxford: Blackwell.

Johnson, Lesley and Justine Lloyd (2004) *Sentenced to Everyday Life: Feminism and the Housewife*, Oxford: Berg.

Jones, Trevor, Monder Ram and Paul Edwards (2006) 'Shades of grey in the informal economy', *International Journal of Sociology and Social Policy*, 26, 9/10, pp. 357–73.

Jütte, Robert (2005) *A History of the Senses: From Antiquity to Cyberspace*, translated by James Lynn, Cambridge: Polity Press.

Kant, Immanuel (1988 [1790]) *The Critique of Judgement*, translated by James Creed Meredith, Oxford: Oxford University Press.

——(2003 [1764]) *Observations on the Feeling of the Beautiful and Sublime*, translated by John T. Goldthwait, Berkeley: University of California Press.

Katz, Jack (1999) *How Emotions Work*, Chicago: University of Chicago Press.

Keay, Douglas (1987) 'Aids, Education and the Year 2000: Interview with Margaret Thatcher', *Woman's Own*, 13 October, pp. 8–10.

Keep, Christopher (1997) 'The Cultural Work of the Type-Writer Girl', *Victorian Studies*, 4, 3, pp. 401–26.

Kern, Steven (1983) *The Culture of Time and Space 1880–1918*, Cambridge, MA: Harvard University Press.

Kiaer, Christina (2005) *Imagine No Possessions: The Socialist Objects of Russian Constructivism*, Cambridge, MA: MIT Press.

Korsmeyer, Carolyn ed. (2005) *The Taste Culture Reader: Experiencing Food and Drink*, Oxford: Berg.

Kracauer, Siegfried (1926) 'Cult of Distraction: On Berlin's Picture Palaces', in *The Mass Ornament: Weimar Essays*, translated by Thomas Y. Levin, Cambridge, MA: Harvard University Press, 1995, pp. 323–28.

——(1995 [1963]) *The Mass Ornament: Weimar Essays*, translated by Thomas Y. Levin, Cambridge, MA: Harvard University Press.

——(1998 [1930]) *The Salaried Masses: Duty and Distraction in Weimar Germany*, translated by Quintin Hoare, London: Verso.

Kristeva, Julia (1981) 'Women's Time', translated by Alice Jardine and Harry Blake, *Signs: Journal of Women in Culture and Society*, 7, 1, pp. 13–35.

Laplanche, Jean (1985 [1970]) *Life and Death in Psychoanalysis*, translated by Jeffrey Mehlman, Baltimore, MD: Johns Hopkins University Press.

Laplanche, Jean and J-B. Pontalis (1983 [1967]) *The Language of Psycho-Analysis*, translated by Donald Nicholson-Smith, London: Hogarth Press.

Latham, Alan (1999) 'The power of distraction: distraction, tactility, and habit in the work of Walter Benjamin', *Environment and Planning D: Society and Space*, 17, pp. 451–73.

Latour, Bruno (1992) 'Where are the Missing Masses? The Sociology of a Few Mundane Artifacts', in *Shaping Technology/Building Society: Studies in Sociotechnical Change*, edited by Wiedee E. Bijker and John Law, Cambridge, MA: MIT Press, pp. 225–58.

Lefebvre, Henri (1984 [1968]) *Everyday Life in the Modern World*, translated by Sacha Rabinovitch, New Brunswick, NJ: Transaction Publishers.

——(1991 [1958]) *Critique of Everyday Life: Volume 1*, translated by John Moore, London: Verso.

——(1995 [1962]) *Introduction to Modernity* translated by John Moore, London: Verso.

Levine, George, ed. (1994) *Aesthetics and Ideology*, New Brunswick, NJ: Rutgers University Press.

Linhart, Robert (1981) *The Assembly Line*, translated by Margaret Crosland, London: John Calder.

Locke, John (2008 [1690]) *An Essay Concerning Human Understanding* (abridged), Oxford: Oxford University Press.

Lonitz, Henri ed. (1999) *Theodor W. Adorno and Walter Benjamin: The Complete Correspondence, 1928–1940*, translated by Nicholas Walker, Cambridge, MA: Harvard University Press.

Lowell, Robert (1974) *Robert Lowell's Poems: A Selection*, London: Faber.

Lowry, Suzanne (1980) *The Guilt Cage: Housewives and a Decade of Liberation*, London: Elm Tree Books.

Lukács, Georg (1971) *History and Class Consciousness: Studies in Marxist Dialectics*, translated by Rodney Livingstone, London: Merlin Press.

Lupton, Ellen (1993) *Mechanical Brides: Women and Machines: From Home to Office*, Princeton, NJ: Princeton Architectural Press.

Mackenzie, Henry (2001 [1771]) *The Man of Feeling*, Oxford: Oxford University Press.

Macpherson, C. B. (1962) *The Political Theory of Possessive Individualism*, Oxford: Oxford University Press.

Marcus, Greil (2006) *Like a Rolling Stone: Bob Dylan at the Crossroads*, London: Faber.

Marcus, Laura (1994) *Auto/Biographical Discourses: Criticism, Theory, Practice*, Manchester: Manchester University Press.

Mass-Observation (1937) *Mass Observation*, introduction by Julian Huxley, London: Fredrick Muller.

Mauss, Marcel (1934) 'Techniques of the Body' translated by Ben Brewster, *Economy and Society*, 2, 1 (1973), pp. 70–88.

McCarthy, Anna (2001a) *Ambient Television: Visual Culture and Public Space*, Durham, NC: Duke University Press.

——(2001b) 'From Screen to Site: Television's Material Culture, and Its Place', *October*, 98, pp. 93–111.

——(2007) 'Reality Television: a Neoliberal Theatre of Suffering', *Social Text*, (93) 25, 4, pp. 17–41.

McIntyre, Jane L. (1989) 'Personal Identity and the Passions', *Journal of the History of Philosophy*, 27, 4, pp. 545–57.

McKenzie, Alan T. (1990) *Certain, Lively Episodes: The Articulation of Passion in Eighteenth-Century Prose*, Athens, GA: University of Georgia Press.

McKernan, Luke (2007) 'Diverting Time: London's Cinemas and their Audiences, 1906–14', *The London Journal*, 32, 2, pp. 125–44.

McLaughlin, Kevin (2005) *Paperwork: Fiction and Mass Mediacy in the Paper Age*, Philadelphia: University of Pennsylvania Press.

McLuhan, Marshall (1997 [1964]) *Understanding Media: The Extensions of Man*, Cambridge, MA: MIT Press.

McNamara, Brooks (1974) 'The Scenography of Popular Entertainment', *The Drama Review*, 18, 1, pp. 16–24.

Mead, George Herbert (2002 [1932]) *The Philosophy of the Present*, Amherst, MA: Prometheus Books.

Merleau-Ponty, Maurice (1964 [1948]) *Sense and Non-Sense*, translated by Hubert L. Dreyfus and Patricia Allen Dreyfus, Evanston, IL: Northwestern University Press.

——(2000 [1968]) *The Visible and the Invisible*, translated by Alphonso Lingis, Evanston, IL: Northwestern University Press.

Meyer, Michel (2000) *Philosophy and the Passions: Towards a History of Human Nature*, translated by Robert F. Barsky, University Park: Pennsylvania State University Press.

Miller, Daniel (1998) *A Theory of Shopping*, Cambridge: Polity.

——(2008) *The Comfort of Things*, Cambridge: Polity.

Minson, Jeffrey (1985) *Genealogies of Morals: Nietzsche, Foucault, Donzelot and the Eccentricity of Ethics*, Basingstoke: Macmillan.

Molotch, Harvey (2003) *Where Stuff Comes From*, New York: Routledge.

Monroe, Jo (2005) *Star of India: The Spicy Adventures of Curry*, Chichester: John Wiley.

Moores, Shaun (2000) *Media and Everyday Life in Modern Society*, Edinburgh: Edinburgh University Press.

Morris, Meaghan (1998) *Too Soon, Too Late: History in Popular Culture*, Bloomington: Indiana University Press.

Morse, Margaret (1998) *Virtualities: Television, Media Art, and Cyberculture*, Bloomington: Indiana University Press.

Mulvey, Laura (1992) *Citizen Kane*, London: BFI.

Munt, Sally R. (2007) *Queer Attachments: The Cultural Politics of Shame*, Aldershot: Ashgate.

Murphy, Patricia (2001) *Time is of the Essence: Temporality, Gender, and the New Woman*, Albany: State University of New York Press.

Narayan, Uma (1995) 'Eating Cultures: Incorporation, Identity and Indian Food', *Social Identities*, 1, 1, pp. 63–86.

——(1997) *Dislocating Cultures: Identities, Traditions and Third-World Feminism*, New York: Routledge.

Nasaw, David (1999) *Going Out: The Rise and Fall of Public Amusements*, Cambridge, MA: Harvard University Press.

Neruda, Pablo (1994a) *Selected Poems: Pablo Neruda*, translated by Ben Belitt, New York: Grove Press.

——(1994b) *Odes to Common Things*, translated by Ken Krabbenhoft, New York: Bulfinch Press.

Neville, Michael R. (1974) 'Kant's Characterization of Aesthetic Experience', *Journal of Aesthetics and Art Criticism*, 33, 2, pp. 193–202.

Oakley, Ann (1974a) *Housewife*, Harmondsworth: Penguin.

——(1974b) *The Sociology of Housework*, London: Martin Robertson.

Oldenburg, Claes (1961) 'I am for an Art', in *Art in Theory 1900–1990: An Anthology of Changing Ideas*, edited by Charles Harrison and Paul Wood, Oxford: Blackwell, 1992, pp. 727–30.

Orwell, George (1945) 'London Letter to *Partisan Review*', in *The Collected Essays, Journalism and Letters of George Orwell, Volume 3: As I Please, 1943–1945*, Harmondsworth: Penguin, 1970, pp. 431–37.

Palmer, Richard E. (1969) *Hermeneutics: Interpretation Theory in Schleiermacher, Dilthey, Heidegger, and Gadamer*, Evanston, IL: Northwestern University Press.

Panayi, Panikos (2002) 'The Spicing up of English Provincial Life: The History of Curry in Leicester', in *Food in the Migrant Experience*, edited by Anne J. Kershen, London: Ashgate, pp. 42–76.

——(2008) *Spicing Up Britain: The Multicultural History of British Food*, London: Reaktion.

Peel, John and Sheila Ravenscroft (2005) *Margrave of the Marshes*, London: Corgi Books.

Petro, Patrice (1989) *Joyless Streets: Women and Melodramatic Representation in Weimar Germany*, Princeton, NJ: Princeton University Press.

——(1991) 'Kracauer's Epistemological Shift', *New German Critique*, 54, pp. 127–38.

——(1993) 'After Shock / Between Boredom and History', *Discourse: Journal of Theoretical Studies in Media and Culture*, 16, 2, pp. 77–99.

——(2002) *Aftershocks of the New: Feminism and Film History*, New Brunswick, NJ: Rutgers University Press.

Phillips, Adam and Barbara Taylor (2009) *On Kindness*, London: Hamish Hamilton.

Phillips, Barty (1984) *Conran and the Habitat Story*, London: Weidenfeld and Nicolson.

Pinch, Adela (1996) 'Emotion and History: A Review Article', *Comparative Studies in Society and History*, 37, 1, pp. 100–109.

Probyn, Elspeth (2000) *Carnal Appetites: FoodSexIdentities*, London: Routledge.

——(2005) *Blush: Faces of Shame*, Minneapolis: University of Minnesota Press.

Procida, Mary A. (2003) 'Feeding the Imperial Appetite: Imperial Knowledge and Anglo-Indian Discourse', *Journal of Women's History*, 15, 2, pp. 123–49.

Quant, Mary (1967) *Quant by Quant*, London: Pan.

Rabinovitz, Lauren (1998) *For the Love of Pleasure: Women, Movies, and Culture in Turn-of-the Century Chicago*, New Brunswick: Rutgers University Press.

Radcliffe, Mark (2009) *Thank You For the Days: A Boy's Own Adventure in Radio and Beyond*, London: Simon and Schuster.

Ram, Monder, Tahir Abbas, Balihar Sanghera and Guy Hillin (2000) '"Currying favour with the locals": Balti owners and business enclaves', *International Journal of Entrepreneurial Behaviour and Research*, 6, 1, pp. 41–55.

Ram, Monder, Trevor Jones, Tahir Abbas and Balihar Sanghera (2002) 'Ethnic Minority Enterprise in its Urban Context: South Asian Restaurants in Birmingham', *International Journal of Urban and Regional Research*, 26, 1, pp. 24–40.

Rancière, Jacques (1989) *The Nights of Labor: The Workers' Dream in Nineteenth-Century France*, translated by Donald Reid, Philadelphia, PA: Temple University Press.

——(1999) *Disagreement: Politics and Philosophy*, translated by Julie Rose, Minneapolis: University of Minnesota Press.

——(2000a) 'Cinematographic Image, Democracy, and the "Splendor of the Insignificant" (Interview)', *Sites*, 4, 2, pp. 249–58.

——(2000b) 'Jacques Rancière: History and the Art System' (interview with Yan Ciret), *Art Press*, 258, pp. 18–23.

——(2002) 'The Aesthetic Revolution and its Outcomes', *New Left Review*, 14, pp. 133–51.

——(2003) 'Politics and Aesthetics (an Interview)', *Angelaki*, 8, 2, pp. 191–211.

——(2004) *The Politics of Aesthetics: The Distribution of the Sensible*, translated by Gabriel Rockhill, London: Continuum.

——(2005) 'From Politics to Aesthetics?' *Paragraph*, 28, pp. 13–25.

——(2006) 'Thinking Between Disciplines: An Aesthetics of Knowledge', translated by Jon Roffe, *Parrhesia*, 1, pp. 1–12.

——(2007) *The Future of the Image*, translated by Gregory Elliott, London: Verso.

——(2008) 'Aesthetics against Incarnation: An Interview by Anne Marie Oliver', *Critical Inquiry*, 35, pp. 172–190.

——(2009a) *Aesthetics and its Discontents*, Cambridge: Polity.

——(2009b) 'A Few Remarks on the Method of Jacques Rancière', *Parallax*, 15, 3, pp. 114–23.

Reeves, Maud Pember (1979 [1913]) *Round about a Pound a Week*, London: Virago.

Rind, Miles (2002) 'The Concept of Disinterestedness in Eighteenth-Century British Aesthetics', *Journal of the History of Philosophy*, 40, 1, pp. 67–87.

Rorty, Amélie Oksenberg (1982) 'From Passions to Emotions and Sentiments', *Philosophy*, 57, 220, pp. 159–72.

Rutsky, R. L. (2002) 'Pop-up Theory: Distraction and Consumption in the Age of Meta-information', *Journal of Visual Culture*, 1, 3, pp. 279–94.

Scannell, Paddy (1996) *Radio, Television and Modern Life*, Oxford: Blackwell.

Schiller, Friedrich (2004 [1795]) *On the Aesthetic Education of Man*, translated by Reginald Snell, New York: Dover.

Schutz, Alfred (1972 [1932]) *The Phenomenology of the Social World*, translated by George Walsh and Frederick Lehnert, Evanston, IL: Northwestern University Press.

Schwartz, Frederic J. (2005) *Blind Spots: Critical Theory and the History of Art in Twentieth-Century Germany*, New Haven, CT: Yale University Press.

Schwartz, Vanessa R. (1999) *Spectacular Realities: Early Mass Culture in Fin-de-Siècle Paris*, Berkeley: University of California Press.

Sedgwick, Eve Kosofsky (2003) *Touching Feeling: Affect, Pedagogy, Performativity*, Durham, NC: Duke University Press.

Sen, Colleen Taylor (2009) *Curry: A Global History*, London: Reaktion.

Serres, Michel (2007 [1980]) *The Parasite*, translated by Lawrence R. Schehr, Minneapolis: University of Minnesota Press.

——(2008 [1985]) *The Five Senses: A Philosophy of Mingled Bodies*, translated by Margaret Sankey and Peter Cowley, London: Continuum.

Shaftesbury, Anthony A. C. (Earl of) (1711) 'Soliloquy: Or, Advice to an Author', in Characteristicks of Men, Manners, Opinions, Times (volume 1), Indianapolis: Liberty Fund, 2001, pp. 154–364.

Shaw, Jenny (1998) '"Feeling a List Coming On": Gender and the Pace of Life', *Time & Society*, 7, 2, pp. 383–96.

Sheridan, Dorothy, Brian Street and David Bloome (2000) *Writing Ourselves: Mass-Observation and Literacy Practices*, Cresskill: Hampton Press.

Shove, Elizabeth and Dale Southerton (2000) 'Defrosting the Freezer: From novelty to convenience – A narrative of normalization', *Journal of Material Culture*, 5, 3, pp. 301–19.

Shove, Elizabeth, Matthew Watson, Martin Hand and Jack Ingram (2007) *The Design of Everyday Life*, Oxford: Berg.

Shusterman, Richard (1992) *Pragmatist Aesthetics: Living Beauty, Rethinking Art*, Oxford: Blackwell.

——(1997) 'The End of Aesthetic Experience', *Journal of Aesthetics and Art Criticism*, 55, 1, pp. 29–41.

Silverman, Kaja (1980) 'Masochism and Subjectivity', *Framework*, 12, pp. 2–9.

——(1992) *Male Subjectivity at the Margins*, New York: Routledge.

Silverstone, Roger (1994) *Television and Everyday Life*, London: Routledge.

Simmel, Georg (1991 [1896]) 'The Berlin Trade Exhibition', translated by Sam Whimster, *Theory, Culture and Society*, 8, 3, pp. 119–23.

——(1903) 'The Metropolis and Mental Life', in *On Individuality and Social Forms*, Chicago: University of Chicago Press, 1971, pp. 324–39.

Slavin, Martin (1987) 'Colour Supplement Living', *Ten: 8*, 23, pp. 2–25.

Smith, Adam (2007 [1759]) *The Theory of Moral Sentiments*, Minneapolis: Filiquarian.

Smith, Roger (1997) *The Human Sciences*, New York: W. W. Norton.

——(2007) *Being Human: Historical Knowledge and the Creation of Human Nature*, New York: Columbia University Press.

Solomon, Robert C. (1993 [1976]) *The Passions: Emotions and the Meaning of Life*, Indianapolis: Hackett Publishing.

——(2003) *Not Passion's Slave: Emotions and Choice*, Oxford: Oxford University Press.

Spacks, Patricia Meyer (1995) *Boredom: The Literary History of a State of Mind*, Chicago: University of Chicago Press.

Spigel, Lynn (1992) *Make Room for TV: Television and the Family Ideal in Postwar America*, Chicago: University of Chicago Press.

——(2001) *Welcome to the Dreamhouse: Popular Media and Postwar Suburbs*, Durham, NC: Duke University Press.

Spinoza, Benedict de (1996 [1677]) *Ethics*, translated by Edwin Curley, London: Penguin.

Stanley, Liz (1992) *The Auto/Biographical I*, Manchester: Manchester University Press.

Steedman, Carolyn (1988) *The Radical Soldier's Tale: John Pearman, 1819–1908*, London: Routledge.

Stewart, Kathleen (2007) *Ordinary Affects*, Durham, NC: Duke University Press.

Stolnitz, Jerome (1961) 'On the Origins of "Aesthetic Disinterestedness"', *The Journal of Aesthetics and Art Criticism*, 20, 2, pp. 131–43.

Strom, Sharon Harman (1992) *Beyond the Typewriter: Gender, Class, and the Origins of Modern American Office Work, 1900–1930*, Urbana: University of Illinois Press.

Tamen, Miguel (2001) *Friends of Interpretable Objects*, Cambridge, MA: Harvard University Press.

Taussig, Michael (1992) *The Nervous System*, New York: Routledge.

Terkel, Studs (2004 [1972]) *Working*, New York: The New Press.

Thomas, Nicholas (1991) *Entangled Objects: Exchange, Material Culture, and Colonialism in the Pacific*, Cambridge, MA: Harvard University Press.

Townsend, Dabney (1982) 'Shaftesbury's Aesthetic Theory', *Journal of Aesthetics and Art Criticism*, 41, 2, pp. 205–13.

——(1987) 'From Shaftesbury to Kant: The Development of the Concept of Aesthetic Experience', *Journal of the History of Ideas*, 48, 2, pp. 287–305.

Trotsky, Leon (1975) *Trotsky's Writings on Britain*, Volume 2, London: New Park Publications.

Turco, Luigi (1999) 'Sympathy and Moral Sense: 1725–40', *British Journal for the History of Philosophy*, 7, 1, pp. 79–101.

Turkle, Sherry ed. (2007) *Evocative Objects: Things We Think With*, Cambridge, MA: MIT Press.

Turner, Victor (1986) 'Dewey, Dilthey, and Drama: An Essay in the Anthropology of Experience', in *The Anthropology of Experience*, edited by Victor Turner and Edward Bruner, Urbana: University of Illinois Press, pp. 33–44.

Turner, Victor and Edward Bruner, eds (1986) *The Anthropology of Experience*, Urbana: University of Illinois Press.

Valentine, Gill (2002) 'In-corporations: Food, Bodies and Organizations', *Body & Society*, 8, 2, pp. 1–20.

Vidler, Anthony (2000) *Warped Space: Art, Architecture, and Anxiety in Modern Culture*, Cambridge, MA: MIT Press.

Visram, Rozina (2002) *Asians in Britain: 400 Years of History*, London: Pluto Press.

Visser, Margaret (1992) *The Rituals of Dinner: The Origins, Evolution, Eccentricities, and Meaning of Table Manners*, New York: Penguin.

Ward, Janet (2001) *Weimar Surfaces: Urban Visual Culture in 1920s Germany*, Berkeley: University of California Press.

Warnke, Georgia (1987) *Gadamer: Hermeneutics, Tradition and Reason*, Stanford, CT: Stanford University Press.

Waters, Lindsay (2003) 'Come Softly, Darling, Hear What I Say: Listening in a State of Distraction – A Tribute to the Work of Walter Benjamin, Elvis Presley, and Robert Christgau', *boundary 2*, 30, 1, pp. 201–12.

Watson, James L. and Melissa L. Caldwell, eds (2005) *The Cultural Politics of Food and Eating*, Oxford: Blackwell.

Wershler-Henry, Darren (2005) *The Iron Whim: A Fragmented History of Typewritting*, Ithaca, NY: Cornell University Press.

Wessell, Leonard P. Jr. (1972) 'Alexander Baumgarten's Contribution to the Development of Aesthetics', *Journal of Aesthetics and Art Criticism*, 30, 3, pp. 333–42.

West, Cornel (1989) *The American Evasion of Philosophy: A Genealogy of Pragmatism*, Houndmills: Macmillan.

Williams, Raymond (1958) 'Culture is Ordinary', in *Resources of Hope: Culture, Democracy, Socialism*, London: Verso, 1987, pp. 3–14.

——(1976) *Keywords: A Vocabulary of Culture and Society*, London: Fontana.

——(1990 [1975]) *Television: Technology and Cultural Form*, edited by Ederyn Williams, London: Routledge.

——(1992 [1961]) *The Long Revolution*, London: Hogarth Press.

Winder, Robert (2004) *Bloody Foreigners: The Story of Immigration to Britain*, London: Little Brown.

Winnicott, D. W. (1951) 'Transitional Objects and Transitional Phenomena', in *Playing and Reality*, Harmondsworth: Penguin, 1974, pp. 1–30.

——(1964) *The Child, The Family, and The Outside World*, Harmondsworth: Penguin.

——(1974) *Playing and Reality*, Harmondsworth: Penguin.

Winocur, Rosalía (2005) 'Radio and Everyday Life: Uses and Meanings in the Domestic Sphere', *Television & New Media*, 6, 3, pp. 319–32.

Wise, Amanda and Adam Chapman (2005) 'Introduction: Migration, Affect and the Senses', *Journal of Intercultural Studies*, 26, 1–2, pp. 1–3.

Wise, J. Macgregor (2004) '"An Immense and Unexpected Field of Action": Webcams, Surveillance and Everyday Life', *Cultural Studies*, 18, 2–3, pp. 424–42.

Woolf, Virginia (1920) 'Solid Objects' in *Selected Short Stories*, Harmondsworth: Penguin, 2000, pp. 61–67.

Zelizer, Viviana A. (2005) *The Purchase of Intimacy*, Princeton, NJ: Princeton University Press.

Index